THE WORLD'S GREATEST FOOTBALL MATCHES

Norman Giller

OCTOPUS BOOKS

Published in 1989 by Octopus Books Limited
Michelin House, 81 Fulham Road,
London SW3 6RB

Typeset and designed
by Norman Giller Enterprises
Shoeburyness, Essex, England

First published in 1989

ISBN 0 7064 3890 6

Printed by Bath Press, England

Contents

This book is dedicated to the memory of 'Wor Jackie' Milburn, the idol of Tyneside, who died on October 9, 1988. Shortly before his death, the most popular player ever to pull on the famous black and white shirt of Newcastle United recalled his greatest match for Editor Norman Giller, a friend of more than 25 years. He said:

❛ I would have to select the 1951 FA Cup final against Blackpool when I managed to score both Newcastle's goals in a 2-0 victory. The first goal came early in the second half when I took possession on the halfway line. It felt as if the whole world was snapping at my heels as I dashed towards goal. Thirty yards out I made up my mind that I was going to try to score. I changed feet a couple of times to throw goalkeeper George Farm off balance, and then I side-footed the ball home from about 16 yards. Five minutes later little Ernie Taylor back-heeled the ball into my path and I scored from 25 yards with a rising drive. We retained the Cup the following year by beating Arsenal 1-0, and I scored with a header inside the first minute in 1955 when we won the Cup again by beating Manchester City 3-1. What was particularly satisfying about my three FA Cup final goals was that I scored with my left foot, right foot and my head. But it's the match against Blackpool that stands out in my memory because that was my first final. ❜

Wor Jackie has passed on, but his name will always live on in the world of football that he illuminated with his style, smile and sportsmanship.

ACKNOWLEDGEMENTS

Editor Norman Giller picked a lot of brains before arriving at the list of matches featured in this book. He is making a donation to the *Children In Need* Fund in return for all the help received. Among the people to whom he would like to offer his sincere thanks for their inspiration during his compilation of the match reports are:

Alan Ball, Gordon Banks, John Barnes, Peter Beardsley, Franz Beckenbauer, Peter Bonetti, Liam Brady, Sir Matt Busby, George Best, Trevor Brooking, Johnny Byrne, Raich Carter, Mike Channon, Bobby Charlton, Jack Charlton, Martin Chivers, Allan Clarke, Brian Clough, Johann Cruyff, Kenny Dalglish, Alfredo di Stefano, Tommy Docherty, Derek Dougan, Ted Drake, George Eastham, Alex Ferguson, Tom Finney, Trevor Francis, Archie Gemmill, Charlie George, Bobby Gould, George Graham, Andy Gray, Ron Greenwood, John Greig, Tommy Harmer, Tony Hateley, Johnny Haynes, Steve Heighway, Jimmy Hill, Glenn Hoddle, Don Howe, Alan Hudson, Emlyn Hughes, Roger Hunt, Geoff Hurst, Tommy Hutchison, Cliff Jones, Kevin Keegan, Howard Kendall, Joe Jordan, Denis Law, Tommy Lawton, Francis Lee, Billy Liddell, Nat Lofthouse, Malcolm Macdonald, Jimmy McIlroy, Frank McLintock, Billy McNeill, Wilf Mannion, Rodney Marsh, Sir Stanley Matthews, Bertie Mee, Jim Montgomery, Bobby Moore, Stan Mortensen, Dennis Mortimer, Terry Neill, Bill Nicholson, Peter Osgood, Pele, Steve Perryman, Martin Peters, David Pleat, Ferenc Puskas, Sir Alf Ramsey, Cyrille Regis, John Richards, Bobby Robson, Bryan (Pop) Robson, Don Rogers, Joe Royle, Ron Saunders, Len Shackleton, Peter Shilton, Tommy Smith, Alex Stepney, Nobby Stiles, Bob Stokoe, Gordon Strachan, Alan Sunderland, Bobby Tambling, John Toshack, Dennis Tueart, Terry Venables, Ricardo Villa, Tony Waiters, Charlie Wayman, Sir Walter Winterbottom, Frank Worthington, Billy Wright.

The Editor also thanks David Edwards for his striking illustrative work, the Football Writers of England and Scotland for the lists of their annual award winners, Michael Giller for his Apple-a-day computer skills, Leigh Jones for his design advice, Piers Murray Hill and David Ballheimer for their motivating powers, and, of course, Greavsie for kicking off the book...

It's a marvellous old game, says Greavsie

This book is a treasure chest for anybody who loves football. No matter where you dip into it you will find a gem of a game that has been reconstructed to give you an eye-witness account of some of the greatest moments in footballing history.

The hardest job that Editor Norman Giller had when compiling the book was deciding which matches to feature because he was restricted to just one game for each post-war season. He was guided finally by his many contacts in the game, and as you will see from his acknowledgements on the facing page his list reads like a who's who of football.

In each match that is spotlighted there was either an outstanding individual performance, a stunning team display or a magical moment that makes the game stand out in the memory. To add feelings to the facts of the matches Norman quotes the players who featured in the games.

There is obviously a strong British bias to the selection, but there is a sprinkling of an international flavour in the list with action-replay reports of World Cup matches featuring teams such as Brazil, West Germany, Argentina and Holland, and—perhaps the greatest club match of them all—the 1960 European Cup final extravaganza between Real Madrid and Eintracht Frankfurt.

I am often asked which is the greatest game in which I played. But just how do you define a great match? For instance, I once watched a reserve match at Southend United that had more twists and turns than an Alfred Hitchcock thriller and when my son, Danny, banged in a late winner I reacted as if he had just knocked in a World Cup final goal. That to me was a great match.

Beauty is in the eye of the beholder. When Norman asked Brian Clough to recall his greatest match he came up with a game he played in 1952 for Middlesbrough against Wolves in a junior match at Molineux. It stuck in Brian's mind because he scored a spectacular goal after taking the ball on a run from deep in his own half. It would not win a place in anybody's list of great matches, but for Brian it was something very special.

The two most *memorable* rather than greatest matches in which I played are both featured in this book. For England, there was the 1961 international against Scotland at Wembley when we slaughtered them 9-3. I was lucky enough to get a hat-

7

trick that day against a Scottish team that included my old pals Denis Law, Dave Mackay and that rascal Ian St John. I never allow them to forget that game even though in my heart of hearts I know it was a freak result. The only choker for me was that it was not freakish enough for us to have got ten goals!

At club level, the match I remember above all others is when Tottenham became the first British club to win a major European trophy. We beat Atletico Madrid 5-1 in the European Cup Winners' Cup in Rotterdam. I scored two of the goals, but the real star of the night was tiny Terry Dyson who netted two goals and ran rings round the Madrid defence. Another match featured in which I had close interest is the 1966 World Cup final, and, as you will read, it has given me the opportunity to put the record straight about my feelings for Sir Alf Ramsey, the manager who left me out of the England team for what would have been the game of a lifetime.

One of the strong appeals of this book apart from the match memories is that it gives you a complete breakdown of all the major champions and cup winners in post-war football. You will not find these sort of facts and figures outside a fat records book, and there are dozens of lists that will help you settle all sorts of arguments. Did you know, for instance, that Stanley Matthews was the first player to be elected European Footballer of the Year? And did you know that Kenny Dalglish was Scottish Footballer of the Year before winning the same honour in England? It's all in here along with potted biographies of

every player given top billing in the Greatest Matches.

You are in knowledgeable company with Editor Norman Giller. He is a walking record book on all sports, and we have produced 12 books together since 1973 when he tunnelled his way out of the *Daily Express* where he was chief football reporter. I don't argue with him because one of his mates is Frank Bruno, with whom he wrote the best-selling book *Know What I Mean?* Among his other writing partners have been Gordon Banks, Tommy Docherty, Henry Cooper, Jim Watt, Brendan Foster, John Newcombe and Tom Graveney. These days he is a prolific television writer. He devised the argument-provoking sports series *Who's the Greatest?*, wrote and co-created *The Games of '48* with his good friend Brian Moore and he is number two scriptwriter to Roy Bottomley on *This Is Your Life*.

I have to say nice things about Norman because he pays well, but if he wasn't looking over my shoulder while I hack out this introduction I would tell you he is one of the all-time bores. Dear old Eric Morecambe, with whom he used to write a regular 'Sports Smile' column in the *Daily Express*, always introduced him as, 'This is Norman Giller, a man I have known and avoided for many years.'

I couldn't put it better myself. But he does write a good book, and I think this one about the Great Football Matches will enlighten and entertain you. It will be hard to match.

1946-47 Shackleton, a six-shooting Clown Prince of soccer

Scoreline: Newcastle United 13, Newport County 0
Venue: St James' Park **Date:** October 5, 1946

THE SETTING: There has never been a club debut quite like the one Len Shackleton made for Newcastle United against Newport County in a Second Division game in the immediate post-war season. But then, there has never been another footballer quite like Shackleton. For him, the football field was a stage and he cast himself in the role of entertainer extraordinary.

'Shack'—as he was known and idolised throughout the north-east—believed football should be fun, and he had a vast repertoire of tantalising tricks that bemused the opposition, amused the fans, and often confused his own team-mates.

When he took his football seriously there were few more explosive exponents of the game as he proved in his first match for Newcastle. His presence in the side lured a crowd of 52,137 to Tyneside as witnesses of what was not so much a match as a massacre.

THE TEAMS: **Newcastle United** Garbutt, Cowell, Graham, Harvey, Brennan, Wright, Milburn, Bentley, Wayman, Shackleton, Pearson. **Newport County** Turner, Hodge, Oldham, Rawcliffe, Low, Cabrie, Davies, Wookey, Craddock, McNab, Bowen.

THE ACTION: Shack stepped into a forward line of attacking aristocrats for his debut in the famous black and white striped shirt of Newcastle. The all-star attack—in the days when teams used to play with five forwards—read: Jackie Milburn, Roy Bentley, Charlie Wayman, Shackleton, Tommy Pearson. Shack had been bought just three days earlier from

Len Shackleton, the Clown Prince

Bradford Park Avenue for £13,000, which was then the Football League's third highest fee. The game got off to a stunning start with Wayman shooting a second-minute penalty wide. By half-time, the same wayward Wayman had helped himself to a hat-trick and Shack had scored four goals, including three in a sensational six-minute spell.

Newport's outclassed defenders had no answer to Shackleton's skill and pace. They tried double marking him, but Shack relished the challenge of taking two players out of position with clever decoy moves that opened yawning gaps through which his colleagues were able to run free. Shackleton gave the fans a treat by digging deep into his treasure chest of footballing tricks. He manipulated the ball like a circus juggler, dribbling 'through' tackles and chipping over goalkeeper Charlie Turner's head with either foot; and he found his team-mates with a stream of corkscrew passes, giving the ball the sort of bias usually seen only on the snooker table or bowls green. There was also the inevitable clowning from Shackleton, who at one stage teased his exhausted opponents by sitting on the ball and beckoning for them to come and try to get it. He was trying for humour, not humiliation.

Jackie Milburn and Roy Bentley got into the scoring act in the second half, adding two goals apiece. But the stage belonged to Shackleton and he lifted his goals contribution to six as Newport caved in to a 13-0 defeat that equals the heaviest loss in League history. If anything, the scoreline flattered Newport. They might easily have conceded 20 goals but for a sequence of courageous saves by Turner.

THE WITNESSES: Goalkeeper Turner said: 'It was like facing a firing squad. With Shackleton in their attack, Newcastle are now certainties for promotion. There is not a defence in the League that could contain them if they continue to play like that.'

Newport manager Tom Bromilow, a formidable Liverpool and England half-back in the 1920s: 'I think they're going to have to get a cricket scoreboard mounted at St James's. The next time we play against Newcastle I've got a way to stop Shackleton. We're going to lock him in the dressing-room and throw away the key. What's he going to be like when he settles into the side?'

'Wor' Jackie Milburn, who over the next decade was to become the king of Tyneside: 'When we missed the penalty in the second minute I thought to myself, 'Oh, no—it's going to be one of those days.' I think it was the only time we missed all afternoon. I could not help feeling sorry for Newport. They were chasing shadows for 90 minutes. Shack was just unstoppable.'

THE SIX SHOOTER: Born in Bradford on May 3, 1922, Shackleton was capped for England schoolboys while at Carlton High School. He joined Arsenal's groundstaff in 1938 and played Saturday football for London Paper Mills and Enfield. Arsenal released him just before the outbreak of war in 1939 because of his frail physique. Shack started his

League career with his local club Bradford, and was snapped up by Newcastle after playing only seven League matches. Despite the dream debut against Newport, he was never completely content at St James' Park and Newcastle surprisingly sold him to local rivals Sunderland the following season for £20,000. He became a legendary hero at Roker Park where he lived up to his title of the Clown Prince of Football. Shack spent the rest of his career on Wearside where he had a memorable partnership with clever Ivor Broadis. Welsh international centre-forward Trevor Ford was the considerable striking force feeding off them.

Shack would have won many more than his five England international caps but for being a rebel without a pause. He never made any secret of his lack of respect for the authority of the football establishment. After his startling debut, he became more of a maker than a taker of goals but still managed to amass 126 League goals in 384 matches before a knee injury forced his retirement in 1957. He later became a respected football writer with the *Sunday People* in the north-east. In his autobiography, *Clown Prince of Soccer*, Shack revealed his anarchic attitude when he deliberately left blank a chapter titled, The average director's knowledge of football.

QUOTE: Len Shackleton: 'We should be shot for not having scored 20. It was one of those games when I could have found the net with my eyes shut. I hope the fans aren't going to expect six goals from me every week!'

FOR THE RECORD: In the last match of the season Newcastle went to Newport for the return match needing a win to clinch promotion. They were beaten 4-2 by a Newport team already doomed to relegation.

JIMMY GREAVES: 'Shack was my hero when I was a schoolkid. I was attracted by his skill and also his irreverent attitude. He was a conjuror. I doubt if there has been a more skilful inside-forward in the history of British football. His unpredictable and sometimes impudent play frightened the life out of the England selectors. The proof is there in that he won only five caps. Players with a tenth of his ability have won twice as many caps. The man was a footballing genius.'

THE CHAMPIONS OF '47

First Division: Liverpool, 57 pts. Runners-up: Manchester United, 56 pts
Second Division: Manchester City, 62 pts. Runners-up: Burnley, 58pts
Third Division (South): Cardiff City, 66 pts. Runners-up: QPR, 57pts
Third Division (North): Doncaster R, 72 pts. Runners-up: Rotherham U, 64 pts
FA Cup final: Charlton Athletic 1, Burnley 0
Top First Division marksman: Derek Westcott (Wolves), 37 goals
Scottish champions: Rangers, 46 pts. Runners-up: Hibernian, 44 pts
Scottish Cup final: Aberdeen 2, Hibernian 1

1947-48 The day that cultured Carey made Blackpool rock

Scoreline: Manchester United 4, Blackpool 2
Venue: Wembley Stadium **Date:** April 24, 1948

THE SETTING: Sir Matt Busby moulded and managed four great Manchester United teams during a glorious 25-year reign at Old Trafford. Many consider the first Busby-built team was the best, and their impressive impact on the immediate post-war years gives powerful weight to the argument. Like all Busby teams, they played football with the accent on attack and lured massive crowds to Maine Road, which they shared with Manchester City for three years while bomb-damaged Old Trafford was being rebuilt. United pulled in a League record crowd of 82,950 when they played Arsenal in a First Division game at Maine Road on January 17, 1948. But it was another match that season for which Busby's team of '48 is best remembered by veteran United fans. For those lucky enough to have seen it, the 1948 FA Cup final against Blackpool still rates as one of the classics of the century.

The Manchester idols went into the match as favourites because their League form had been more consistent than Blackpool's. They had finished runners-up for the First Division title behind Arsenal and eight points clear of their Lancashire rivals. But nobody would have been foolish enough to write off a Blackpool team that included in their attack the two 'Super Stanleys' of British football—Matthews and Mortensen.

United also had an all-star forward line, and their defence was under the command of one of the most versatile players ever to pull on a pair of football boots in skipper Johnny Carey. The day that Carey led Manchester United out at Wembley for the 1948 FA Cup final against Blackpool terrace tickets cost just 3s. 6d. (17.50p). Ticket touts were demanding and receiving £20 a ticket, but by the end of

Johnny Carey, a gentleman of football

a breath-taking match nobody thought they had been overcharged.

THE TEAMS: **Blackpool** Robinson, Shimwell, Crossland, Johnston, Hayward, Kelly, Matthews, Munro, Mortensen, Dick, Rickett.
Manchester United Crompton, Carey, Aston, Anderson, Chilton, Cockburn, Delaney, Morris, Rowley, Pearson, Mitten.

THE ACTION: There have rarely been two teams meeting at Wembley so committed to playing adventurous, open football. From the first moments the ball was being played forward deep into the goal areas and there were narrow misses at both ends before the game was ten minutes old. Blackpool, the underdogs, were first to score in the 14th minute, Eddie Shimwell slotting in the ball from the penalty spot after Stan Mortensen's charge for goal had been ended by a mistimed tackle from the over-enthusiastic Allenby Chilton.

Jimmy 'Old Bones' Delaney darted down the right wing to set up an equaliser for centre-forward Jack Rowley in the 28th minute, but within five minutes Blackpool had regained the lead when Mortensen scored with a cross shot to join the exclusive club of players who have scored in every round of the FA Cup.

Johnny Carey's whole philosophy of football was captured in a one-line order issued as United prepared to leave the dressing-room for the start of the second half. 'Just keep playing football, lads,' he said in his soft Irish brogue. United did exactly that and gradually and smoothly took control

of the match after Rowley had caught the Blackpool defenders napping as he raced forward to meet a quickly taken Johnny Morris free-kick with a spectacular diving header.

In a breakaway raid 12 minutes from the end Mortensen threatened to lift Blackpool into the lead for a third time, but Jack Crompton stretched himself across the goal to make a magnificent save. The ball was immediately transferred into the Blackpool half where John Anderson found Stan Pearson who fired a rising 20-yard drive into the net off a post.

Stanley Matthews, bidding to end his first season in Blackpool colours with an FA Cup winners' medal, tried to make his mark on the match but was stifled by the tight marking of John Aston. United clinched a memorable victory in the 82nd minute when Anderson's shot was deflected out of Robinson's reach.

THE WITNESSES: Stan Mortensen: 'It was a privilege to have been part of the game even though we finished up the losers. The turning point was when Jack Crompton saved my shot when it was 2-2. Within seconds the ball was in the back of our net. If I had blasted the ball over the bar instead of forcing Jack to make that save who knows what might have happened...'

Matt Busby: 'There were a few moans and groans about Blackpool's penalty at half-time but Johnny Carey had a great calming influence and told the players not to waste breath talking about what was history. I did not have to say much because I knew the way they were playing goals would come. We had a very experienced team, and

13

every player knew exactly what was expected of him. From first ball to last the Final was an absolute classic.'

THE GENTLEMAN: Johnny Carey, born in Dublin on February 23, 1919, was a man for all positions, at home in any role and in any company. United featured him in every position except outside-left during his 17 years at Old Trafford. The Irishman, one of the great gentlemen of the game, even filled in as goalkeeper during an emergency, but it was as a cultured full-back that he won world recognition. A measure of his mastery of the soccer arts was his selection as captain of Europe against Great Britain in a prestige international at Hampden Park in 1947. He played for both Northern Ireland and Eire, appearing for each within three days in two matches against England in the first post-war season. At the end of his eventful playing career he was a manager with Blackburn Rovers, Everton, Leyton Orient and Barrow.

QUOTE: Johnny Carey: 'It was the sort of match that you dream about. We were determined to maintain our composure, and we knew that if we just kept playing our natural game we would eventually come out on top. The proudest moment for me was climbing the Wembley steps to accept the FA Cup from King George VI who told me he had enjoyed every moment of the match. I think that went for every-body at Wembley.'

FOR THE RECORD: The FA Cup victory laid the foundation for a United run of success that lasted more than 20 years. In the six years immediately after the war United won the League championship once (1951-52) and were runners-up four times. It was a team that kept United in the honours hunt until a new crop of players—the Busby Babes—came along.

JIMMY GREAVES: 'I remember listening to the wireless commentary on the 1948 final when I was a kid, and it helped increase my appetite for football. That United team was a cracker, and I doubt if there has ever been a centre-forward who could match Jack Rowley's shooting power. Old pros used to tell me that it was like the shot from an elephant gun.'

THE CHAMPIONS OF '48

First Division: Arsenal, 59 pts. Runners-up: Manchester United, 52 pts
Second Division: Birmingham City, 59 pts. Runners-up: Newcastle U, 56 pts
Third Division (South): QPR, 61 pts. Runners-up: Bournemouth 57 pts
Third Division (North): Lincoln City, 60 pts. Runners-up: Rotherham U, 59 pts
FA Cup Final: Manchester United 4, Blackpool 2
Top First Division marksman: Ronnie Rooke (Arsenal) 33 goals
Footballer of the Year: Stanley Matthews (Blackpool)
Scottish champions: Hibernian, 48 pts. Runners-up: Rangers, 46 pts
Scottish Cup Final: Rangers 1, Morton 0 (after a 1-1 draw)

1948-49 'The other Stanley' makes a fine mess of Italy's defence

Scoreline: Italy 0, England 4
Venue: Stadio Municipali, Turin **Date:** May 16, 1948

THE SETTING: The Stadio Munici-pali in Turin was formerly the Stadio Mussolini until the dictator's disgrace following the capitulation of Italy in the Second World War. The Italians much preferred football to war and an excited, capacity crowd gathered to watch their idols try to prove they were still kings of world soccer. Italy had won the World Cup in 1934 and again in 1938, the last time it had been played. They knew they could still claim to be football's rulers if they could master one of the most powerful sides England had ever paraded on a foreign field.

Team manager Walter Winter-bottom was barely able to make himself heard above the din of the spectators as he gave his last-minute tactical talk in the England dressing-room deep in the bowels of the sta-dium.

England were being captained for the first time by goalkeeper Frank Swift, the Blackpool-born giant who stood 6ft 3in tall, weighed 14 stone and had hands the size of shovels. As he prepared to lead the team out of the dressing-room for a match that was to be played in sweltering hot conditions, Swiftie turned to his for-wards and shaped his right hand into a massive fist. 'Give us an early goal, lads,' he said, in a short, sharp sum-mary of all that Winterbottom had been saying. 'We've got to shut that crowd up.'

Most of the players were unable to hear what their skipper said because of the increasing volume of noise from Italian fans whose anticipation of their first major international since the war years had lifted them to fever pitch. One person who did hear was Black-pool inside-forward Stan Mortensen, 'the *other* Stanley'...

Stan Mortensen, a bomber in boots

THE TEAMS: **Italy** Bacigalupo, Ballarin, Eliani, Anrovazzi, Parola, Grezar, Menti, Loik, Gabetto, Mazzola, Carapellese.
England Swift, Scott, Howe, Wright, Franklin, Cockburn, Matthews, Mortensen, Lawton, Mannion, Finney.

THE ACTION: The game was into its fourth minute when Mortensen answered Swiftie's call for a quick goal. Stanley Matthews, his right wing partner for club as well as country, dropped back into the England half to collect a pass out of defence from Billy Wright. As the Italian defenders tensed themselves ready to face one of the dribbling runs for which Matthews was famed and feared he quickly transferred the ball low down the right wing into the space where Mortensen was racing like a hare. Italian centre-half Carlo Parola moved across to challenge as Mortensen reached the ball in full stride. He checked as if to change direction and as Parola tackled his shadow he kept running in a straight line parallel with the touchline. Right-back Ballarin was next to be beaten by a sudden burst of acceleration and as Mortensen approached the corner flag the Italian defenders hurried to take up marking positions in the middle. They were waiting for a pass that never came. Mortensen cut in along the dead-ball line and ended his 40-yard sprint with a curling shot into the roof of the net from the tightest of angles. As the England players celebrated an astonishing goal that stunned the crowd into silence Mortensen gave a half bow in the direction of skipper

Swift, who was punching his huge fists into the air in delight. He was then forced to use his enormous hands for much more than just applauding.

For the next 20 minutes it became Italy v Frank Swift as the Manchester City custodian produced a succession of stupendous saves that provided all the necessary evidence as to why to this day many good judges rate him the greatest goalkeeper ever to have pulled on an England jersey. Even the frustrated Italian fans had to applaud in appreciation as Swift made blinding saves in quick succession from shots by centre-forward Gabetto and left-winger Carapellese. Just as it looked as if Italy's pressure would have to spawn an equaliser that man Mortensen struck again. In the 25th minute he made an identical spurt through the Italian defence but this time when he reached the dead-ball line he squared a pass back into the path of centre-forward Tommy Lawton, who almost broke the net with the power of a right foot shot that sent the ball screaming wide of goalkeeper Bacigalupo's right hand.

Italy continued to play neat, constructive football for the rest of the first half but on the two occasions they managed to get the ball past the defiant Swift full-backs Laurie Scott and Jack Howe took it in turns to clear the shots off the line. The spirit of the Italians was finally punctured early in the second half when Spanish referee Pedro Escarpin ruled that a header by Gabetto from a free-kick had not crossed the England line after hitting the under-side of the bar.

Following the disallowed goal, the usually disciplined Italian defenders

became exposed to the perils of panic as wingers Matthews and Finney started to take control with weaving runs that left their markers confused and bemused. It was two clinically taken goals by Finney late in the game that clinched one of the finest victories ever registered by an England team in an overseas international.

THE WITNESSES: England half-back Billy Wright: 'Morty's goal gave us just the motivation we needed. Everybody in the stadium expected Stan to pass the ball back and we just couldn't believe it when he managed to get it into the net from that acute angle. Then big Frank took over with one of the greatest goal-keeping displays I have ever seen. There was no way in the world he was going to let them get the ball past him and his performance inspired the rest of us.'

Team manager Walter (now Sir Walter) Winterbottom: 'I don't think I have ever known a stadium go quite so deathly quiet as when Stan Mortensen found the net. It was as if 80,000 Italians had suddenly been gagged. I was urging Stan to lay the ball back for Tommy Lawton. A goal just did not seem possible from that angle. Frank Swift was very nervous about being the first England goal-keeper to captain the team and was anxious to show that he was up to the job. He gave one of the finest displays of his career.'

MAGICAL MORTY: Stan Mortensen powered through a highly productive playing career proud rather than peeved to be known as 'the *other* Stanley'. His prolific partnership with Stanley Matthews produced many memorable moments both for Blackpool and England. While Matthews did all the clever, intricate work as he dismantled defences with his dribbling runs, it was 'the other Stanley' who was always on hand to do what mattered most...put the ball into the back of the net. Morty, as he was lovingly labelled by the fans, had as his main strength exceptional speed and dramatic acceleration plus deadly shooting accuracy when he arrived at his destination.

Morty had a career story right out of *Boys' Own* fiction. He was lucky to survive the war when the Wellington bomber he was piloting crash-landed. He was lifted out of the wreckage with severe head and back injuries and doctors said he would be lucky to live, let alone play football again. Two years later giant-hearted Stan—a bomber in football boots—made his international debut in extraordinary circumstances. He went to Wembley as an England reserve and finished up playing for injury-hit Wales. England won this war-time international 8-3.

His first game for England was even more remarkable. It was against a highly rated Portugal side in Lisbon in 1947, and it was the first match in which the selectors dared to play both Matthews and Finney in the same attack. They ran riot on the wings and Mortensen and Tommy Lawton each helped themselves to four goals as outplayed Portugal slumped to a 10-0 defeat. Morty netted 23 goals in 25 full internationals for England, and during ten post-war seasons with Blackpool averaged two goals every three games including a record 30 in FA Cup ties. He finished with a club record 197 goals in 317 League matches for Blackpool before winding down his distinguished playing League career with Hull City and Southport. After appearing in non-League football with Bath City and then Lancaster City, Morty had three up-and-down seasons as Blackpool's manager before leaving football to concentrate on a business career.

QUOTE: Stan Mortensen: 'My intention had been to centre the ball for Tommy Lawton but I noticed that the Italian goalkeeper had not positioned himself properly, so I shot on the run and could have jumped over the roof of the stadium when the ball curled out of his reach and into the net. I scored a few more spectacular goals for Blackpool during my career, but I think this one has pride of place in my England collection. What made it particularly satisfying was that just a few minutes earlier that smashing bloke Frank Swift had asked for a quick goal. I was delighted to oblige!'

FOR THE RECORD: Tragically, the two captains in this match were later to die in air crashes. Italy's skipper Valentino Mazzola, father of the famous Mazzola brothers, was killed along with all his Torino team-mates when their plane crashed into a hillside just outside Turin in 1949. Frank Swift, one of the most popular footballers of his era, was killed in the Munich air disaster of 1958 when he was travelling with Manchester United as a journalist attached to the *News of the World.*

JIMMY GREAVES: 'If anybody captured the spirit of English football in the 1940s and 1950s it was Stan Mortensen. He played it hard but fair, never giving less than 100 per cent and really grafting for his goals with a boldness that was typical of a man who had flown wartime bombers. He was never once lost in the giant shadow cast by the other Stanley, the wizard of dribble. In fact he helped make Matthews a better player because a lot of his clever work might have come to nothing but for Morty's deadly finishing touch. He was the hero of thousands of schoolkids.'

THE CHAMPIONS OF '49

First Division: Portsmouth, 58 pts. Runners-up: Manchester United, 53 pts
Second Division: Fulham, 57 pts. Runners-up: West Bromwich Albion, 56 pts
Third Division (South): Swansea, 62 pts. Runners-up: Reading, 55 pts
Third Division (North): Hull City, 65 pts. Runners-up: Rotherham U, 62 pts
FA Cup Final: Wolverhampton Wanderers 3, Leicester City 1
Top First Division marksman: Willie Moir (Bolton Wanderers), 25 goals
Footballer of the Year: Johnny Carey (Manchester United)
Scottish champions: Rangers, 46 pts. Runners-up: Dundee, 45 pts
Scottish Cup Final: Rangers 4, Clyde 1

1949-50 The Old Masters humbled by a star-spangled goal

Scoreline: United States of America 1, England 0
Venue: Belo Horizonte, Brazil **Date:** June 29, 1950

THE SETTING: England, the Old Masters of football, had beaten Chile 2-0 in their first ever World Cup match in the 1950 tournament staged in Brazil. They now looked forward with confidence to clinching a place in the second stage of the finals by accounting for a nondescript United States team. To those following the competition closely, it seemed the Americans had just a walk-on part in the tournament like extras on a film-set about to be cut down by John Wayne and the other big names. Before the match at Belo Horizonte, Scottish-born American coach Bill Jeffrey said: 'Obviously there's no way we can expect to beat England, but we hope to give a good account of ourselves and learn something about the way the game should be played. Our main objective will be to keep the score against us as low as possible.' Nobody in the world doubted that his expectation of defeat would be well founded.

Apart from the absence of Stanley Matthews, England were close to full strength, while the United States team was made up of a mixture of over-the-hill veterans and novices new to the international stage. It was wrongly and unfairly reported at the time that the United States players had come *en masse* from Ellis Island and did not

Alf Ramsey, got his revenge

include a single American-born member. In fact all but three of their team were United States citizens by birth. Their three 'imports' were Belgian Joe Maca, Larry Gaetjens of Haiti and their captain Eddie McIlvenny, a Scottish right-half who had been given a free transfer by Wrexham and who, after the World Cup, signed for Manchester United.

Just 16 days before the World Cup duel England, with Matthews in the line-up, struggled to a 1-0 victory over the United States in an unofficial international match in New York. But even this close encounter provided no warning of the shock waiting for England in Belo Horizonte—'Beautiful Horizon'. The Indians were about to up and massacre John Wayne and his men.

THE TEAMS: **England** Williams, Ramsey, Aston, Wright, Hughes, Dickinson, Finney, Mortensen, Bentley, Mannion, Mullen.
United States Borghi, Keough, Maca, McIlvenny, Colombo, Bahr, Wallace, Pariani, Gaetjens, Ed Souza, Clarkie Souza.

THE ACTION: England struggled to get any pattern to their play on a cramped, rutted pitch that was hardly conducive to the sort of ball control and skill that had made players like Tom Finney and Wilf Mannion world-respected forwards. The United States were under prolonged pressure but showed tremendous determination and enthusiasm as they competed for every ball. Finney and Mannion smacked shots against the post before centre-forward Larry Gaetjens dived to deflect a shot wide of Wolves goalkeeper Bert Williams in a rare first-half raid in the 37th minute to give the Americans a shock lead.

Team manager Walter Winterbottom, his hands tied by an outdated selection-committee system, tried to inject some bite into the England attack for the start of the second half by switching Finney into the middle, but the United States grew in composure and confidence and fought an intelligent and industrious rearguard action. England's chances of salvag-

ing even a draw disappeared as Mullen hit a post and Mortensen the bar before the referee turned down strong appeals for a penalty after a blatant handling offence right in front of the American goal. Mortensen was rugby tackled inside the penalty area in the closing minutes, but all England got was a free-kick. Ramsey hammered the ball right footed towards the top corner of the net but as England arms went up in celebration of an equaliser, goalkeeper Borghi—a professional baseball catcher—somehow stretched himself across the goal to claw the ball away.

THE WITNESSES: Skipper Billy Wright : 'As long as I live I will never know how we lost the game. It was like one long nightmare. We were just not meant to win. Everything went against us. Even their goal was a freak effort. We were all speechless in the dressing-room after the match. We just couldn't believe what had happened to us.'

Harry Keough, the United States right-back who later became a respected coach: 'Of course we had no business beating a team like England, but it's what makes soccer such a great game that these things can sometimes happen. We did not feel the British press gave us the credit we deserved. Yes, we had luck on our side, but we worked damned hard for our victory. I must say, though, that the England players took the defeat like true sportsmen.'

THE GOAL SCORER: The name Larry Gaetjens is like a knife-thrust in the history of English football. His winning goal in Belo Horizonte caused

the biggest upset of the century, rivalled as a giant-killing only by Italy's defeat by North Korea in the 1966 World Cup finals. Gaetjens, a centre-forward born in Haiti, used his head to deflect the ball wide of a despairing dive by England goalkeeper Bert Williams. Some reports described it as an opportunist header; others that the ball had merely struck him and gone into the net. Efforts to trace Gaetjens for the true story foundered in 1970 when, in his native Haiti, it was reported that he had 'disappeared in mysterious circumstances'. Later unconfirmed reports stated that he had died in a Haitian jail after helping to organise a guerilla movement against the island's dictator, 'Papa' Doc. His name will live on in football history.

FOR THE RECORD: England needed to beat Spain in their third match to qualify for the second stage of the finals. Stanley Matthews, Jackie Milburn and the effervescent Eddie Baily were drafted into the side, but morale was so low after the shock of the United States defeat that the team never got into their stride.

Spain won 1-0 and England's first World Cup challenge had ended in humiliation. A world record crowd of 199,854 gathered for the deciding match in the 1950 World Cup finals between Uruguay and Brazil in Rio de Janeiro, with Englishman George Reader as the referee. Brazil needed only a draw to take the trophy in front of their fanatical supporters, but Uruguay came from a goal down to win 2-1 and so take the World Cup for a second time. Sweden beat Spain 3-1 to clinch third place.

JIMMY GREAVES: 'I was a ten-year-old schoolkid when the 1950 World Cup was played and I remember everybody being as choked by that defeat by the United States as if somebody had died. We thought England were unbeatable. To lose to the Yanks was just mind-numbing. From then on we had to accept that we were no longer the masters. I cannot think of a result in the history of the game that has been greeted with such disbelief. Alf Ramsey was manager of England when they beat the USA 10-0 in 1964, so he got some sort of revenge.'

THE CHAMPIONS OF '50

First Division: Portsmouth, 53 pts. Runners-up: Wolves, 53 pts.
Second Division: Tottenham, 61 pts. Runners-up: Sheffield Wednesday, 52 pts
Third Division (South): Notts Co, 58 pts. Runners-up: Northampton T, 51 pts
Third Division (North): Doncaster R, 55 pts. Runners-up: Gateshead, 53 pts
FA Cup Final: Arsenal 2, Liverpool 0
Top First Division marksman: Dick Davis (Sunderland), 25 goals
Footballer of the Year: Joe Mercer (Arsenal)
Scottish champions: Rangers, 50 pts. Runners-up: Hibernian, 49 pts
Scottish Cup Final: Rangers 3, East Fife 0
World Cup deciding match: Uruguay 2, Brazil 1

1950-51 Fit-as-a-fiddle Liddell puts the pride back into Scotland

Scoreline: England 2, Scotland 3
Venue: Wembley Stadium **Date:** April 14, 1951

THE SETTING: Scotland were still smarting from their 1-0 defeat by England at Hampden the previous season in a match that decided which country should represent Britain in the World Cup. It was the contention of every soul o'er the border that Scotland would have been better suited to carry the British banner on the World Cup stage than an England team that hardly covered itself in glory. The Scots were determined to prove their point by beating England on their own territory at Wembley.

The Scottish selectors put their faith at the feet of home-based players, and selected only one Anglo-Scot—Billy Liddell, the left winger whom many people, particularly in shouting distance of Anfield, considered the most potent player in Britain.

THE TEAMS: **England** Williams, Ramsey, Eckersley, Johnston, Froggatt, Wright, Matthews, Mannion, Mortensen, Hassall, Finney.
Scotland Cowan, Young, Cox, Evans, Woodburn, Redpath, Waddell, Johnstone, Reilly, Steel, Liddell.

THE ACTION: England were in trouble after just 11 minutes when inside-right Wilf 'Golden Boy' Mannion was carried off with a fractured cheekbone. The ten-man England team in these pre-substitute days

Billy Liddell,the king of the Kop

battled with a bravery and determination that rocked the Scots back on their heels and it was debutant Harold Hassall who gave the English a 25th minute lead when he fired the ball wide of goalkeeper Jimmy Cowan after receiving a square pass from Stan Mortensen.

Bobby Johnstone, making his debut in the Scottish attack, equalised eight minutes later from a Lawrie Reilly pass. There were more problems for England four minutes before half-time when Mortensen was knocked out in a goalmouth collision. He was brought round by the 'magic sponge' and refused to go off although obviously still in a daze. As the players came off at half-time he had to be supported by team-mates as he reeled from side to side.

England started the second half with nine men and the Scots quickly took full advantage of the acres of space. Reilly, a bundle of dynamite from Hibernian who was always at his best against 'the auld enemy,' swivelled to score with a shot on the turn in the 47th minute. As the ball flew into the net English voices in the crowd were heard above the roar of the Scottish supporters as they reacted to the sight of Mortensen bravely returning to the fray. This had an uplifting effect on England and, with Matthews and Finney operating as emergency right wing partners, they penned Scotland in their own half under a battery of attacks that did everything but produce a goal.

It was Scotland who scored during a breakaway raid when the tearaway Reilly kicked the ball out of the hands of goalkeeper Bert Williams and the fit-as-a-fiddle Liddell moved at lightning speed to whip the ball into the net.

Ten minutes later Finney drew goalkeeper Cowan off his line before chipping the ball into the net to give England hope of salvaging a draw, but it was too high a mountain for ten men to climb and the Scots clung on to their lead and claimed revenge for the defeat at Hampden.

THE WITNESSES: Rangers winger Willie Waddell (who later became Editor Norman Giller's football reporting colleague on the *Daily Express*): 'I rarely knew a Scottish team so determined to win a match. For us, it was like a World Cup final. The unfortunate injury to Wilf Mannion made it that much harder for us to get control because, as was often the case with teams reduced to ten men, England suddenly lifted their game. Lawrie Reilly played a blinder and Billy Liddell, as usual, gave excellent support. It was his goal that finally put the game beyond England's reach, but it was never easy.'

Tom Finney: 'There were about 20 minutes in the second half when I honestly thought we were going to win the match. We had the Scottish defence at sixes and sevens but just couldn't apply the vital finishing touch. Morty deserved a medal for bravery. He was out on his feet at half-time, but they couldn't keep him in the dressing-room. He insisted on rejoining the game, and for quite a while we had the Scots clinging desperately to their lead. The winner could not have come from a nicer man than Billy Liddell. He was one of the greats of the game.'

THE FLYING SCOT: Billy Liddell, scorer of the victory-clinching goal against England, monopolised so many matches with Liverpool that for many seasons the club was known as 'Liddellpool.' The sturdy Scot came close to being the *perfect player*. He was skilful, fast, intelligent, could shoot powerfully with either foot and he once bulleted a header into the net from outside the penalty area. His favourite position with Liverpool and Scotland was as a left winger, but he was equally effective at centre-forward. Born in Dunfermline on January 10, 1922, he was the son of a miner and the eldest of six children. He first came to international prominence during the war while serving as an RAF navigator and played in the same Scottish side as Matt Busby and Bill Shankly. It was Matt Busby who recommended him to the directors at Anfield.

Throughout his career Liddell was a part-time professional, concentrating on a job away from football as an accountant, and following his retirement in 1961 he became bursar at Liverpool University. He was appointed a Justice of the Peace and he has been a tireless worker for charity organisations on Merseyside where he will always have hero status.

QUOTE: Billy Liddell: 'The credit for my goal really has to go to Lawrie Reilly, whose perseverance and quick reflexes paved the way for me to score. It was an important victory for everybody connected with Scottish football because it restored our pride after the disappointment of the World Cup qualifying match defeat by England at Hampden the previous year. We felt we had put the record straight.'

FOR THE RECORD: Billy made his League debut in a 7-4 defeat of Chelsea in 1946 and he finished the season with a League Championship medal. He scored 216 goals in 492 League matches for Liverpool, and served them for 15 years. He scored six goals in his 28 appearances for Scotland.

JIMMY GREAVES: 'Billy Liddell was a credit to football on and off the pitch, a true gentleman of the game. I was lucky enough to see him play several times for Liverpool against Spurs when I was a kid and he was always a handful for Alf Ramsey, who was no mean full-back. Few wingers got the better of Alf, but he always looked uncomfortable against Liddell—as did most full-backs. He had superb ball control and tremendous physical power mixed in with his skill.'

THE CHAMPIONS OF '51

First Division: Tottenham, 60 pts. Runners-up: Manchester United, 56 pts
Second Division: Preston NE, 57 pts. Runners-up: Manchester City, 52 pts
Third Division (South): Nottm Forest, 70 pts. Runners-up: Norwich C, 64 pts
Third Division (North): Rotherham U, 71 pts. Runners-up: Mansfield T, 64 pts
FA Cup Final: Newcastle United 2, Blackpool 0
Top First Division marksman: Stan Mortensen (Blackpool), 30 goals
Footballer of the Year: Harry Johnston (Blackpool)
Scottish champions: Hibernian, 48 pts. Runners-up: Rangers, 38 pts
Scottish Cup Final: Celtic 1, Motherwell 0

1951-52 Lofthouse the Lionheart is a knockout in Vienna

Scoreline: Austria 2, England 3
Venue: Prater Stadium, Vienna **Date:** May 25, 1952

THE SETTING: It was with some justification that the 1952 meeting between England and Austria in Vienna was being described before the kick-off as 'the unofficial championship of Europe'. Austria had scored 57 goals in their last 16 matches while England, the Old Masters, had regained pride and prestige with a sequence of eight games without defeat following their 1950 World Cup humiliation when they lost to the United States.

Vienna was still an occupied city and there were many British servicemen in the 65,000 crowd shoe-horned into the sprawling Prater Stadium.

It was a meeting of two worlds, the old and the new. Austria, with the versatile Ernst 'Clockwork' Ocwirk conducting the team from midfield, were experimenting with a fresh, flowing style of soccer soon to be perfected by the magical Magyars of Hungary. England were still sticking to the effective but old-fashioned 2-3-5 formation.

THE TEAMS: **Austria** Musil, Roeckl, Happel, Schleger, Ocwirk, Brink, Melchior, Hanappi, Dienst, Huber, Haummer.
England Merrick, Ramsey, Eckersley, Wright, Froggatt, Dickinson; Finney, Sewell, Lofthouse, Baily, Elliott.

THE ACTION: England survived a heavy opening onslaught from the Austrians and took the lead against the run of play in the 21st minute with an incisive counter attack. A penetrating pass by skilful Spurs schemer Eddie Baily triggered a breakthrough at the heart of the Austrian defence and Lofthouse finished off the move with a left foot volley deep into the net. The cheers of the British soldiers were still

Nat Lofthouse, the Lion of Vienna

25

filling the Prater Stadium when Jack Froggatt conceded a penalty from which Huber side-footed an equaliser. The Portsmouth centre-half quickly made amends with a pass that opened the way for Jackie Sewell to score a spectacular goal. With a sudden swerve and dummy that wrong-footed his marker, Sewell showed just why Sheffield Wednesday had paid Notts County a record £35,000 for him. Then, feinting to go left, he sent another defender the wrong way before scoring with a lethal shot. Austria pulled level again just before half-time through centre-forward Diego, who shrugged off a challenge from Billy Wright before forcing the ball past Gil Merrick.

Eight minutes from the end with the game deadlocked at 2-2, goalkeeper Merrick collected a corner and threw the ball quickly to Finney out on the right. It would have been tempting for this marvellous ball player to have kept possession while England got forward in numbers, but his shrewd football brain told him that a quick pass was called for and he delivered a superbly judged ball that set Lofthouse clear just inside the Austrian half on a lone raid.

He galloped 45 yards with a pack of Austrian defenders hunting at his heels. Musil advanced off his line to block the England centre-forward and it was obvious to all onlookers that there would be a collision if one of them did not give way. Both brave men continued on their paths and Lofthouse managed to release a low shot at the moment that they collided 12 yards from the Austrian goal. Lofthouse was flat out unconscious

and did not see the ball roll slowly into the net. He was carried off on a stretcher but came hobbling back for the last five minutes, and he hammered a shot against a post to ease pressure on an overworked England defence. From this memorable match on, Lofthouse was known as The Lion of Vienna.

THE WITNESSES: England right-back Alf Ramsey: 'The courage Nat showed in the match against Austria was typical of him as a man and as a player. The way he insisted on coming back into the match lifted the heart of every Englishman in the stadium. It made us redouble our efforts to keep the Austrians out.'

England skipper Billy Wright: 'If you were ever in trouble, Nat was the sort of iron man you would have selected to be alongside you. We could only stand and watch his lonely run into the Austrian half and as the goalkeeper came out it was obvious there was going to be a collision. But Nat didn't check his stride. He just kept going. It was unbelievable bravery.'

THE LION: Nat Lofthouse was born in Bolton on August 27, 1925. He was the youngest of four sons of the head horsekeeper of Bolton Corporation and attended the same Castle Hill School as Tommy Lawton, his predecessor as England centre-forward.

Lofty served Bolton for more than 40 years, first as a player and later as a coach, scout and, briefly, as manager. It was somehow fitting that Rocky Marciano was ruling as the world heavyweight champion when Nat was at his mightiest. He was the Marciano

of football, playing with clenched fists and crashing through defences with brute force and little concern for his or anybody else's physical welfare. And like The Rock, Lofthouse away from the sporting arena was a gentle person who was never boastful or arrogant. He scored a club record 256 goals in 452 League matches for Bolton between 1946 and 1960. In 33 England matches he scored 30 goals and he was elected Footballer of the Year in 1953.

He was captain of the Bolton team that beat Manchester United 2-0 in the 1958 post-Munich FA Cup final. He refued to let sentiment get in his way as he hammered the two goals that gave Bolton victory. The second came when he charged goalkeeper Harry Gregg and the ball into the net. It was a physical gesture that summed up his approach to the game: 'Get out of the way…Nat Lothouse is here!'

QUOTE: Nat Lofthouse: 'The Austrian goalkeeper was in two minds and hesitated about coming out and was a split-second too late to stop me shooting. I went out like a light when we collided but our trainer Jimmy Trotter told me I had scored when he brought me round with the magic sponge. They tried to tell me I couldn't go back on but wild horses couldn't have kept me off the pitch.'

FOR THE RECORD: England lost only one of their next 12 internationals with Lofty scoring 15 goals. He was missing from the England attack for the first time in 18 matches when England played Hungary at Wembley on November 25, 1953. Hungary won 6-3 to sow the seeds of a revolution in English football.

JIMMY GREAVES: 'Nat was not all muscle, like his reputation suggested. He also had a lot of method. His positional sense made him an ideal centre-forward who was always finding room so that his colleagues could find him with passes. To supplement his driving power he had a cracking shot in both feet, and few centre-halves got the better of him in the air even though at just a fraction over five foot nine he was not particularly tall. He may have been lacking in inches, but he was unquestionably one of the giants of the game.'

THE CHAMPIONS OF '52

First Division: Manchester United, 57 pts. Runners-up: Tottenham, 53 pts.
Second Division: Sheffield Wednesday, 53 pts. Runners-up: Cardiff C, 51 pts
Third Division (South): Plymouth A, 66 pts. Runners-up: Reading, 61 pts
Third Division (North): Lincoln C, 69 pts. Runners-up: Grimsby T, 66 pts
FA Cup Final: Newcastle United 1, Arsenal 0
Top First Division marksman: George Robledo (Newcastle U), 33 goals
Footballer of the Year: Billy Wright (Wolves)
Scottish champions: Hibernian, 45 pts. Runners-up: Rangers, 41 pts
Scottish Cup Final: Motherwell 4, Dundee 0

1952-53 | Wizard of Dribble conjures Cup winners' medal at last

Scoreline: Blackpool 4, Bolton Wanderers 3
Venue: Wembley Stadium **Date:** May 2, 1953

THE SETTING: Stanley Matthews, the world's most famous footballer, was 38 years old when Blackpool reached the FA Cup final for the third time in five years. They had been runners-up in 1948 and 1951, and the 1953 final against Bolton Wanderers was seen as the last chance for the 'Wizard of Dribble' to collect the FA Cup winners' medal that had always eluded him during a distinguished 21-year career. Nobody could have guessed that 12 years later Matthews would still be weaving his magic on the First Division stage at the age of 50.

Stanley Matthews, Wizard of Dribble

Standing in the way of Matthews and his Wembley dream were Blackpool's Lancashire neighbours Bolton Wanderers, a formidable team inspired by the barnstorming performances of England centre-forward Nat Lofthouse who spearheaded an all-international attack. On the flanks were England wingers Doug Holden and Bobby Langton, and skilfully feeding Lofthouse at inside-forward were Scotland's Willie Moir and England's Harold Hassall.

Both defences had shown signs of brittleness under pressure during the 1952-53 First Division campaign when Blackpool finished seventh and Bolton fourteenth, so plenty of goals were anticipated.

Blackpool went into the match as favourites and all attention was centred on Wembley as Old Master Matthews ran out on to the sacred pitch for what would surely be the last time in an FA Cup final.

The match was televised and it is estimated that ten million viewers crowded round the country's two million sets watching in black and white and on average screen sizes of ten inches. The classic contest they were about to witness deserved to grace a giant, panoramic screen in full, living colour.

What few of the watching millions knew is that Matthews almost missed

what was to be the game of a lifetime because of problems with a pulled muscle. He had a pain-killing injection on the morning of the match before deciding to play.

Could he at last collect a winners' medal? The nation held its breath.

THE TEAMS: **Blackpool** Farm, Shimwell, Garrett, Fenton, Johnston, Robinson, Matthews, Taylor, Mortensen, Mudie, Perry.
Bolton Wanderers Hanson, Ball, Banks, Wheeler, Barrass, Bell, Holden, Moir, Lofthouse, Hassall, Langton.

THE ACTION: It was Bolton and Lofthouse instead of Blackpool and Matthews who took instant command of the match. Lofthouse tried a speculative shot after just 75 seconds that caught Blackpool's Scottish international goalkeeper George Farm cold and he allowed the ball to slip from his grasp and into the net. Blackpool skipper and centre-half Harry Johnston was finding Lofthouse hard to pin down, and in the 20th minute the Bolton flier almost made it 2-0 with a shot that cannoned off a post. Blackpool's forwards were making little impact on the match, and just as it seemed as if Bolton were going to dominate a one-sided game their left-half Eric Bell pulled a muscle. Bolton had gambled on playing him because the injury—similar to the one troubling Matthews—had caused him concern during the build-up to the match. The gamble failed, and Bell, with no substitutes allowed, was reduced to the role of a limping passenger on the left wing. Harold

Hassall was pulled back into defence in an emergency reshuffle of the Bolton team and ten minutes before half-time he deflected a left foot shot from Stan Mortensen into his own net to make it 1-1. Four minutes later Farm was slow to come off his line to a cross from Langton and Moir dived across him to divert the ball into the net to give Bolton a 2-1 lead at the interval. Ten minutes into the second half the Matthews' Cup-winning dream seemed to have disintegrated when the hobbling Bell—left unmarked by the Blackpool defence—defied the pain from his leg and leapt to head in a cross from Holden to give Bolton what looked to be a match-winning 3-1 lead. No team in any of the previous 71 FA Cup finals had managed to come back from being two goals down. But then, enter stage right Stanley Matthews...

For an hour, Matthews had been on a tight rein. It was almost as if he was saving himself for a final burst. The moment Bolton scored their third goal he rolled up the sleeves of his orange shirt and clapped his hands to attract the attention of his colleagues. It was the signal that he wanted the ball to his feet. Little Ernie Taylor, the orchestrator of the Blackpool attacks, responded by sending a stream of passes to Matthews who for 30 golden minutes turned on the finest individual display ever witnessed at Wembley.

He ran the Bolton defence ragged with his slow-slow-quick-quick-slow dribbling, and harassed left-back Ralph Banks made so many turns trying to keep in contact with his tormentor that he became a cramp victim. Matthews sent over a cross in

the 68th minute that hung tantalis-
ingly in the air. Goalkeeper Stan
Hanson failed to collect it cleanly and
Mortensen came charging in to force
the loose ball over the line, colliding
with a post as he put the finishing
touch. Blackpool 2, Bolton 3.

Matthews was pushing his play to
new dimensions that lifted him into
the land of legend. He continually
tricked his way past the luckless
Banks who was totally perplexed by
his feints and changes of pace. But
time was running out for Blackpool
and four scoring chances laid on by
Matthews were wasted before, with
just three minutes to go including
injury time, Mortensen blasted a free-
kick through a poorly constructed
Bolton defensive wall and into the net
from 20 yards for an equaliser. It
completed the one and only FA Cup
final hat-trick at Wembley.

Extra time looked inevitable, but
Matthews had other ideas. There was
one minute left on the watch of referee Mervyn Griffiths when he
dribbled inside Banks for the ump-
teenth time. England international
centre-half Malcolm Barrass came
charging across to try to cover but
Matthews dismissed him from the
action with a dip of the left shoulder
and a shimmy to the right. He took
the ball down to the dead-ball line and
then hooked it back into the path of
South African left winger Bill Perry
who swept it forcefully into the net
from six yards. The goal was Perry's,
but the glory belonged to Matthews
who was chaired around the pitch
alongside skipper Harry Johnston. For
ever more the game would be known
as 'the Matthews final'.

THE WITNESSES: Ernie Taylor,
who also played in FA Cup finals with
Newcastle and Manchester United: 'I
suppose it was understandable that
Stanley Matthews should get all the
publicity because he had waited so
long for his winners' medal, but in my
opinion Morty was the real hero. His
third goal was a belter. I usually took
the free-kicks but Stan said he wanted
a pot at goal. I didn't think he could
get it through the wall, but I'm glad to
say he proved me wrong.'

Stan Mortensen, the hat-trick hero:
'Stanley did his stuff when it mattered
and I didn't mind him getting all the
headlines. All that mattered was that
we won. I have never played in a game
with so many twists and turns. We
should have sewn it up long before the
final whistle, but then it may not have
been such a thrilling classic.'

Johnny Wheeler, Bolton's right-
half: 'Stanley Matthews destroyed us
in that last half-hour. We all knew the
Matthews style—the shuffle, the feint
and then the sudden dart past. But
knowing what he was going to do and
trying to stop him doing it were two
different things.'

THE WIZARD: Stanley Matthews
was born at Hanley, Stoke, on February 1, 1915, the son of a professional
featherweight boxer nicknamed 'The
Fighting Barber of Hanley'. He inher-
ited his father's lightness of foot, his
co-ordination and the ability to feint.
But he did it all with his feet, not his
fists. Matthews ruled the world of
football with his regal skill for an astonishing span of 33 years, and he
represented in the eyes of the world so
much that was legendary about the

England of his time. London Bridge was falling down, Old Father Times kept rolling along and Stanley Matthews was always running defences into dizzy disarray. He was a one-off. A soloist par excellence.

Matthews played 54 matches for England between 1935 and 1957 and made another 30 appearances in wartime internationals. He turned professional with Stoke in 1932, and Blackpool bought him for £11,500 in 1947—a transfer that brought a mass protest march from 3,000 Stoke supporters. He had his greatest triumphs at Blackpool but went home to Stoke in 1961 to add a remarkable new chapter to his legend. Matthews was 48 when he lined up for Stoke's final match of the 1962-63 season against Luton. Stoke needed one point for the Second Division championship. Luton needed a win to avoid relegation. Matthews scored the goal that gave Stoke a 1-1 draw and the title. It was his final goal.

QUOTE: Stanley Matthews: 'The '53 Cup final was my most unforgettable match, but I did not win the game on my own. That's a myth. It was a great team effort. The minute I saw Ralph Banks limping with cramp I knew there was a weak spot in the Bolton defence that we had to exploit. I don't think enough credit has been given to Stan Mortensen. He was a real inspiration with his never-say-die spirit, and I knew that if I could get the ball into the middle I could count on Stan to get the ball into the net.'

FOR THE RECORD: Twice voted Footballer of the Year and the first European Footballer of the Year in 1956, Matthews played a total of 698 League matches and scored 71 goals. He was 17 when he played his first League game for Stoke and 50 when he played his last in 1965 shortly after becoming the first knight of football.

JIMMY GREAVES: 'There will never be another like Stanley Matthews. The Wizard of Dribble was a fitting nickname. He could not only send defenders but the entire crowd the wrong way with one of his clever feints. I had the honour of playing alongside him in his farewell testimonial match at Stoke and that is one of my treasured memories. Even at the age of 50 he could outsprint most people on the pitch.'

THE CHAMPIONS OF '53

First Division: Arsenal, 54 pts. Runners-up: Preston North End, 54 pts
Second Division: Sheffield United, 60 pts. Runners-up: Huddersfield T, 58pts
Third Division (South): Bristol Rovers, 64 pts. Runners-up: Millwall, 62 pts
Third Division (North): Oldham A, 59 pts. Runners-up: Port Vale 58 pts
FA Cup Final: Blackpool 4, Bolton Wanderers 3
Top First Division marksman: Charlie Wayman (Preston North End), 24 goals
Footballer of the Year: Nat Lofthouse (Bolton Wanderers)
Scottish champions: Rangers, 43 pts. Runners-up: Hibernian, 43 pts
Scottish Cup Final: Rangers 1, Aberdeen 0 (after a 1-1 draw)

1953-54 Major Puskas composes a new Hungarian rhapsody

Scoreline: England 3, Hungary 6
Venue: Wembley Stadium **Date:** November 25, 1953

THE SETTING: England had never been beaten in a home international by overseas opposition*. As that proud record stretched back 45 years there was no reason why people with just a surface knowledge of football should have suspected that 1952 Olympic champions Hungary were the team to end the run. But anybody who made a study of how the game was developing abroad—which embraced few in England—would have known that this Hungarian team was something quite special.

The Hungarians, on a run of 29 successive matches without defeat, were professional in everything but name. They were officially soldiers in the Hungarian army, but their parade ground was the football field and the only drills they carried out were designed purely to improve their skills. They were under the command of Major Ferenc Puskas, whose influence on the pitch was so great that he should have held the rank of Field Marshal.

The 'Magical Magyars,' with the portly yet light-footed Puskas plotting their raids with the arrogance of a modern-day Napoleon, had found a way of combining the short passing game of the South Americans with the

Ferenc Puskas, the Galloping Major

long-ball technique that had for so many years been a copyright of the British game. They played to a flexible 4-2-4 formation, inter-changing positions and making England's traditional 2-3-5 pattern seem about as outdated as a hansom cab on a freeway.

As Puskas waited in the centre circle for England skipper Billy Wright to join him for the coin tossing he picked up the match ball and juggled it on his left foot, flicked it

*England were beaten 2-0 by the Republic of Ireland at Goodison in 1949, but they were not considered in the 'overseas' category because nine of their players were based in England.

into the air, caught it on his thigh and then let it run down his shin and back on to the centre spot. There were muted jeers from among the 100,000 spectators who interpreted this as somebody showing off rather than doing what came naturally. Within 40 seconds of the kick-off Puskas was showing that he was much more than just a juggler. It was not the circus that had come to town. It was a football revolution.

THE TEAMS: **England** Merrick, Ramsey, Eckersley, Wright, Johnston, Dickinson, Matthews, Ernie Taylor, Mortensen, Sewell, Robb.
Hungary Grosics, Buzanszky, Lantos, Bozsik, Lorant, Zakarias, Budai, Kocsis, Hidegkuti, Puskas, Czibor. Sub: Geller.

THE ACTION: The Puskas left foot was on display again within the first minute. He delivered the ball through the heart of the England defence like a dagger thrust, and Nandor Hidegkuti quickly brought it under control and then completely deceived centre-half Harry Johnston with a distracting dummy before rifling the ball high into the net from 20 yards.

Johnston was one of four Blackpool players in the England team—along with Matthews, Mortensen and Taylor—who six months earlier had featured in one of the greatest of all FA Cup finals. Against Bolton, Johnston had his hands full with Nat Lofthouse but at least he knew where to find Lofty. He did not have a clue where Hidegkuti was going to pop up next. The Hungarian wore the No 9 shirt, but was one of a new breed of centre-forwards who liked to lie back in a deep position from where he could navigate a path to goal.

The Blackpool skipper, one of the most dependable centre-halves in Britain, was used to playing against robust, English-style centre-forwards who trod on his toes and dug him in the ribs and rarely left the penalty area. He did not know whether to follow Hidegkuti deep into midfield or stay on guard in his usual territory marking nobody. He was so torn by indecision that he finished up giving Hidegkuti the freedom of Wembley.

Johnston got into the game as a creator of a goal in the 15th minute after a hairline offside decision had robbed Hidegkuti a split second before he whipped the ball past advancing goalkeeper Gil Merrick following dazzling approach play by Czibor and Puskas. Johnston raced 30 yards from his own penalty area with the ball at his feet and ended an inspired run with a pinpoint pass to his club-mate Mortensen, who outpaced a defender before transferring the ball to Sewell out on the left. He cut in and beat Groscis with a low, left-foot cross shot.

The 100,000 crowd, bewildered and bemused by the hurricane start Hungary had made, breathed a collective sigh of relief. England, they were convinced, were unbeatable at home and now they would put the cherry-shirted invaders in their place.

Thirteen minutes later the scoreline was England 1, Hungary 4, and by then it had dawned on everybody but the most obstinate spectators that England were being exposed to a new world of football that had left the English style of play looking not only old fashioned but also redundant.

Hidegkuti scored Hungary's second goal from close range and then Puskas stepped imperiously on to the scoring stage with what many consider the finest goal ever scored at Wembley. Let Billy Wright, the England skipper who was closest to the action, describe it: 'Puskas was in the inside-right position when he received the ball. I thought I was perfectly placed to make a tackle, but as I challenged he pulled the ball back with the sole of his left foot and all in the same movement fired a left foot shot inside Gil Merrick's near post. I tackled thin air and the next day that great reporter Geoffrey Green wrote in *The Times* that I was like a fire engine going the wrong way for the fire. It was a perfect summary. Puskas had completely hoodwinked me. In all my 105 internationals for England I did not see a better executed goal.'

Puskas netted goal number four three minutes later when he heel-flicked the ball past Merrick from a free-kick taken by master of the midfield Jozef Bozsik. If nothing else England had fighting spirit going for them and Mortensen battled his way through the Hungarian defence with typical gusto to smash-and-grab a second goal for England just before half-time.

'We can still pull this out of the fire,' Morty said to his club-mate Stanley Matthews as they walked together back to the dressing-rooms. You needed to pin Mortensen to the canvas before he would admit defeat.

Any hope England had of getting back into the game died within ten minutes of the second half when first

Nandor Hidegkuti, deadly finisher

Bozsik scored with a rising drive, and then hat-trick hero Hidegkuti put the finishing touch to a dazzling succession of passes as the Hungarians reduced the match to something of an exhibition that earned them the nickname the 'Magical Magyars'.

Right-back Alf Ramsey pulled one back for England from the penalty spot after Tottenham schoolmaster George Robb, playing his one and only international match, was pulled down by goalkeeper Grosics. At 6-3, the scoreline flattered England.

The Wembley crowd shook off their disappointment at seeing their heroes humbled to acclaim a Hungarian team that had flourished a standard and style of football never before witnessed at Wembley. They showed the Old Masters the way the game could and should be played.

THE WITNESSES: Gil Merrick, England's goalkeeper who had to pick the ball out of his net 13 times in two appearances against the Hungarians: 'Whoever said the Hungarians did not know how to shoot must have been wearing a blindfold. They were the most accurate marksmen I ever faced. Their passing was so accurate and their running off the ball so intelligent that they often seemed to have two players to every one of ours.'

Jozef Bozsik, a member of the Hungarian House of Representatives who played in 100 international matches: 'The victory at Wembley was the greatest moment in the history of our football. England gave the game to the world and to beat them was like winning at the home of football. We were confident that we could cause a surprise but to score six goals at Wembley where no visiting team had ever won was like a dream come true.'

Ron Greenwood, who was a professional footballer with Chelsea watching from the stand: 'It was one of the most exciting days of my life. Tomorrow's world was suddenly opened up to us. It was going to be a long process, but at last it was accepted that we had to start rethinking our tactics and revising the way we approached the game. That defeat for England was the start of a much-needed revolution in our game.'

THE GALLOPING MAJOR: With his stunningly powerful left-foot shot and his ability to be a thought and a deed ahead of most defenders, Ferenc Puskas was the most influential player in the magnificent Hungarian team of the 1950s.

Born in Budapest in 1926, he won 84 international caps and scored 85 goals before his defection from Hungary following the 1956 Uprising. He was leading marksman in the Hungarian League in 1947, 1950 and 1953 when playing for Honved, the team consisting of players who had been commissioned in the Hungarian army. Puskas had the rank of Major and was nicknamed the 'Galloping Major' following his performance against England at Wembley.

After the Hungarian revolution he added to his reputation as one of the greatest players of all time by becoming a front-line master with Real Madrid where he struck up a devastating partnership with Alfredo di Stefano. Puskas was top Spanish League scorer in 1960, 1961, 1963 and 1964. Pancho—as he was affectionately known in Madrid—played for Spain in three World Cup final matches in 1962 but was then 36 and slowed to a stroll by a spreading waistline. At the end of his brilliant and eventful playing career he switched to management and guided Panathanaikos of Athens to the 1971 European Cup final.

QUOTE: Ferenc Puskas: 'To understand how we felt about the match against England in 1953 you first had to appreciate how highly we regarded English football. Players like Stanley Matthews and Billy Wright were giants in our eyes and we were in awe of playing at Wembley. I played in many hundreds of games during my career but no victory gave me greater pleasure than the 6-3 win against England. I don't think anybody will accuse me of exaggeration when I say we could have scored ten goals. We felt ten feet tall when we walked off that famous pitch because we knew that we had given the old masters a lesson.'

FOR THE RECORD: When the Hungarians arrived in Switzerland for the 1954 World Cup finals they were the hottest favourites of all time. They had gone four years without a single defeat, and had followed their 6-3 drubbing of England at Wembley with an even more convincing 7-1 victory in Budapest during the build-up to the World Cup. They also comfortably beat Scotland home and away. Their concentration during the World Cup was interrupted by an ugly dressing-room brawl with the Brazilians after a bad-tempered quarter-final won 4-2 by Hungary. The Hungarians, minus the injured Puskas, had a close call in the semi-final against Uruguay. They led 2-0 at half-time but the Uruguyans pulled back in the second half to force extra time. Hohberg was a coat of paint away from completing a hat-trick for Uruguay before Kocsis

scored two of his typical headers to win Hungary a place in the final against West Germany.

Their unbeaten record finally crashed at the heartbreak hurdle of the World Cup final. A gamble of playing Puskas when half-fit blew up in their faces and the unheralded West Germans, splendidly marshalled by Fritz Walter, became the new champions. But that Hungarian team of the early 1950s will always be remembered as one of the greatest combinations ever to operate on a football pitch.

JIMMY GREAVES: 'I grew up in awe of Ferenc Puskas. I was a 13-year-old schoolboy when Hungary gave us that hiding. It was one of the first matches that I saw on television, a squint-size screen on which I could hardly believe what I was seeing. It was as if the Hungarians had come from another planet. I had the honour of playing against Puskas for England against the Rest of the World at Wembley in 1963. I have never seen a better left foot than his. He could unlock a safe door with it and he also had the power to dynamite it open.'

THE CHAMPIONS OF '54

First Division: Wolves, 57pts. Runners-up: West Bromwich Albion, 53 pts
Second Division: Leicester City, 56 pts. Runners-up: Everton, 56pts
Third Division (South): Ipswich Town, 64 pts. Runners-up: Brighton, 61 pts
Third Division (North): Port Vale, 69 pts. Runners-up: Barnsley 58 pts
FA Cup Final: West Bromwich Albion 3, Preston North End 2
Top First Division marksmen: Jimmy Glazzard (Huddersfield T) and Johnny Nicholls (West Bromwich Albion), 29 goals
Footballer of the Year: Tom Finney (Preston North End)
Scottish champions: Aberdeen, 49 pts. Runners-up: Celtic, 46 pts
Scottish Cup Final: Celtic 2, Aberdeen 1
World Cup Final: West Germany 3, Hungary 2

1954-55 Wright's Wolves Wonders start European ball rolling

Scoreline: Wolverhampton Wanderers 3, Honved 2
Venue: Molineux **Date:** December 13, 1954

THE SETTING: All that glistered on the English soccer scene during the 1950s were the old gold shirts of Wolves as they powered through a startling sequence of success. In nine years from 1952-53 they won the League crown three times including successive Championships, finished out of the first three only once and missed a hat-trick of First Division titles and the FA Cup and League double by just one point in 1959-60. But for all their domestic dominance, this golden Wolves era will be best remembered for their pioneering of European club football under flood-lights.

They mastered the mightiest teams in Europe in a series of unofficial world club championships at Molineux that were staged so successfully that they accelerated the move towards organised European competitions. These midweek evening games—alleged 'friendlies'—were played at full throttle because of the enormous international prestige and pride involved. The matches were screened live on television—a rarity in those days—and the exciting exploits of Wolves captured the nation's interest and imagination.

The game that grabbed most attention was against Honved of Budapest—virtually the Hungarian national team that had hammered 13 goals

Billy Wright, the master of Molineux

against the full England side in two meetings during the previous 14 months. Could Wolves do what England failed to do and conquer Ferenc Puskas and Co? Sixty thousand fans packed into the Molineux ground and armchair viewers at home waited for the answer.

THE TEAMS: **Wolves** Williams, Stuart, Shorthouse, Slater, Wright, Flowers, Hancocks, Broadbent, Swinbourne, Wilshaw, Smith. **Honved** Farago, Sarosi, Kovaks, Boszik, Lorant, Banyai, Budai, Kocsis, Machos, Puskas, Czibor.

37

THE ACTION: After throwing bouquets to the crowd, the Hungarians started to deflower the Wolves defence masterminded by England skipper Billy Wright. Honved might easily have scored three goals in the opening ten minutes as they skipped lightly over the muddy Molineux turf to test goalkeeper Bert 'The Cat' Williams. A goal seemed inevitable and it came in the 11th minute when Puskas floated over a free-kick for Kocsis to send a bullet header past Williams to add to the belief that he was the most powerful header of a ball in the world.

Three minutes later goal-taker Kocsis turned goal-maker with a defence-splitting pass to Machos, who drove the ball firmly past the oncoming Williams. These two knife thrusts would have been enough to kill off most sides, but Wolves—characterising the iron will of their demanding manager Stan Cullis—were never a team of quitters. The match settled into a fascinating duel between two worlds—the short passing game of the Hungarians against the thumping long-ball tactics of Wolves. With the pitch becoming heavier and muddier by the minute, it was the Wolves strategy that began to pay dividends and despite going off at half-time two goals in arrears there were definite signs of the game beginning to swing in favour of the Midlanders.

They started a second-half revival movement that had Honved stretched to breaking point. Tiny England winger Johnny Hancocks used his size two right boot to hammer a 49th minute penalty into the net after he had been bundled off the ball by Kovaks. Captain Wright, with nightmare memories of Hungary's 13 goals against England as his motivation for revenge, was giving a Herculean performance in the middle of the defence, and he drove his forwards to new peaks of effort as Wolves set up camp in the Honved half. After half a dozen chances had been made and missed, Wolves finally snatched an equaliser in the 76th minute when Bill Slater and Denis Wilshaw combined to create an opening for centre-forward Roy Swinbourne who nodded the ball wide of Farago's despairing dive.

Honved were suddenly almost visibly drained of spirit and energy, and all resistance was knocked out of them two minutes later when Wilshaw and Swinbourne again got their act together, this time Swinbourne volleying in a centre for the winning goal.

THE WITNESSES: Stan Cullis, the Wolves manager who was the master of Molineux throughout the golden years: 'It was without any question the most exciting match I ever saw. Even when we were two goals down at half-time I was convinced we could win, and I simply told the lads to keep plugging away. It was a magnificent team performance.'

Denis Wilshaw, who later in the season scored four goals for England against Scotland at Wembley: 'There has never been a match quite like it for atmosphere and excitement. The newspapers were calling us the club champions of the world, and I don't think anybody who saw our victory against Honved would have argued.'

Ferenc Puskas: 'Billy Wright is a good friend of mine as well as a re-

spected opponent. I told him after the match that he should be proud to be captain of such an outstanding team. We have not come up against a better club side. Wolves do not have a single weakness.'

THE CAPTAIN: Blond Billy Wright was the heart of the Wolves across a span of 12 years and 491 League games. He was a magnificent general on the pitch, captaining Wolves to a procession of memorable triumphs and leading England 90 times while winning a then record 105 caps. Born at Ironbridge, Shropshire, on February 6, 1924, he started his career as an inside-forward before developing into a driving right-half. Billy switched to centre-half in an emergency for the 1954 World Cup finals and went on to establish himself as one of England's greatest-ever central defenders. He had a spell as England Under-23 and Arsenal manager at the close of his distinguished playing career before becoming an executive with Central Television.

QUOTE: Billy Wright: : 'The win against Honved went some way to making up for the hammerings we experienced against Hungary. It was the greatest night in my club football career. To give a team of Honved's calibre a two-goal start and then beat them 3-2 was like something out of a fairy story.'

FOR THE RECORD: Wolves under Stan Cullis were FA Cup winners in 1949, League champions in 1953-54, 1957-58 and 1958-59, and FA Cup winners again in 1960. In the first 15 post-war years they were only twice out of the top six teams at the end of each season, and in each of the last four League seasons they scored more than 100 First Division goals.

JIMMY GREAVES: 'You would have needed the emotions of a stone statue not to have been moved by those pulsating performances from Wolves in the 1950s. The victory against Honved helped restore our pride and self-confidence after some dodgy results at international level. For somebody like me who came into the professional game in the 1950s, Wolves were among the Great Untouchables.'

THE CHAMPIONS OF '55

First Division: Chelsea, 52 pts. Runners-up: Wolves, 48 pts
Second Division: Birmingham City 54 pts. Runners-up: Luton Town, 54pts
Third Division (South): Bristol City, 70 pts. Runners-up: Leyton Orient, 61pts
Third Division (North): Barnsley, 65 pts. Runners-up: Accrington S, 61 pts
FA Cup Final: Newcastle United 3, Manchester City 1
Top First Division marksman: Ronnie Allen (West Bromwich Albion), 27 goals
Footballer of the Year: Don Revie (Manchester City)
Scottish champions: Aberdeen, 49 pts. Runners-up: Celtic, 46 pts
Scottish Cup Final: Clyde 1, Celtic 0 (after a 1-1 draw)

1955-56 'Tommy the Tank' Taylor delivers the old one-two

Scoreline: England 4, Brazil 2
Venue: Wembley Stadium **Date:** May 9, 1956

THE SETTING: Brazil were on the threshold of the greatest era in their footballing history when they visited Wembley to play the Old Masters England for the first time. The foundation was there for the team that would win the World Cup in 1958 and retain it four years later. Goalkeeper Gylmar and unrelated full-back partners Djalma and Nilton Santos gave stability to the defence, stocky bundle of energy Zozimo was bringing his dynamic power to the midfield and the wonderfully gifted Didi was the composer and arranger of the attack. Nilton Santos, a left-back famed for his adventurous play, was as excited as a schoolboy when he was told that he would be marking the legendary Stanley Matthews, who had been recalled by England at the age of 41. 'Stanley Matthews is a magical name in the world of football,' Nilton said before the kick-off. He was about to discover just why. And central defender Pavao, in an experimental role as a third back, was to find out why Manchester United centre-forward Tommy Taylor was being hailed as 'the new Tommy Lawton.'

THE TEAMS: **England** Reg Matthews, Hall, Byrne, Clayton, Wright, Edwards, Stanley Matthews, Atyeo, Tommy Taylor, Haynes, Grainger **Brazil**: Gylmar, Djalma Santos, Nilton

Tommy Taylor, a thoroughbred

Santos, Zozimo, Pavao, Dequina, Paulinho, Alvaro, Gino, Didi, Chanoteiro

THE ACTION: Tommy Taylor signalled that he meant business in the first minute when he brought Gylmar to his knees with a snap shot.

It was a dress rehearsal for what came moments later when he left Pazao standing with a sudden change of pace before ramming the ball low past Gylmar and into the net. The Brazilians were still shell shocked from this explosive start when Sheffield United left-winger Colin Grainger cut inside at sprint speed to steer the ball into the net to make it 2-0 inside five minutes. England touched peaks of perfection in the first half and the ageing maestro Matthews responded to the enthusiasm of his young team-mates by tormenting Nilton Santos with a succession of his now-you-see-me-now-you-don't dribbling runs.

England learned the hard way that you must never relax against the Brazilians who can turn a match with just a moment's burst of brilliance. It came from Didi, who completely baffled goalkeeper Reg Matthews early in the second half with one of his famous 'falling leaf' free-kicks, the ball spinning slowly out of his reach when he was convinced he had it covered. Paulinho showed that he too could bend the ball with a cross shot that swerved into the England net from 15 yards.

The next dozen minutes were as amazing as any seen in a Wembley international. Brazilian tempers snapped when French referee Michel Guigue awarded a disputed penalty and the players threatened to go on strike in protest. There was the pantomime of one of the Brazilians walking off with the ball stuck up his jersey. When all the fuss was over John Atyeo, the most reliable marksman in the history of Bristol City Football Club, was astonished to find Gylmar

diving to punch his penalty shot over the bar. Ten minutes later, after Taylor had restored England's lead from a measured pass by Matthews, England were awarded a second penalty. This time Manchester United left-back Roger Byrne shot wide. Johnny Haynes, Duncan Edwards and Byrne gave England total supremacy on the left wide of the field, and over on the right Matthews was playing with a real spring in his step. On a count of chances created England should have won by six or seven goals, but they were not able to consider the match safe until Grainger, a nightclub singer when he was not on the soccer stage, netted from close range six minutes from the final whistle.

THE WITNESSES: England schemer Johnny Haynes: 'Even though we won you could see that the Brazilians had the makings of a magnificent team. That was one of the finest England teams I played with, but there was not a moment when we could relax. We knew we had to hit them with an early goal before they settled, and Tommy Taylor and Colin Grainger came up trumps. For me, it was a joy to have Duncan Edwards and Roger Byrne behind me, and the unsinkable Stanley Matthews turned on one of his great exhibitions.'

Nilton Santos, who played in Brazil's World Cup winning teams of 1958 and 1962: 'It was one of the most memorable experiences of my career to face Stanley Matthews. I had grown up hearing stories about his skill and I found out that none of them were exaggerated. He gave me a very hard afternoon but was always a perfect

41

sportsman and it was a pleasure to play against him. We felt that the referee favoured the home side but we could not argue about the result.'

THE BARNSLEY BOMBER: Born at Smithies, near Barnsley, on January 29, 1932, Tommy Taylor joined Manchester United from Barnsley for what was then a British record fee of £29,999 in March 1953. He was snapped up by Matt Busby after he had scored 26 goals in 44 League matches. Soon after moving to United he won the first of his 19 caps, and he was established as England's regular centre-forward at the time of his death in the Munich air crash. He scored 139 goals in 212 League matches, netted 12 in European Cup matches and another 16 in internationals.

QUOTE: Tommy said after his superb performance against Brazil: 'Stanley Matthews gave us the inspiration to lift our game. You could see that the Brazilians were terrified every time he got the ball and they were so busy worrying about him that it gave the

rest of us more space in which to move. We were determined to hit an early goal and that's why I went out with the intention of shooting at every opportunity.'

FOR THE RECORD: England team manager Walter Winterbottom was confident that he had got a quality team for the 1958 World Cup. But by the time of the finals in Sweden the Munich air crash had robbed England of Roger Byrne, Duncan Edwards and Tommy Taylor, and a few months later Birmingham City right-back Jeff Hall was struck down by polio.

JIMMY GREAVES: 'Tommy Taylor had real class and quality and can be bracketed with Tommy Lawton and Nat Lofthouse as the best of England's post-war centre-forwards. He had excellent positional sense, was strong and determined, and difficult to knock off the ball. I was an apprentice professional on Chelsea's books at the time of that match against Brazil and the stylish way England won made everybody walk a little taller.'

THE CHAMPIONS OF '56

First Division: Manchester United, 60 pts. Runners-up: Blackpool, 49 pts
Second Division: Sheffield Wednesday, 55 pts. Runners-up: Leeds U, 52pts
Third Division (South): Leyton Orient, 66 pts. Runners-up: Brighton, 65pts
Third Division (North): Grimsby T, 68 pts. Runners-up: Derby Co, 63 pts
FA Cup Final: Manchester City 3, Birmingham City 1
Top First Division marksman: Nat Lofthouse (Bolton Wanderers), 33 goals
Footballer of the Year: Bert Trautmann (Manchester City)
Scottish champions: Rangers, 52 pts. Runners-up: Aberdeen, 46 pts
Scottish Cup Final: Heart of Midlothian 3, Celtic 1
European Cup Final: Real Madrid 4, Stade de Reims 3
European Footballer of the Year: Stanley Matthews (Blackpool)

1956-57 — McParland on a collision course with FA Cup fame

Scoreline: Aston Villa 2, Manchester United 1
Venue: Wembley Stadium **Date:** May 4, 1957

THE SETTING: The second and, arguably, the greatest of the Manchester United teams that Matt Busby built won the League championship in 1955-56 by an overwhelming margin of 11 points. Never had the title been captured so conclusively and never by a younger team—the average age was under 23, and they were nicknamed the Busby Babes. They were champions again the following year, this time by eight points. In the final match of the season they journeyed to

Wembley scorching-hot favourites to become the first team this century to complete the League and FA Cup double.

The team standing between the Busby Babes and history were Aston Villa, a club with an even finer pedigree than United. But Villa had been living on the memories of what their ancestors had achieved and few people gave them a prayer of beating all-conquering United. Villa had lived dangerously on the way to Wembley. They were taken to replays by Luton in the third round, Burnley in the sixth round and by West Bromwich Albion in the semi-final. Each time it was a late goal by Irish winger Peter McParland that rescued them from defeat. It was hardly the sort of form to suggest that Villa could disunite a United team that had plundered 83 goals on the way to retaining the League title.

THE TEAMS: **Aston Villa** Sims, Lynn, Aldis, Crowther, Dugdale, Saward, Smith, Sewell, Myerscough, Dixon, McParland.
Manchester United Wood, Foulkes, Byrne, Colman, Blanchflower, Edwards, Berry, Whelan, Taylor, Charlton, Pegg.

THE ACTION: The match was virtually won and lost in the sixth minute when United goalkeeper Ray Wood

Peter McParland, the great rescuer

43

was carried off with a fractured cheek-bone following a collision with flying winger Peter McParland. United were forced to shuffle their side, with Jackie Blanchflower taking over in goal and Duncan Edwards switching to centre-half. Even with ten men the Busby Babes were difficult to master and they restricted the Villa forwards to long-range shots that Blanchflower handled with care.

Ray Wood rejoined the game for the second half, providing nuisance value for United as a right winger. Just as United were beginning to dictate the pattern of play Villa snatched the lead when McParland headed in a floating centre from skipper John Dixon. Five minutes later McParland struck again, this time hammering the loose ball into the net after Dixon's shot had crashed against the crossbar with the gallant Blanchflower beaten.

Lesser sides would have conceded defeat, but United raised their pace and pushed Villa back under an avalanche of attacks. Their only reward was a headed goal by Tommy Taylor from a Duncan Edwards corner in the 83rd minute, and the final whistle signalled that the double would have to wait for another day—and another team.

THE WITNESSES: Matt Busby: 'Losing our goalkeeper so early in the match was too great a blow, but I was proud of the way the team battled right up until the end. I honestly felt we were going to at least force a replay until their second goal. That was the one that took the carpet from under our feet. But this team will be back...'

Pat Saward, Villa's Irish interna-tional left-half: 'Everybody dismissed us as having no chance against United, but I had a feeling our name was on the Cup after all the narrow escapes we had on our way to Wembley. And it must have been worth a bet that Peter McParland would score. He has always been the man for the big occasion. It was sad that Ray Wood had to go off injured, but we had to dismiss that from our minds. Wembley is no place to start showing sympathy.'

MAC THE KNIFE: Born in Newry in 1931, Peter McParland developed his goal-scoring talents as a left-winger with Newry Town and Dundalk before joining Aston Villa in 1952. He had come across to England on the ferry at the age of 16 for a trial with Leeds, but was so badly affected by sea sickness that he returned home after just one training session at Elland Road. Making his international debut for Northern Ireland in 1954, he scored with his very first kick against Wales and went on to win 34 caps. In all he scored 123 League goals and ten in international matches, including five in the 1958 World Cup. He was an outstanding success in the World Cup finals in Sweden. He netted a goal against Argentina, both of Ireland's goals against West Germany and again both goals in the play-off victory against Czechoslovakia that clinched a place in the quarter-finals.

Back on the domestic scene he scored the goal that won the League Cup for Aston Villa in the first final in that competition in 1960-61 before playing out his career with Wolves and then Plymouth. Peter briefly played for Worcester City, tried his luck in the

United States with Atlanta, and then returned to Northern Ireland as manager of Glentoran. He led them into the European Cup in 1970 before becoming a freelance football scout.

QUOTE: Peter McParland: 'Our victory at Wembley should have been one of the great days of my life, but the whole day was ruined by my collision with Ray Wood. The United fans never allowed me to forget it. In those days you could challenge a goalkeeper and it was a complete accident when Ray was injured.'

FOR THE RECORD: The Busby Babes were League champions in 1955-56 and 1956-57, topping the table for 41 of their 42 match programme when they retained the title. Real Madrid beat them 5-3 on aggregate in the 1957 European Cup semifinal and they had reached this stage of the competition again at the time of the Munich tragedy. United players Geoff Bent, Roger Byrne, Eddie Colman, Duncan Edwards, Mark Jones, David Pegg, Tommy Taylor and Liam Whelan were among those killed in Munich on the way home from a successful European Cup quarter-final match against Red Star Belgrade. The heart had been ripped out of the team, but the legend of the Busby Babes lives on in the minds and the memories of all those lucky enough to have seen them in action. A rebuilt United team were back at Wembley for the 1958 FA Cup final where they were beaten by Bolton and two goals from the old lionheart, Nat Lofthouse.

JIMMY GREAVES: 'Peter McParland's controversial collision with Ray Wood has sadly been allowed to overshadow his extraordinary goalscoring achievements. There has rarely been a winger to touch him for cutting in and finishing with a deadly accurate shot. He was a superb opportunist who could win a game with one flash of brilliance. I rated that Busby Babes team the greatest British club side in post-war football, and along with everybody else I was devastated by the news of the Munich air disaster. Precious lives were lost and it knocked a great hole in our game.'

THE CHAMPIONS OF '57

First Division: Manchester United, 64 pts. Runners-up:Tottenham, 56 pts
Second Division: Leicester City, 61 pts. Runners-up: Nottingham Forest, 54pts
Third Division (South): Ipswich Town, 59 pts. Runners-up: Torquay U, 59pts
Third Division (North): Derby County, 63 pts. Runners-up: Hartlepools, 59 pts
FA Cup Final: Aston Villa 2, Manchester United 1
Top First Division marksman: John Charles (Leeds United) 38
Footballer of the Year: Tom Finney (Preston North End)
Scottish champions: Rangers, 55 pts. Runners-up: Heart of Midlothian, 53 pts
Scottish Cup Final: Falkirk 2, Kilmarnock 1 (after a 1-1 draw)
European Cup Final: Real Madrid 2, Fiorentina 0
European Footballer of the Year: Alfredo di Stefano (Real Madrid)

1957-58 Juggling boys from Brazil rule the world soccer stage

Scoreline: Sweden 2, Brazil 5
Venue: Rasunda Stadium, Stockholm **Date:** June 29, 1958

THE SETTING: Since the first World Cup finals in 1930 Brazil had been exhibitionists extraordinary who were continually tripped up by their suspect temperament whenever the major prize was within shooting distance. Critics sneered that they were jugglers who became clowns when the pressure was at its peak. In the 1958 World Cup they set out with steely determination to prove they could win as well as entertain.

They came to Sweden not only with new resolve but also new tactics—a 4-2-4 formation that was to revolutionise world football. Their defence, so often undisciplined and disorganised in the past, was built around two rock-hard central defenders in skipper Bellini and the unyielding Orlando. They were flanked by one of the greatest full-back combinations in the history of football in Nilton and Djalma Santos, and they had behind them the safe hands and lightning reflexes of goalkeeper Gylmar. All attacks flowed from their midfield orchestrators Didi and Zito, who provided the passes for four enormously gifted forwards: explosive right winger Garrincha, a 17-year-old wonder boy called Pele, the silky smooth Vava and probing outside-left Zagalo.

Host country Sweden, strengthened by the return home of their 'gipsy'

Garrincha, the Birdman of Brazil

professionals Hamrin, Liedholm, Skoglund, Gren and Gustavsson, all of whom had become highly paid stars on the Italian stage, were waiting to confront them in the final after beating Cup holders West Germany 3-1 in the semi-final. Sweden's English-born manager George Raynor dismissed talk of a Brazilian walkover. 'Just let's wait and see what happens if we score first,' he said. 'My bet is that Brazil will then panic all over the place.'

THE TEAMS: **Sweden** Svensson, Bergmark, Axbom, Borjesson, Gustavsson, Parling, Hamrin, Gren, Simonsson, Liedholm, Skoglund.

Brazil Gylmar, Djalma Santos, Bellini, Orlando, Nilton Santos, Zito, Didi, Garrincha, Vava, Pele, Zagalo.

THE ACTION: Sweden *did* score first. Nils Liedholm—later to become one of the world's finest coaches—drifted through the Brazilian defence on a rain-sodden surface and netted with a powerful shot in the fourth minute. It was the first time Brazil had been behind in the tournament, but there was no sign of the predicted panic. Instead they hit back with purpose, giving full rein to their 'samba soccer' that produced deftly taken goals scored by Vava and created by Garrincha in the ninth and 30th minutes.

Then, ten minutes into the second half, the young prodigy Pele produced a moment of magic that announced to the world that here was a glittering talent for all to enjoy for years to come. Positioned at the heart of the Swedish penalty area, he caught a high, dropping ball on his thigh, hooked it over his head, whirled round close-marking centre-half Gustavsson in time to meet the ball on the volley and send it crashing into the net.

Mario Zagalo, destined to manage the 1970 World Cup winning team, beat two defenders before shooting Brazil's fourth goal in the 77th minute. In the hectic closing stages Agne Simonsson pulled a goal back for the gallant Swedes before Pele put the finishing touch with a magnificent headed goal from Zagalo's centre.

THE WITNESSES: Pele: 'I wept at the end because a dream had come true. We were not only thrilled with our victory but the manner in which we won. It was a sporting contest and all credit to Sweden for the part that they played. They won our respect. My first goal was purely instinctive. You cannot plan a goal like that.'

Swedish manager George Raynor: 'I thought I had seen everything there is to see in football, but this Brazilian team has brought new dimensions to the game. They now have discipline to go with their flair, and I cannot believe more skilful players than Didi, Pele and Garrincha have ever stepped on to a pitch.'

THE BIRD MAN OF BRAZIL: There has never been another footballer quite like Garrincha, a nickname meaning 'Little Bird.' Born Manoel Francisco dos Santos in the mountain village of Pau Grande in 1933, he was a cripple at birth. An operation left one leg shorter than the other and both legs were so bowed you could have run a pig through them without him knowing. After the operation he had what were virtually two left feet, and he used to wear two left boots when playing. This helped him confuse defenders and when there was a ball at his feet he could be the most bewitching, bewildering and stunning winger who ever pulled a defence apart.

He was such an individualist that even Brazilian coaches, with their preaching of freedom of expression, were petrified of his independent spirit. It was only after a deputation of his team-mates had pleaded on his behalf that he was included in the 1958 World Cup match against Russia after being left on the sidelines for the first two games. Garrincha's contribution to the

World Cup victories of 1958 and 1962 was greater than anybody's. He tried to motivate the Brazilians again in 1966 but a cartilage operation and injuries collected in a car smash had robbed him of much of his unique magic. He won 68 caps while playing for Botafogo, Corinthians and Flamengo.

QUOTE: Garrincha: 'As far as I was concerned football was a game to be enjoyed. I hated tactical talks. Coaches should stick to saying: "Here's the ball...there's the pitch...now get on with it." The great Brazilian teams, such as the World Cup winners in 1958, were never over coached. You did not have to tell a Pele, a Didi or a Vava how to play the game. They just followed their instincts, and that was the way I liked to play it.'

FOR THE RECORD: Brazil beat France by an identical 5-2 scoreline in the semi-final, with Pele contributing a hat-trick. France, inspired by the skill and precision of Raymond Kopa, ham-mered West Germany 6-3 in the third-place play-off. Just Fontaine, Kopa's Marrakesh-born clubmate at Reims, scored four of the goals to lift his tally for the tournament to a record 13. France scored 23 goals in their six matches but conceded 15. Brazil netted a total of 16 goals but, with their new discipline in defence, conceded goals only in the semi-final and final.

JIMMY GREAVES: 'I was in the England World Cup team that Garrincha destroyed with his amazing skill in the 1962 quarter-finals in Chile. The man was a genius. Full stop. He beat our goalkeeper Ron Springett twice, first with a thumping header and then with a viciously swerving 20-yard shot that spun into the net like a Jim Laker off-break. Garrincha was an animal-loving country boy who among other things kept 80 birds in his village home. I doubt if there has been a better attacking team than the 1958 World Cup championship-winning side, with Garrincha and Pele the unbeatable aces in the pack.'

THE CHAMPIONS OF '58

First Division: Wolves, 64 pts. Runners-up: Preston North End, 59 pts
Second Division: West Ham United, 57 pts. Runners-up: Blackburn Rovers, 56 pts
Third Division (South): Brighton, 60 pts. Runners-up: Brentford, 58 pts
Third Division (North): Scunthorpe, 66 pts. Runners-up: Accrington S, 59 pts
FA Cup Final: Bolton Wanderers 2, Manchester United 0
Top First Division marksman: Bobby Smith (Tottenham), 36 goals
Footballer of the Year: Danny Blanchflower (Tottenham)
Scottish champions: Heart of Midlothian, 62 pts. Runners-up: Rangers, 49 pts
Scottish Cup Final: Clyde 1, Hibernian 0
European Cup Final: Real Madrid 3, AC Milan 2 (after extra time)
European Footballer of the Year: Raymond Kopa (Real Madrid)
World Cup Final: Sweden 2, Brazil 5

1958-59 Harmer the Charmer serves gourmet 10-goal banquet

Scoreline: Tottenham Hotspur 10, Everton 4
Venue: White Hart Lane **Date:** October 11, 1958

THE SETTING: On the morning of Saturday, October 11, 1958, Bill Nicholson was officially appointed manager of Tottenham Hotspur. In the afternoon he was given the most remarkable start there has ever been to a manager's career.

Tottenham were in the transition period between their push-and-run triumphs of the early 1950s and the 'Super Spurs' of the early 1960s. Everton, with Bobby Collins—the 'Wee Master'—as their midfield marshal, were struggling three from the bottom of the First Division, a point behind 16th placed Spurs.

The first decision Bill Nicholson made as manager was to recall Tottenham's impish inside-forward Tommy Harmer, known to the Spurs fans as 'The Charmer.' But that afternoon Everton found him more like 'The Harmer' as he pulled them apart with an astounding individual performance. He had a hand—or rather a well-directed foot—in nine goals and scored one himself.

THE TEAMS: **Tottenham Hotspur** Hollowbread, Baker, Hopkins, Blanchflower, Ryden, Iley, Medwin, Harmer, Smith, Stokes, Robb. **Everton** Dunlop, Sanders, Bramwell, King, Jones, Harris (B), Fielding, Harris (J), Hickson, Collins, O'Hara.

THE ACTION: Spurs took the lead in the second minute through Alfie Stokes after an inch-perfect diagonal

Danny Blanchflower, in total command

pass from Harmer had split the Everton defence. The Merseysiders equalised eight minutes later when Jimmy Harris side footed in a Dave Hickson centre. The unfortunate Albert Dunlop, deputising in goal for the injured Jimmy O'Neill, then suffered a nightmare 30 minutes as Spurs ruthlessly smashed five goals past him through skipper Bobby Smith (2), George Robb, Stokes again and Terry Medwin.

The foundation for all the goals was being laid in midfield where Harmer and Danny Blanchflower, both masters of ball control, were in complete command. Jimmy Harris gave Everton brief hope of a revival with a headed goal to make it 6-2 just after half-time, but bulldozing Bobby Smith took his personal haul to four and the irrepressible Harmer helped himself to a goal that was as spectacular as any scored during this gourmet's feast. Bobby Collins lost possession just outside the Everton penalty area. The ball bobbled in front of Harmer who struck it on the half volley from 20 yards and watched almost in disbelief as it rocketed into the roof of the net. It was the first time Tommy had scored a League goal from outside the penalty area.

Everton refused to surrender and the industrious Harris completed his hat-trick from a centre by dashing centre-forward Dave Hickson. Then Bobby Collins, just an inch taller than Harmer, showed that this was a magical match for the wee people when he hammered in a 25-yard drive as both teams crazily pushed everybody forward in all-out attack.

All the goals were scored by forwards until Spurs centre-half John Ryden, limping on the wing, scrambled in Tottenham's tenth goal—the 14th of the match and the seventh of the second-half—in the closing minutes.

THE WITNESSES: Bill Nicholson, who went on to become the greatest manager in Tottenham's history: 'I have never believed in fairy tales in football, but this came close to making me change my mind. In many ways it was a bad advertisement for football because so many of the goals were a result of slip-shod defensive play. But I have to admit it was magnificent entertainment. Little Tommy Harmer played the game of his life. On his day he was as clever a player as I have

ever seen, but he was too often handicapped by his small physique. On this day, he was a giant.'

Danny Blanchflower, equally eloquent with tongue and feet: 'Everton had no idea how to contain Tommy, so we kept feeding the ball to him. It was one of those days when I would have backed him to pass the ball through the eye of a needle. You could say it was a match in which defences did not dominate.'

Albert Dunlop, Everton's battered goalkeeper: 'It ended a nightmare week for me. On the Wednesday I had taken injured Jimmy O'Neill's place in a friendly against a South African international touring team at Goodison Park. We scored seven goals but I let in four. So by the time the Spurs match was over I had picked the ball out of the net 14 times in 180 minutes. I honestly didn't feel that I played that badly against Tottenham. It was one of those crazy games when shots that usually crept past the post crept in, and a game in which everything ran for Spurs. Our biggest mistake was giving Tommy Harmer too much room.'

Jimmy Harris: 'It was a good news-bad news day for me. I was able to tell people that I had scored a hat-trick against Spurs, and then I would mumble the bad news that we had lost 10-4. It was an astonishing game. It's no exaggeration to say we could have had at least four more goals. I don't know who were the more bewildered by it all—the players or the spectators, who got incredible value for their money. Tommy Harmer was the man who won it for Tottenham. It was as if he had the ball on a piece of string.'

THE CHARMER: Tommy Harmer was the 'Tom Thumb' character of football. He stood just 5ft 2in tall and was a bantamweight who looked as if

he could be blown away by a strong wind. But he had mesmeric control of the ball and when conditions suited him he could dominate a match with his passing and dribbling. Born in Hackney on February 2, 1928, he joined Tottenham from amateur club Finchley in 1951 and over the next eight years played 205 League games and scored 47 goals. He lost his place in the first team when John White was bought from Falkirk and he moved on to Watford before winding down his career with Chelsea. It was his goal— a rebound that went in off his groin— that clinched Chelsea's promotion back to the First Division in 1963.

QUOTE: Tommy Harmer: 'I had been out of the League team for the previous four matches and was half expecting to be left out again when I reported to White Hart Lane for the match with Everton. But Bill Nick told me I was in, and everything went right for me that day. I particularly remember my goal because it was about the only time I ever scored from that sort of range. As we came off the pitch I said to Bill Nick, "I hope you're not going to expect ten goals from us every week, boss...!"'

FOR THE RECORD: Only three players from the Spurs team that scored the knockout ten goals against Everton survived as regular members of the 'double' winning side of 1960-61—right-back Peter Baker, artistic right-half Danny Blanchflower and the bulldozing Bobby Smith. The 14 goals scored equalled the aggregate First Division record set in 1892 when Aston Villa hammered Accrington Stanley 12-2.

JIMMY GREAVES: 'I remember that day because I was sitting in the bath at Stamford Bridge soaking out my bruises after Chelsea had been beaten by Bolton—the Bolton defence in those days always left you with bruises—when the Tottenham score was announced on the wireless. I thought I had misheard the result, but the announcer repeated it. Little Tommy Harmer was one of the most under-rated players in the League. He could almost make the ball sit up and talk. If he'd had just a little more power he would have won a cup-boardful of caps.'

THE CHAMPIONS OF '59

First Division: Wolves, 61pts. Runners-up: Manchester United, 55 pts
Second Division: Sheffield Wednesday, 62 pts. Runners-up: Fulham, 60 pts
Third Division: Plymouth Argyle, 62pts. Runners-up: Hull City, 61 pts
Fourth Division: Port Vale, 64 pts. Runners-up: Coventry City, 60 pts
FA Cup Final: Nottingham Forest 2, Luton Town 1
Top First Division marksmen: Jimmy Greaves (Chelsea) and Bobby Smith (Tottenham Hotspur), 32 goals
Footballer of the Year: Syd Owen (Luton Town)
Scottish champions: Rangers, 50 pts. Runners-up: Heart of Midlothian, 48 pts
Scottish Cup Final: St Mirren 3, Aberdeen 1
European Cup Final: Real Madrid 2, Stade de Reims 0
European Footballer of the Year: Alfredo di Stefano (Real Madrid)

1959-60 Alfredo the Great produces the Real thing at Hampden

Scoreline: Real Madrid 7, Eintracht Frankfurt 3
Venue: Hampden Park, Glasgow **Date:** May 18, 1960

THE SETTING: The footballing aristocrats of Real Madrid had dominated
the European Cup since its inception
in 1955, and they were bidding to win
the trophy for a fifth successive year
when they journeyed to Glasgow for
the 1960 final against Eintracht
Frankfurt. Hampden Park was
heaving with 127,621 spectators,
many of them Rangers fans who
believed they were gathering to see
the end of the Real Madrid reign.
They were still flabbergasted by the
way Eintracht had blasted Rangers to
defeat on an aggregate of 12-4 in the
semi-finals, and they were convinced
that any team capable of twice scoring
six goals against their Ibrox idols
could topple the old masters of
Madrid.

Alfredo di Stefano, an Untouchable

Real were a team of soccer merce-
naries, drawn from all points of the
compass to give them punch and panache. Their formidable defence was
shaped around intimidating Uru-
guayan centre-half Santamaria and
Argentinian goalkeeper Dominguez,
but it was for their attacking prow-
ess that they were acclaimed. The
forward line was under the intox-
icating influence of Alfredo di
Stefano, who had come from Colom-
bia via his native Argentina and, at
34, was still one of the world's premier purveyors of the footballing arts.
He pulled the strings for an attack that
included the whiplash shooting of the
incomparable Hungarian Ferenc
Puskas, the pace and dribbling skills
of home-grown heroes Luis Del Sol
and Paco Gento and the invention of
Brazilian winger Canario.

An indication of Real's riches is
that they were able to leave another
Brazilian, 1958 World Cup star Didi,
on the bench. Eurovision was a new
enterprise that brought the game
'live' to an armchair audience of
millions, and across Europe viewers
watched in awe as Real and Eintracht

conjured one of the greatest foot-balling classics of all time.

THE TEAMS: **Real Madrid** Domin-guez, Marquitos, Pachin, Vidal, Santamaria, Zarraga, Canario, Del Sol, di Stefano, Puskas, Gento.
Eintracht Frankfurt Loy, Lutz, Hoefer, Wellbaecher, Eigenbrodt, Stinka, Kress, Lindner, Stein, Pfaff, Meier.

THE ACTION: For 19 minutes the two teams sparred like stylish boxers looking for an opening for the knock-out punch, and then Richard Kress scored for Eintracht to open the flood-gates—and it was goals from Real that came pouring through.

Di Stefano, gliding across the Hampden turf like a Nureyev on grass, equalised eight minutes later at the end of a five-man passing movement that had the spectators purring. It was Scottish teams who first pioneered the measured, 'along-the-carpet' passing game, and the crowd were treated to a perfect exhibition of this sophisti-cated style of play. By half-time di Stefano and Puskas had made it 3-1 to Real, the Puskas goal being a thing of wonder when he somehow managed to fire a rising shot into the net from what seemed an impossible angle.

For 30 minutes in the second half Real produced football so majestic and so artistic that it could have been set to music. By the 70th minute it was Real 6, Eintracht 1—and the peerless Puskas had lifted his personal tally to four goals, including a penalty. Eintracht were playing much more than a walk-on part and after hitting the woodwork twice got the goal they

deserved when centre-forward Erwin Stein scored with a stinging shot in the 72nd minute.

Almost from the restart di Stefano scored Real's seventh goal and what a goal. He moved imperiously from a deep-lying position, exchanging passes with colleagues and always demanding the return of the ball until he ended his advance with a deadly accurate shot that beat goalkeeper Loy all ends up. It was Stein who had the final word in the ten-goal extravaganza when he intercepted a rare mishit pass by Real defender Vidal and rounded goal-keeper Dominguez before scoring.

The breathless crowd gave both teams an ovation that lasted a full 15 minutes after a magnificent match that has been preserved on film as evidence of how the game of football can be played at the highest level.

THE WITNESSES: Puskas: 'Stef and I have our names on the scoresheet, but this match was a triumph for every-body on the pitch—including the Eintracht players. I must also pay tribute to the spectators. Most were neutral but they encouraged us to keep raising the standard of our play.'

Walter Winterbottom, England team-manager who watched the match on Eurovision in Budapest where he was in charge of a tour squad: 'We could not quite believe what we were seeing. It has to be the nearest thing there has ever been to perfection on a football pitch. There was so much to wonder at—the finishing of Puskas, the pace of Gento, the delicate touches from Del Sol but it was di Stefano who left a lasting impression with his display. He is the *complete* player.'

ALFREDO THE GREAT: Capped by his native Argentina and Spain, this legendary centre-forward scored more than 500 goals in 11 years with Real Madrid including 49 in 58 European Cup ties. Surprisingly he never played in a World Cup final series. He travelled with Spain to the 1962 finals in Chile but was injured in a pre-tournament club match. The son of a bus conductor, Alfredo was born in Buenos Aires on July 4, 1926. He was a worshipped member of the River Plate team in Argentina when he shocked his home fans by signing for the then outlawed Colombian club Los Millionarios in 1949. Three years later he was involved in a transfer tug of war between Barcelona and Real Madrid. Real's victory in the battle for his signature coincided with the start of the greatest period in their history, and there was no doubt that it was Alfredo the Great who generated the success.

As moody off the pitch as he was magnificent on it, father-of-six di Stefano wound down his playing career with Espanol before becoming a successful manager with Boca Juniors in his homeland. He then returned to Spain as manager-coach of Valencia and later had a spell in charge at Real.

QUOTE: Di Stefano: 'I played in many fine matches, but none greater than the 1960 European Cup final. Everything we tried worked to perfection. It was an honour and a privilege to be part of it.'

FOR THE RECORD: Real Madrid scored 112 goals and conceded 42 in 37 European Cup matches from 1955 to 1960 during which they won all five finals. They were beaten finalists in 1962 and 1964 and won the Cup for a sixth time in 1966 when beating Partizan Belgrade 2-1 in Brussels.

JIMMY GREAVES: 'I was among the millions who watched the 1960 European Cup Final on Eurovision, and I have often seen it since on video. Everytime I watch it I am astonished at the football. It was a real feast, with di Stefano as the master chef. He is one of the few players who can be put on the same pedestal as Pele.'

THE CHAMPIONS OF '60

First Division: Burnley, 55pts. Runners-up:Wolves, 54 pts
Second Division: Aston Villa, 59 pts. Runners-up: Cardiff City, 58 pts
Third Division: Southampton, 61 pts. Runners-up: Norwich City, 59 pts
Fourth Division: Walsall, 65 pts. Runners-up: Notts County, 60 pts
FA Cup Final: Wolves 3, Blackburn Rovers 0
Top First Division marksman: Dennis Viollet (Manchester United), 32 goals
Footballer of the Year: Bill Slater (Wolves)
Scottish champions: Heart of Midlothian, 54 pts. Runners-up: Kilmarnock, 50 pts
Scottish Cup Final: Rangers 2, Kilmarnock 0
European Cup Final: Real Madrid 7, Eintracht Frankfurt 3
European Nations Cup Final: USSR 2, Yugoslavia 1 (after extra time)
European Footballer of the Year: Luis Suarez (Barcelona)

1960-61 Haynes sends England one over the eight as Scots reel

Scoreline: England 9, Scotland 3
Venue: Wembley Stadium **Date:** April 15, 1961

THE SETTING: England team manager Walter Winterbottom pledged at the start of the 1960-61 season that he would make only injury-forced changes to his side throughout the campaign. He wanted to see what could be achieved by fielding a settled side of players not burdened with the worry that a mistake or brief loss of form could cost them their international place. Overwhelming evidence that the plan worked is that England won all their five matches, scoring 32 goals and conceding eight.

It was one of the best balanced teams ever to represent England, and their newly introduced 4-2-4 formation allowed for boldness and adventure in attack from a springboard of a disciplined and defiant defence. The new system revolved around the precise passing skill in midfield of skipper Johnny Haynes and his versatile side-kick Bobby Robson.

Their dual role was to provide the ball for a four-man firing line that featured the dribbling talent of Bryan Douglas on the right wing and the pace and the power of young blond Bobby Charlton on the left wing. In the middle bulldozing centre-forwad Bobby Smith was striking up an understanding with Chelsea's 20-year-old cheeky chappie Jimmy Greaves, a partnership that was later to prove stunningly productive for Tottenham.

In their first four matches together England hammered Northern Ireland 5-2, Luxembourg 9-0, a star-spangled Spanish team 4-2 and Wales 5-1. But according to many people in the game—particularly north of the border—the real test would come at Wembley from a Scottish side studded with the skills of players of the calibre of Denis Law, Ian St John and wing

Johnny Haynes, the pass master

wizards John McLeod and Davie Wilson. And England, it was claimed, would not find goals easy to come by against a defence that included three of the finest defenders in British football in Eric Caldow, Billy McNeill and the granite-tough Dave Mackay, who during the season just ending had been a main driving force behind Tottenham's historic League and Cup double triumph.

THE TEAMS: **England** Springett, Armfield, McNeil, Robson, Swan, Flowers, Douglas, Greaves, Smith, Haynes, Charlton.
Scotland Haffey, Shearer, Caldow, Mackay, McNeill, McCann, McLeod, Law, St John, Quinn, Wilson.

THE ACTION: Celtic goalkeeper Frank Haffey was like a man in a nightmare as he faced an England attack determined to prove their supremacy over 'the auld enemy.' His positioning was questionable with all three goals carved out by England in the first half, Robson (nine minutes) and Greaves (20 and 29 minutes) putting the finishing touches to moves masterminded by Haynes. Scotland were filled with false optimism that they could get back into the match when Mackay and Wilson pulled it back to 3-2 early in the second half, but they pushed forward suicidally and left themselves wide open to counter attacks.

There were great gaps for Haynes to fill with a procession of paralysing passes, and England sank the Scots without trace under a storm of five goals in 11 minutes. Douglas, Greaves, Smith and two goals from

Haynes himself did the damage, with Motherwell inside-left Quinn interrupting the torture before Bobby Smith hammered goal number nine. Johnny Haynes was carried off shoulder-high by the celebrating England players, while inconsolable goalkeeper Frank Haffey—cruelly dubbed 'Slap-Haffey' by the headline writers—slumped off the Wembley pitch in tears.

THE WITNESSES: Bobby Robson: 'This was Walter Winerbottom's reward for keeping a settled England side together. We had a tremendous team understanding while the Scots were totally disorganised. We were just sad at the end that we had not managed to reach double figures. That would have looked great in the record books. Greavsie and Johnny Haynes were unbelievable that day. They were poetry in motion.'

Denis Law: 'No self respecting Scot would want to talk about this match. I would not dream of putting the blame on any one player, but Frank Haffey himself admitted that on any other day he would have stopped at least five of the goals. Johnny Haynes and Jimmy Greaves could not believe their luck. We gave them the freedom of Wembley.'

THE PASS MASTER: They should put a plaque on the wall down at Fulham's Craven Cottage with the inscription: 'Johnny Haynes passed this way, 1952-1970'. For all those 18 years Haynes was the pass master of English football. His accuracy at distances up to 70 yards was unmatched. He could take a defence apart with one stunning crossfield pass, usu-

ally struck with his right foot. Johnny was the midfield general for England in 56 internationals, 22 of them as captain. He would have collected many more caps but for a car smash in the summer of 1962 that put him out of action for a year.

His unswerving loyalty to Fulham was rewarded in 1961 when chairman Tommy Trinder made him Britain's first £100-a-week footballer. Born in Kentish Town on October 17, 1934, Johnny was a schoolboy international who helped England beat a Scotland team including Dave Mackay 8-2 at Wembley in 1950. He had 17 days as Fulham player-manager in 1968 but gave up the job because he reckoned it was turning his Brylcreemed hair grey before its time. He held his passing out parade with Durban City before returning to Britain to concentrate on a business career. And where did he base himself? In Scotland!

QUOTE: Johnny Haynes: 'There have been few—if any—better England teams than the one I was privileged to lead in that 9-3 win over Scotland. They made poor Frank Haffey the scapegoat but I am convinced we would have run away with the match regardless who was in goal that day.'

FOR THE RECORD: England stretched their unbeaten run to eight matches with an 8-0 victory against Mexico, a 1-1 draw in Portugal and a 3-2 win in Italy before going down 3-1 against Austria in Vienna. They had scored 45 goals and conceded 14 in nine games.

JIMMY GREAVES: 'We paraded the great Haynesie around the Wembley pitch as if he was the FA Cup at the end of a match in which he touched perfection. My abiding memory is of Dave Mackay charging murderously at any Englishman in possession in the closing stages. My Scottish mates in the game like Dave, Denis Law and, of course, the Saint, carry the scar of that demoralising defeat to this day.'

THE CHAMPIONS OF '61

First Division: Tottenham, 66pts. Runners-up:Sheffield Wednesday, 58 pts
Second Division: Ipswich Town, 59 pts. Runners-up: Sheffield United, 58 pts
Third Division: Bury, 68 pts. Runners-up: Walsall, 62 pts
Fourth Division: Peterborough U, 66 pts. Runners up: Crystal Palace, 64 pts
FA Cup Final: Tottenham 2, Leicester City 0
League Cup Final: Aston Villa 3, Rotherham United 2 (0-2, 3-0 after extra time)
Top First Division marksman: Jimmy Greaves (Chelsea), 41 goals
Footballer of the Year: Danny Blanchflower (Tottenham)
Scottish champions: Rangers, 51 pts. Runners-up: Kilmarnock, 50 pts
Scottish Cup Final: Dunfermline Athletic 2, Celtic 0 (after a 0-0 draw)
European Cup Final: Benfica 3, Barcelona 2
European Cup Winners' Cup Final: Fiorentina 4, Rangers 1 (2-0, 2-1)
Inter-Cities Fairs Cup Final: Birmingham City 2, AS Roma 4 (2-2, 0-2)
European Footballer of the Year: Omar Sivori (Juventus)

1961-62 Understudy Amarildo takes a World Cup starring role

Scoreline: Brazil 3, Czechoslovakia 1
Venue: National Stadium, Santiago, Chile **Date:** June 17, 1962

THE SETTING: How do you replace Pele, the greatest footballer on earth? That was the question Brazil had to answer after the jewel in their crown had limped off with a pulled muscle during the early stages of the 1962 World Cup finals. Their answer was to promote Pele's 21-year-old understudy Amarildo and he functioned with such stunning style and skill that by the time the final shots of the tournament had been fired he was being hailed as 'the new Pele.'

Waiting to challenge Amarildo and his gifted team-mates in the World Cup final were Czechoslovakia, a strong, unyielding side that based their success on a physically intimidating defence and fleet-footed forwards who were continually on the look out for the opportunity to launch rapier-quick counter attacks.

Brazil, defending the world title they had captured with memorable flair in Sweden, knew they could not lightly dismiss the Europeans. Countering Brazil's fluid 4-2-4 system with a cautious 3-3-4 formation, the Czechs had managed to smother the South Americans in a goalless first round match during which Pele had collected his injury.

Now the world watched to see if Czechoslovakia could repeat the contain-and-counter tactics against Brazil in the final in Santiago.

Amarildo, starred as the understudy

THE TEAMS: **Brazil** Gylmar, Djalma Santos, Mauro, Zozimo, Nilton Santos, Zito, Didi, Garrincha, Vava, Amarildo, Zagalo.
Czechoslovakia—Schroif, Tichy, Novak, Pluskal, Popluhar, Masopust, Pospichal, Scherer, Kvasniak, Kadraba, Jelinek.

THE ACTION: As in the 1958 final Brazil were stunned by an early goal. Josef Masopust ghosted through the unsuspecting Brazilian defence in the 15th minute to get on the end of a precise pass from Adolf Scherer and

he struck a firm shot left footed past goalkeeper Gylmar. Brazil kept their heads and quickly gained control with their inimitable samba-rhythm football that was being choreographed by Botafogo clubmates Didi, Zagalo, the amazing Amarildo and the extraordinarily inventive Garrincha, who was lucky to be allowed into the final after being sent off for the first time in his career during a spiteful semi-final with Chile.

Within minutes Brazil were level thanks to a superb solo goal by Amarildo. He worked his way down to the bye-line and feinted as if to pass into the centre before sending a shot curling round goalkeeper Wilhelm Schroif.

For nearly an hour the game was evenly balanced, Czechoslovakia battling with grit and determination against a side of superior skills. The Czechs, with European Footballer of the Year Masopust causing problems with his probing runs from midfield, were just beginning to get the confidence to be more adventurous when Brazil struck a killer blow. Zito made a rare strike forward into the opposition half in the 69th minute, exchanged passes with Amarildo and got goal-side of the massive balding figure of centre-back Jan Popluhar to head a swinging cross into the net.

Suddenly all doubts about Brazil's ability to retain the World Cup disappeared, and they started to move with the majesty of true champions. Schroif, one of the safest goalkeepers in European football, now felt as exposed as a nudist in a hailstorm, and 12 minutes from the final whistle he dropped a teasing lob from Djalma Santos and that electric-reflexed centre-forward Vava swept the loose ball into the net before any other Czech defender could move a muscle for his third goal in two finals.

THE WITNESSES: Ramos Mauro, Brazil's captain: 'This is the proudest day of my life. The performance of our team in the 1958 World Cup was a difficult act to follow, but we achieved our one and only aim of retaining the trophy. We were handicapped by the injury to Pele, but Amarildo was almost in Pele's class. There can be no higher praise. Pele has encouraged us every step of the way since his injury and has remained an invaluable member of the squad with his advice and support.'

Wilhelm Schroif, Czechoslovakia's goalkeeper: 'What other team in the world could come up with a player like Amarildo to replace Pele? I know I am being criticised because he beat me at the near post with the first goal. But who would have expected him to curl a shot in from his position? I accept that I should have held the ball that led to the third goal, but all the credit for the first goal must go to Amarildo. It was a magnificent shot.'

THE DEPUTY: As understudy to the one and only Pele, Tavares Amarildo thought he was going to the 1962 finals just for the ride. Suddenly he was promoted to the key position in Brazil's attack and he answered the challenge by scoring two goals against Spain in his World Cup debut. He was little known outside Brazil, but he had earned his place in the squad with a series of outstanding performances for

Botafogo during the previous domestic season when his goals helped lift them to the national championship. His number one fan in Chile was the great man himself, Pele. He was so excited by his deputy's two-goal debut against Spain that he jumped fully clothed into the team bath after the match to congratulate him! Amarildo's flame did not flare for long on the international scene. He was out of the Brazilian squad by the time the 1966 World Cup came round, but his performances in the 1962 tournament assured him of a lasting place in World Cup history.

QUOTE: Amarildo: 'The most memorable moment for me was my goal in the final. I realised that everybody was expecting me to centre, but I knew I could bend the ball around the goalkeeper. Pele was wonderful to me throughout the World Cup tournament and gave me lots of encouragement and advice. He is a gentleman as well as a genius of a footballer.'

FOR THE RECORD: Brazil topped Group 3 in the qualifying rounds, beating Mexico 2-0, Spain 2-1 and drawing 0-0 with group runners-up Czechoslovakia. In the quarter-finals they eliminated England 3-1, while the Czechs beat Hungary 1-0. Host country Chile beat Yugoslavia 1-0 in the third place play-off.

JIMMY GREAVES: 'I recall how relieved we England players were in Chile when we heard that Pele would be missing the quarter-final against us because of his injury. Amarildo was an unknown quantity, but we realised on our way to a 3-1 defeat that Brazil had unearthed yet another gem of a player. He was almost in Pele's class. Just to think, if it hadn't been for Pele's injury he would not even have got a game in the World Cup! He would have walked into any other side.'

THE CHAMPIONS OF '62

First Division: Ipswich Town, 56 pts. Runners-up: Burnley, 53 pts
Second Division: Liverpool, 62 pts. Runners-up: Leyton Orient, 54pts
Third Division: Portsmouth, 65 pts. Runners-up: Grimsby Town, 62pts
Fourth Division: Millwall, 56 pts. Runners-up: Colchester United, 55 pts
FA Cup Final: Tottenham 3, Burnley 1
League Cup Final: Norwich City 4, Rochdale 0 (3-0, 1-0)
Top First Division marksmen: Ray Crawford (Ipswich Town) and Derek Kevan (West Bromwich Albion), 33 goals
Footballer of the Year: Jimmy Adamson (Burnley)
Scottish champions: Dundee, 54 pts. Runners-up: Rangers, 51 pts
Scottish Cup Final: Rangers 2, St Mirren 0
European Cup Final: Benfica 5, Real Madrid 3
European Cup Winners' Cup: Atletico Madrid 3, Fiorentina 0 (after 1-1 draw)
Inter-Cities Fairs Cup: Valencia 7, Barcelona 3 (6-2, 1-1)
European Footballer of the Year: Josef Masopust (Dukla Prague)
World Cup Final: Brazil 3, Czechoslovakia 1

1962-63 Danny's pre-match blarney spurs a remarkable victory

Scoreline: Tottenham Hotspur 5, Atletico Madrid 1
Venue: Feyenoord Stadium, Rotterdam **Date:** June 17, 1962

THE SETTING: No British team had won a major trophy in Europe when Tottenham travelled to Rotterdam for the European Cup Winners' Cup final, and hopes of Spurs breaking the duck were diminished considerably when key man Dave Mackay failed a fitness test on the day of the match. For two years Spurs had been the dominant team on the domestic front, becoming in 1961 the first winners this century of the League Championship

Jimmy Greaves, Old King Goal

and FA Cup double with fluent, flowing football that earned them the appropriate nickname 'Super Spurs.'

The absence of Mackay was a devastating blow because he had been a major force in Tottenham's success, and when the rest of the players realised they had to perform without his battering-ram backing they became less than confident about their chances of mastering an outstanding Atletico Madrid side who were the holders of the Cup Winners' Cup. Manager Bill Nicholson added to their depression when he ran through the strengths of the opposition during a tactical team talk. Skipper Danny Blanchflower was so concerned about the mood of gloom and doom that descended on the team when Mackay gave the thumbs-down that he summoned all the players to a private meeting and made what winger Cliff Jones later described as 'one of the most inspiring speeches I have ever heard.'

Word master Blanchflower, using a mixture of fact and blarney, pumped confidence back into the players and made them believe in their ablity to win. He countered every point that Bill Nicholson had made about the Madrid players by underlining Tottenham's strengths, and he convinced his team-mates that they were superior in every department to the Spaniards. One of his most telling points was to indicate Jimmy Greaves and say: 'Look, we've got Greavsie—the best finisher in the business and playing in the best attack in football. It's Atletico Madrid who have got to do the worrying, not us.'

THE TEAMS: **Tottenham** Brown, Baker, Henry, Blanchflower, Norman, Marchi, Jones, White, Smith, Greaves, Dyson.
Atletico Madrid Madinabeytia, Rivilla, Rodriguez, Ramiro, Griffa, Glaria, Jones, Adelardo, Chuzo, Mendonca, Collar.

THE ACTION: Manager Bill Nicholson, one of the finest tacticians in the game, deserves the credit for the fact that Tottenham took the lead in the 16th minute. He had spotted during a spying mission to Madrid that the Atletico defence were slow to cover down the left side and he instructed that full use should be made of the blistering speed of Cliff Jones. The Welsh international, moving with the pace and determination of a rugby wing-threequarter, sprinted to meet a neatly placed pass from Bobby Smith and his accurate centre was deftly guided left footed into the net by Jimmy Greaves, the Fagin of the penalty area who plucked goals out of nowhere like a pickpocket.

It was on the wings where Tottenham were monopolising the match, with Jones and tiny Terry Dyson running the Spanish full backs into dizzy disorder. They combined to set up goal number two in the 32nd minute, exchanging passes before releasing the ball to Smith who laid it back for John White to rifle a low shot into the net.

Atletico Madrid revived their flickering flame of hope in the first minute of the second half when Collar scored from the penalty spot after Ron Henry had fisted the ball off the goal-line. For 20 minutes Tottenham lost their way as the Cup holders forced a series of corner-kicks, but Tottenham's defence—with Tony Marchi giving a solid display in place of injured Mackay—managed to stifle the Spanish storm. It was Dyson who dynamited the Atletico comeback when his hanging cross was fumbled into the net by goalkeeper Madinabeytia. Dyson became a man inspired and laid on a goal for Greavsie before putting the seal on a memorable performance with a scorching shot at the end of a weaving 30-yard run. His first goal was a fluke, but his second was a masterpiece.

THE WITNESSES: Bill Nicholson: 'Terry Dyson played better that night than at any time in his life. To be honest, I did not think he could turn on a performance like that. I have to admit that I was worried for about 20 minutes in the second half, and it took a fluke goal for us to regain control.'

Terry Dyson: 'I enjoyed every second of the match, and was determined that we should win. Danny Blanchflower pumped us all full of confidence before the game and we went out determined to win. The second goal I scored was the best of my life. Greavsie said I should hang up my boots and retire because I couldn't top it!'

Danny Blanchflower: 'I just simply persuaded the team to adopt a positive

attitude. It struck me that Bill Nicholson, a marvellous manager, had allowed himself to become a little too obsessed by the strengths of Atletico. He did such a thorough job cataloguing their skills that he got us worrying whether we could live with them. I decided to balance all that Bill said by pointing out our many assets.'

THE MASTER: Jimmy Greaves was arguably the greatest finisher of all time. He exploded on the First Division scene with Chelsea in 1957, a spiky-haired 17-year-old prodigy who pumped in goals with astonishing ease. He scored in every major debut match throughout his career. After four unhappy months in Italy with AC Milan in 1960 he was signed by Spurs for a then record fee of £99,999. He had the best years of his footballing life at Tottenham, first as a plundering partner to the barnstorming Bobby Smith and then in double harness with the elegant Alan Gilzean. After nine

seasons at Spurs he wound down his League career with West Ham before retiring from top-flight football at the relatively young age of 31. By then he had amassed 357 First Division goals and 44 in 57 internationals for England. He conquered a well-publicised drink problem to fashion a new career for himself as a television personality noted for the same sort of cheeky, entertaining output that marked his days as the incomparable artful dodger of the penalty area.

JIMMY GREAVES: 'It should be Terry Dyson or Danny Blanchflower featuring in this chapter rather than me. Terry played out of his skin against Atletico, but it was Danny who won the match for us before a ball was kicked. I wish I'd got what he said on a tape recorder because it was in the Churchill class as a rallying speech and would have served as a lesson to all football managers and coaches on how to motivate a team.'

THE CHAMPIONS OF '63

First Division: Everton, 61 pts. Runners-up: Tottenham, 55 pts
Second Division: Stoke City, 53 pts. Runners-up: Chelsea, 52pts
Third Division: Northampton Town, 62 pts. Runners-up: Swindon Town, 58 pts
Fourth Division: Brentford, 62 pts. Runners-up: Oldham Athletic, 59 pts
FA Cup Final: Manchester United 3, Leicester City 1
League Cup Final: Birmingham City 3, Aston Villa 1 (3-1, 0-0)
Top First Division marksman: Jimmy Greaves (Tottenham), 37 goals
Footballer of the Year: Stanley Matthews (Stoke City)
Scottish champions: Rangers, 57 pts. Runners-up: Kilmarnock, 48 pts
Scottish Cup Final: Rangers 3, Celtic 0 (after 1-1 draw)
European Cup Final: AC Milan 2, Benfica 1
European Cup Winners' Cup Final: Tottenham 5, Atletico Madrid 1
Inter-Cities Fairs Cup Final: Dynamo Zagreb 1, Valencia 4 (1-2, 0-2)
European Footballer of the Year: Lev Yashin (Moscow Dynamo)

1963-64 England are pulverised as King Pele runs riot in Rio

Scoreline: Brazil 5, England 1
Venue: Maracana Stadium, Rio de Janeiro **Date:** May 30, 1964

THE SETTING: Which of the hundreds of matches touched with the magic of Pele—Brazil's superman for all seasons—should be featured? It is like trying to choose the best of Beethoven or the greatest work of Van Gogh. The Aladdin's Cave of choices was made easier by the evidence of the players who witnessed his first ever performance against England during a prestige international tournament in Brazil in the summer of 1964. Even by Pele's skyscraping standards it was an exhibition of exceptional brilliance. Brazil were the current world champions and in opponents England they were facing the team that would take over their crown two years later.

Pele, the King

Manager Alf Ramsey was still searching for his 1966 players and formation. Only four of the players selected for the match against Brazil would survive for the World Cup final at Wembley Stadium—fullbacks George Cohen and Ray Wilson, skipper Bobby Moore and Manchester United striker Bobby Charlton, who was yet to make the transition to a scheming role. Surprisingly for such a crucial contest, Ramsey decided to leave regular first-choice goalkeeper Gordon Banks on the sidelines and to call in debutant Tony Waiters, who was a lifeguard on Blackpool beach when not keeping goal for the local club. Brazil relied on a mixture of the old and the new. Goalkeeper Gylmar and gifted striker Vava were survivors of the 1958 and 1962 World Cup winning squads along with the incomparable Pele, and among the newcomers were full-backs Carlos Alberto and Brito, and a gazelle of a forward called Gerson, all of whom would write their names into World Cup history in the 1970 finals.

THE TEAMS: **Brazil** Gylmar, Carlos Alberto, Brito, Diaz, Joel, Rildo, Julinho, Gerson, Vava, Pele, Rinaldo.

England Waiters, Cohen, Wilson, Milne, Norman, Moore, Thompson, Greaves, Byrne, Eastham, Charlton.

THE ACTION: Alf Ramsey decided not to give any detailed marking instructions for Pele. 'Whoever is closest to him at set pieces can take responsibility for him,' Alf said in a team meeting before the kick-off. 'Let's try to stop the ball getting through to him and if it does whichever defender is nearest must pick him up.' There was plenty of time for tactical talking because Brazil arrived at the ground an hour late with a fuming Ramsey about to call the match off. He saw it as a deliberate ploy to unsettle the England players before they had to go out in front of 100,000 frenzied fans who were filling the night air with rockets and firecrackers.

Ramsey's plan of virtually ignoring Pele seemed to work in the first half during which centre-forward Johnny Byrne had a shot cleared off the goal-line and Jimmy Greaves was just a coat of paint off target with a shot on the turn. At half-time only a goal by left winger Rinaldo separated the two teams, but the fact that it had been created by a run from Pele in which he glided past four tackles was a warning of what was to come.

Greavsie gave England brief hope of taking command when he stole a typical goal from close range midway through the second half, but then Pele took over and pulverised England with a purple patch that produced three goals in five minutes. Twice he earned free-kicks just outside the penalty area while dancing through the England defence juggling the ball like a circus performer. Waiters was completely deceived by swerving free-kicks that brought spectacular goals from wingers Rinaldo and Julinho. Pele also contributed a magical goal of his own, pushing the ball through the legs of first Bobby Moore and then Maurice Norman before sending a shot screaming into the England net from 25 yards. Suddenly a scoreline that had read a healthy 1-1 was now a Pele-inspired 4-1. Still the master was not finished. He ran the England defence to such confusion that they failed to spot Diaz coming through from a deep position to score goal number five two minutes from the end.

THE WITNESSES: Bobby Moore: 'The only difference between the two teams was Pele. But what a difference! He played as if he was from another planet. I made the mistake of trying to tackle him out on the touchline. He waited for me to commit myself and was then away and past me like the wind. I had been completely hoodwinked by a dip from his shoulder. The man is a magician.'

Tony Waiters, manager of Canada in the 1986 World Cup finals: 'What a match for my England debut! For an hour I thought we were going to get a draw or even a victory. Then Pele suddenly moved up a gear and had us at sixes and sevens. I have never seen ball control like it. We had some great defenders in that team but they just could not get near him. It would have been marvellous stuff to watch if we had not been on the receiving end.'

George Eastham: 'For 20 minutes Pele played us almost on his own. It was an incredible performance. We forwards dropped back to try to help out in defence but the more people he had in front of him the more inspired he became. We could have put a parade of guards in front of him and he would still have run rings round them. It was heart breaking for us because we had been the better team for much of the game. The 5-1 score-line was really flattering to Brazil. We had given them a fright until Pele took command.'

Johnny Byrne: 'What people have never realised about Pele is the speed of the man. He had unbelievable skill that we could all see but it was only when you were chasing him that you realised that he could motor like an Olympic sprinter. I was running back after him when he was on a run through the England defence and it was all I could do to keep pace with him—and he had the ball at his feet. He had left two of our defenders standing and then fired a right footed shot while in full stride. The ball whistled into the net from 25 yards and as it left him Pele shouted, "G-o-a-l!" He was as enthusiastic about his football as a young kid. I felt it a privilege to be on the same pitch.'

THE KING: Edson Arantes do Nascimento—the one and only Pele—was born in near poverty in Tres Coracoes (Three Hearts), Bauru, on October 23, 1940. He came under the influence of former Brazilian World Cup player Waldemar de Brito while playing for his local team, Noroeste. De Brito recommended him to Santos, where he quickly emerged as an international star, making his debut for Brazil at the age of 16 and getting world acclaim

the following season for his magnificent performances in the 1958 World Cup finals.

Wearing the number 10 shirt that was to become his trademark, Pele averaged 94 goals a season in his first three years with Santos and rival coaches tried to mark him out of games by putting as many as four defenders on him. Santos, using Pele as their calling card, toured the world playing exhibition matches.

His World Cup record is second to none. He is the only player to have been a member of three World Cup winning teams (1958, 1962 and 1970), although he missed the final stages of the 1962 tournament because of a pulled muscle. His total World Cup appearances including his two matches in 1966 were 14, and he scored in the 1958 and 1970 finals. He was brutally hacked out of the 1966 tournament, the victim of the sort of vicious tackling that he had to contend with throughout his career.

Although usually a sporting opponent, he had a touchpaper temperament if defenders deliberately fouled him and there were several times in his career when he was guilty of retaliating against players with lesser ability who tried to literally chop him down to size. The worst demonstration of Pele's ugly temper came in Brazil's second match of the 1964 tournament after the 5-1 victory over England. Brazil were playing arch rivals Argentina and right from the first whistle defender Messiano made it clear that his one intention was to stop Pele from playing. He kicked him, tripped him, spat at him, wrestled him to the floor and pulled his shirt anytime he seemed likely to get

past. Finally, after about 30 minutes of this treatment, Pele completely lost his temper. He took a running jump at Messiano and butted him full in the face. The Argentinian was carried off with a broken nose and, incredibly, the Swiss referee—fearing a violent crowd reaction—let Pele play on. Pele scored 1,216 goals in 1,254 matches from 1956 until his retirement in 1974. His peak year for goals was 1958 when he scored 139 times. In 1975 he made a comeback with New York Cosmos, giving soccer in the United States the kick of life. He made a farewell appearance against Santos in New Jersey on October 1, 1977. It was his 1,363rd match and he naturally marked it with a goal to bring his career total to 1,281.

FOR THE RECORD: The four-nation international tournament was won by Argentina, with three victories from three matches. Brazil finished second

and England and Portugal—who drew 1-1—were equal third with one point each. Argentina beat Brazil 3-0 and England 1-0 in a match in which their skipper Antonio Rattin was the outstanding player. Two years later he was sent off against England at Wembley in the 1966 World Cup quarter-finals when England won 1-0.

JIMMY GREAVES: 'In a word, Pele was a genius. I'm sure he could have been a world-class gymnast. He had wonderful spring, perfect balance, could shoot with either foot, was as brave as a lion and had tremendous vision. If Maradona is valued at £6 million, Pele at his peak today would be worth £10 million. We held the Brazilians for an hour in Rio and were just beginning to think in terms of trying to win the game when Pele ran riot. He sold our defence more dummies than Mothercare and won the match on his own.'

THE CHAMPIONS OF '64

First Division: Liverpool, 57 pts. Runners-up: Manchester United, 53 pts
Second Division: Leeds United, 63 pts. Runners-up: Sunderland, 61 pts
Third Division: Coventry City, 60 pts. Runners-up: Crystal Palace, 60 pts
Fourth Division: Gillingham, 60 pts. Runners-up: Carlisle United, 60 pts
FA Cup Final: West Ham United 3, Preston North End 2
League Cup Final: Leicester City 4, Stoke City 3 (1-1, 3-2)
Top First Division marksman: Jimmy Greaves (Tottenham), 35 goals
Footballer of the Year: Bobby Moore (West Ham United)
Scottish champions: Rangers, 55 pts. Runners-up: Kilmarnock, 49 pts
Scottish Cup Final: Rangers 3, Dundee 1
European Cup Final: Inter Milan 3, Real Madrid 1
European Cup Winners' Cup: Sp. Lisbon 1, MTK Budapest 0 (after 3-3 draw)
Inter-Cities Fairs Cup: Real Zaragoza 2, Valencia 1
European Nations Cup Final: Spain 2, USSR 1
European Footballer of the Year: Denis Law (Manchester United)

1964-65 Moore the Majestic reigns as Sealey seals victory

Scoreline: West Ham United 2, Munich 1860 0
Venue: Wembley Stadium **Date:** May 19, 1965

THE SETTING: West Ham's contribution to football in the mid-60s stretched far beyond the boundaries of the domestic scene. They won the FA Cup and the European Cup Winners' Cup with stylish soccer that was tactically a decade ahead of its time. The three main motivators—Bobby Moore, Geoff Hurst and Martin Peters—knitted West Ham-designed moves into the England playing pattern and they were massively influential in the 1966 World Cup triumph.

There have been more successful and resilient sides than Ron Greenwood's Hammers but rarely one as attractive and entertaining. Their peak performance came, fittingly, in front of their biggest audience when 100,000 spectators at Wembley and millions more watching on Eurovision saw West Ham come close to perfection in a memorable European Cup Winners' Cup final against Munich 1860.

Manager Greenwood selected a side showing four changes from the team that had pipped Second Division Preston 3-2 in a thrilling FA Cup encounter in 1964. Joe Kirkup replaced the veteran John Bond at right-back. The elegant Martin Peters took Eddie Bovington's place in midfield and virtual unknowns Alan Sealey and Brian Dear came into the attack for injured England internationals Johnny

Bobby Moore, the motivator

Byrne and Peter Brabrook. Munich, who eliminated Cup favourites Torino in the semi-final, had just finished third in the fiercely contested Bundesliga and fielded four West German internationals. It looked an evenly balanced contest, and Greenwood told his players: 'We must adopt a positive attitude. Let's go out there to win and *to win in style.*' Across the concrete corridor separating the dressing-rooms at Wembley respected Munich coach Max Merkel was giving almost identical instructions. He wanted victory *in style.*

THE TEAMS: **West Ham United**
Standen, Kirkup, Burkett, Peters, Brown, Moore, Sealey, Boyce, Hurst, Dear, Sissons.
Munich 1860 Radenkovic, Wagner, Kohlars, Bena, Reich, Luttrop, Heiss, Kuppers, Brunnenmeier, Grosser, Rebele.

THE ACTION: West Ham fans feared that their attack would not be firing on all cyclinders because of the absence of dribbling wingman Peter Brabrook and highly skilled centre-forward Johnny 'Budgie' Byrne, but within minutes their home-produced stand-ins Alan Sealey and Brian Dear were making daring inroads deep into the Munich defence. Radenkovic, a colourful goalkeeper from Yugoslavia, made a string of superb saves for Munich, and at the opposite end the immaculate Bobby Moore shepherded his defence into keeping composed under the pressure of swift counter attacks. Hammers goalkeeper Jim Standen, a summertime cricketer with Worcestershire, held two magnificent catches from point-blank snap shots by Rudi Brunnenmeier, Munich's roving German international centre-forward and skipper.

From first kick to last, both teams produced bold, adventurous and imaginative football and there could have been a shoal of goals at either end before Sealey at last broke the deadlock in the 69th minute. It was Ron Boyce, nicknamed 'Ticker' because his non-stop running in midfield made the team tick, who set the goal up moments after the jinking John Sissons had crashed a shot against a post to interrupt a tide of Munich raids. Boyce sent a defence-splitting pass arrowing through to Sealey who instantly converted it into a goal with a low right-footed shot from 12 yards. Sealey, born within goal-kicking distance of West Ham's Upton Park ground, cartwheeled with delight and just 90 seconds later had even more reason for celebration. Moore flighted a free-kick to Martin Peters who smartly flicked it into the goalmouth where Sealey charged forward to force the ball over the goal-line from two yards. In the final moments of a glorious game Sissons again smashed a shot against the woodwork. It was sad for the gifted winger but justice for Munich, who were certainly not deserving of a three-goal defeat. They had played a proud part in a classic contest. Bobby Moore led his team up the Wembley steps to collect the trophy a year and 17 days after making the same journey to receive the FA Cup. He would complete an historic hat-trick in 1966.

THE WITNESSES: Ron Greenwood: 'If anybody wants to know what my thinking on football is all about I would like to be judged on this match. It was close to perfection and presented the game in the best possible light. We had worked for this for four years and for us it was like reaching the summit of Everest.'

Alan Sealey: 'I had to pinch myself to make sure it was all true. I had got married just four days earlier and my wife was watching from the stands. In the previous season I had scored only three goals, and I would have been happy with just one. I did a somersault when I scored the first goal. I wanted to jump over the stand when the second goal went in.'

THE CAPTAIN: There has rarely been a better 'big occasion' player than Bobby Moore, who collected a record 108 caps for England and equalled the Billy Wright record of captaining the team in 90 matches. The one and only Pele paid him the ultimate compliment of calling him 'the greatest defender in the world.' Born in Barking on April 12, 1941, Bobby skippered the England youth team while winning a record 18 caps. He made his West Ham debut in 1958, replacing his great pal Malcolm Allison whose career was cut short by tuberculosis. In 1962 he succeeded Bobby Robson in the England team and he took over from Jimmy Armfield as captain in 1963-64. He played 545 League matches for West Ham before switching to Fulham late in his career. In his first season at Craven Cottage he played a major part in steering Fulham to their first ever FA Cup final. Ironically they were beaten at Wembley by West Ham.

FOR THE RECORD: West Ham and Munich 1860 shared a United Nations Fair Play Award for their sportsmanship and skill in the 1965 Wembley classic. Hammers went for a Cup hattrick in 1966 but were beaten 5-3 by West Bromwich Albion in a two-leg League Cup final.

JIMMY GREAVES: 'West Ham produced one of the finest footballing displays ever seen at Wembley, and a lot of the credit must go to Munich for matching West Ham's spirit of adventure. Mooro was his usual reliable and ice-cool self. England have not had a finer servant. He was an immaculate defender, stamping his authority on every match, and he read the game better than any other player.'

THE CHAMPIONS OF '65

First Division: Manchester United, 61 pts. Runners-up: Leeds United, 61 pts
Second Division: Newcastle U, 57 pts. Runners-up: Northampton T, 56 pts
Third Division: Carlisle United, 60 pts. Runners-up: Bristol City, 59 pts
Fourth Division: Brighton, 63 pts. Runners-up: Millwall, 62 pts
FA Cup Final: Liverpool 2, Leeds United 1 (after extra time)
League Cup Final: Chelsea 3, Leicester City 2 (3-2, 0-0)
Top First Division marksmen: Jimmy Greaves (Tottenham Hotspur) and Andy McEvoy (Blackburn Rovers), 29 goals
Footballer of the Year: Bobby Collins (Leeds United)
Scottish champions: Kilmarnock, 50 pts. Runners-up: Heart of Midlothian, 50 pts
Scottish Cup Final: Celtic 3, Dunfermline 2
Scottish Player of the Year: Billy McNeill (Celtic)
European Cup Final: Inter-Milan 1, Benfica 0
European Cup Winners' Cup: West Ham United 2, Munich 1860 0
Inter-Cities Fairs Cup Final: Juventus 0, Ferencvaros 1
European Footballer of the Year: Eusebio (Benfica)

1965-66 | The Wingless Wonders rule the world at Wembley

Scoreline: England 4, West Germany 2 (after extra-time)
Venue: Wembley Stadium **Date:** July 30, 1966

THE SETTING: England team manager Alf Ramsey, who was usually as mean with his quotes as a miser with his money, stepped out of character six months before the 1966 World Cup finals when he stated quite categorically: 'England will win the World Cup.' He had tossed aside his customary cloak of caution to go against history because it was 32 years since the host country had won the tournament. Outsiders found it difficult to understand Ramsey's confidence during the group matches when England made heavy work of a goalless draw with Uruguay, and hardly set the world alight with victories over Mexico and France.

In a bitterly fought quarter-final England accounted for a talented but temperamental Argentinian side 1-0 after skipper Antonio Rattin had been ordered off because of his contemptuous attitude towards the referee.

The winning goal against Argentina was scored by West Ham striker Geoff Hurst, who was making his World Cup debut because of an injury to Jimmy Greaves. For the first time in the tournament England played without a recognised winger. England's 'Wingless Wonders' were born and their 4-3-3 formation was to change the face of football.

Ramsey's 'We will win' prediction gathered a bandwagon of support when England sparkled to a 2-1 victory over Eusebio-inspired Portugal in a high quality semi-final that erased the memory of much of the tedium and tantrums of the early matches. This was the performance that convinced Ramsey that he should select the same side for the final,

Geoff Hurst, hat-trick hero

71

which meant there was no place for fit-again Jimmy Greaves who was arguably the greatest goal striker of modern times. It was a gamble by Ramsey... a calculated gamble launched against a powerful West German team that had reached the final with a quarter-final elimination of Uruguay and a semi-final win over the USSR.

In Uwe Seeler, Ziggy Held and Helmut Haller the Germans had a striking force that could devastate any defence if given freedom of movement, and lurking out on the left was the tricky but unpredictable Lothar Emmerich who had one of the fiercest left foot shots in the game.

Motivating the team from midfield were the composed, 20-year-old Franz Beckenbauer and elegant, left-footed pass master Wolfgang Overath. They had strength in depth in defence with Horst Höttges and Karl-Heinz Schnellinger giving them flair at full-back while Willie Schulz and Wolfgang Weber were solid and reliable partners at the heart of the defence. The one big question mark was against goalkeeper Hans Tilkowski, whom the England players had nicknamed 'Dracula' because he seemed so frightened of crosses.

THE TEAMS (both in 4-3-3):
England Banks, Cohen, Jack Charlton, Moore, Wilson, Stiles, Bobby Charlton, Peters, Ball, Hunt, Hurst.
West Germany Tilkowski, Höttges, Schulz, Weber, Schnellinger, Haller, Beckenbauer, Overath, Seeler, Held, Emmerich.

THE ACTION: Two sharp showers just before the kick-off made the surface of the Wembley pitch quick and treacherous. Players on both sides showed nerves that were as exposed as barbed wire on a wall, and there was so much tension around that it was inevitable that a goal was going to be born out of an error. What nobody expected was that the mistake would be made by the most reliable of all England's players—the cool, commanding Ray Wilson, who had not put a foot wrong throughout the tournament.

The game was into its 13th minute when Wilson looked to have time and room in which to clear a Ziggy Held cross. But instead of his usual pinpoint accuracy, he pushed the ball to the feet of Helmut Haller, a deadly enough marksman without need of such charitable assistance. He turned and gleefully squeezed a low shot just inside the left post from 12 yards. England 0, West Germany 1. The home fans tried to console themselves with the fact that the World Cup had not been won by the side which scored first in any of the four post-war finals.

It was after this startling goal that England revealed the discipline and determination that Alf Ramsey had drilled into them during the build-up to the finals. There was no hint of panic or loss of composure. The unflappable Wilson carried on in his usual immaculate style with a poker-face manner that was to serve him well in his later profession as a funeral director.

If anything, the goal acted as an inspiration to England and they began

Alan Ball, the marathon man

semi-final and had been so impressed by a phenomenal display from Bobby Charlton that he delegated Beckenbauer to a man-to-man marking job on the Manchester United schemer. This meant that the two most creative players on the pitch were cancelling each other out.

Roger Hunt squandered a good chance to give England the lead and thoughts briefly came to the surface that Ramsey had been wrong to leave Greavsie on the sidelines, but England were gradually getting on top—particularly down the right side of the pitch where Alan Ball, the 21-year-old 'baby' of the England team, was providing action to go with his words. He had told room-mate Nobby 'The Toothless Tiger' Stiles before the match in that Clitheroe Kid voice of his: 'That Schnellinger's made for me. I'll give him such a chasing that he won't know what day it is.'

It was fitting that the red-shirted, red-haired Ball—covering every inch of the right side of the Wembley pitch like the fire from a flamethrower—should set up what most people thought was the match-winning goal 12 minutes from the end. His shot was pushed out by Tilkowski for a corner that the Blackpool marathon runner took himself. The ball dropped at the feet of Hurst whose shot was deflected by Höttges into the path of Martin Peters. He almost had enough time to pick his spot as he clinically buried the ball into the back of the net from six yards.

The Germans looked out on their feet and there was a growing victory roar rolling around Wembley. The cheers died in thousands of throats

to settle into their stride. They were rewarded for their professional attitude with an equaliser just six minutes later. Overath tripped Bobby Moore and the England skipper took an instant free-kick while the German defenders were still regrouping. He floated the ball in from the left and his West Ham team-mate Geoff Hurst drifted behind the German defence to glide a header wide of Tilkowski, who was still feeling the effects of an early collision with Hurst in which he was knocked out.

The action was fast and fluctuating with neither side able to claim domination. West German team manager Helmut Schöen had watched England's victory against Portugal in the when, with less than a minute to go, Swiss referee Gottfried Dienst harshly ruled that Jack Charlton had fouled Germany's spring-heeled skipper Uwe Seeler.

Emmerich, who had hardly been allowed a kick by his marker George Cohen, crashed the free-kick towards goal with his feared left foot. The ball was deflected—Bobby Moore argued that it was by a German hand—to Held, who half hit the ball across the face of the goal. Gordon Banks, the outstanding goalkeeper in the tournament, was wrong footed because he had reacted for a clean shot from Held. The ball bobbled loose to defender Wolfgang Weber who bundled it into the England net with the last kick of ordinary time.

Players of both sides tumbled to the ground in exhaustion as the referee's whistle signalled extra time. Alf Ramsey came striding purposefully on to the pitch and did a quick walkie-talkie tour of his players, offering them encouragement and advice. He pointed to the drained West German players. 'Look at them,' he said. 'They're finished. You've beaten them once. Now go and do it again.'

The fiercely competitive Nobby Stiles, socks rolled down to his ankles and teeth removed, flourished a fist at his team-mates. 'Come on, lads,' he said in his broad Mancunian accent . 'Let's stoof the boogers.' Battling Alan Ball responded with a run and a shot in the second minute of extra time that brought a fine save from Tilkowski, who had shaken off his early indecision.

Eight minutes later, after a Bobby

Charlton shot from a pass by brother Jack had been turned on to a post, Ball tore past the exhausted Schnellinger yet again. This time his centre found Geoff Hurst who spun round and crashed a shot against the underside of the bar. As the ball bounced down, Roger Hunt—the England player closest to the net—immediately whirled round in celebration of a goal. His opinion was supported by Russian linesman Tofik Bakhramov who signalled that the ball had crossed the line, a decision disputed to this day by the Germans.

Skipper Seeler called for one more effort from team-mates who had run themselves to the edge of exhaustion. Beckenbauer, at last released from his negative containment of Bobby Charlton, pushed forward from midfield and was shaping to shoot when he was dispossessed by a tigerish tackle from the resolute Stiles who was displaying the brand of courage and willpower for which medals are awarded in the field of battle.

Then Haller battled his way through the middle only to be foiled by the long legs of Jack Charlton. The Germans were so committed to all-out attack that they were leaving inviting gaps in their own penalty area.

Celebrating England fans were trespassing over the touchline in anticipation of the final whistle when hero-of-the-hour Hurst ended all arguments in the closing seconds of the match. He chased a measured pass from the majestic Moore and hammered in a left foot shot that left Tilkowski rooted in front of his goal like a man facing a firing squad. With

the last kick of the match Hurst had become the first man to complete a World Cup hat-trick, and for the first time the World Cup had come to the birthplace of organised football.

THE WITNESSES: Alf Ramsey: 'Every player did England proud. They showed tremendous character in extra time and thoroughly deserved their victory. It was not an easy decision to leave out Jimmy Greaves, but I felt that this was the right team for the job we faced. Yes, it was difficult having to omit Greaves — just as it was tough having to leave out ten other players in the squad. They have all played their part simply by being here. Our team spirit on and off the pitch has been a key factor in our success. It has been suggested that I seemed less than happy at the final whistle, but I could not leap to my feet simply because I was pinned down by trainer Harold Shepherdson and team doctor Alan Bass who were so busy congratulating me that I was unable to get off the bench.'

Helmut Schöen: 'We could argue that Geoff Hurst's second goal did not cross the line, but why waste breath? The referee and linesman said it was a goal so that is all there is to it. It would be a pity to have controversey spoil an occasion in which the game of football was a winner. It was a splendid match and I concede that England on the day were just that little bit better than us.'

Alan Ball: 'I died several times out on that pitch. It was really exhausting, but I kept telling myself that this was the most important match of my life and that we had to win it.'

Martin Peters: 'I will never forget the goal I scored. I had time to place my shot and knew it was going into the net from the moment I made contact. It was the greatest moment of my career, and I thought it was going to be the winner until that last-minute equaliser. Geoff went on to complete his hat-trick and few people were able to recall who scored our other goal. But for me it will always be a treasured memory.'

THE HAT-TRICK HERO: West Ham manager Ron Greenwood transformed Geoff Hurst's career—and his life—when he switched him from the role of 'just another' half-back to a striker who demolished defences with his pace and power. The son of a non-League professional, Hurst was born in Ashton-under-Lyne, Lancashire, on December 8, 1941. He was selected for the England squad for the first time in the 1965-66 season, making his debut in a 1-0 victory over West Germany in a friendly international at Wembley on February 23, 1966. He scored 24 goals in 49 matches for England. His League goals haul for West Ham was 180. He added 22 League goals for Stoke before closing his career with West Bromwich Albion. He became player-manager of Telford United, assisted Ron Greenwood with the coaching of the England team and then managed Chelsea until 1981 before going into the world of insurance along with his old West Ham and England team-mate Martin Peters. As thrilled as he was by his World Cup final hat-trick, Geoff selects as his most memorable goal his winner against Argentina in the quarter-final. 'That gave me more satisfaction than any other goal I ever scored,' he says.

QUOTE: Geoff Hurst: 'I was not sure whether my third goal counted until I saw it go up on the scoreboard. I noticed some fans running on the pitch as I shot and I wondered if the final whistle had gone. I am completely overwhelmed by what has happened. A couple of weeks ago I didn't think I was going to get a game in the World Cup. Now this. It's just incredible. My heart bleeds for Jimmy Greaves because by rights he should have been out there on the pitch.'

FOR THE RECORD: Alf Ramsey was honoured with a knighthood and Bobby Moore an OBE in the honours list following England's victory. Other players who took part in early matches in the tournament were wingers Terry Paine, Ian Callaghan and John Connolly and Jimmy Greaves, who played in the first three games. Eusebio was top scorer with nine goals, including four in the quarter-final against North Korea when he inspired a comeback from 3-0 down to a 5-3 victory. Portugal beat the USSR 2-1 in the third-place play-off.

JIMMY GREAVES: 'I was obviously choked not to be in the team for the final, and I would not pretend otherwise. Long before a ball was kicked in the tournament I was convinced England were going to win and I wanted to be part of it. But I have never held it against Alf Ramsey for not selecting me, in fact I am happy to go on record as saying that he has been the best of all the England managers. He made what he thought was the right decision and Geoff's three goals put an end to all arguments. It was England's finest hour in football.'

THE CHAMPIONS OF '66

First Division: Liverpool, 61 pts. Runners-up: Leeds United, 55 pts
Second Division: Manchester City, 59 pts. Runners-up: Southampton, 54 pts
Third Division: Hull City, 69 pts. Runners-up: Millwall, 65 pts
Fourth Division: Doncaster Rovers, 59 pts. Runners-up: Darlington, 59 pts
FA Cup Final: Everton 3, Sheffield Wednesday 2
League Cup Final: West Bromwich Albion 5, West Ham United 3 (1-2, 4-1)
Top First Division marksman: Roger Hunt (Liverpool), 30 goals
Footballer of the Year: Bobby Charlton (Manchester United)
Scottish champions: Celtic, 57 pts. Runners-up: Rangers, 55 pts
Scottish Cup Final: Rangers 1, Celtic 0 (after a 0-0 draw)
Scottish Player of the Year: John Greig (Rangers)
European Cup Final: Real Madrid 2, Partizan Belgrade 1
European Cup Winners' Cup Final: Borussia Dortmund 2, Liverpool 1 (aet)
Inter-Cities Fairs Cup Final: Barcelona 4, Real Zaragoza 3 (0-1, 4-2)
European Footballer of the Year: Bobby Charlton (Manchester United)
World Cup Final: England 4, West Germany 2 (after extra time)

1966-67 The team that Jock built takes Europe by storm

Scoreline: Celtic 2, Inter-Milan 1
Venue: National Stadium, Lisbon **Date:** May 25, 1967

THE SETTING: Celtic's record under the mesmerising management of Jock Stein is unparalleled in British football. In his first six full seasons in charge at Parkhead the Glasgow club won six Scottish League titles and lost only 17 of 204 League games while scoring 597 goals. They reached five Scottish FA Cup finals, winning three; and they won five out of six League Cup finals. Celtic polished and perfected their teamwork in a Scottish League where they were so dominating that even Rangers fans had to applaud their achievements.

There were dismissive remarks heard south of the border that the Scottish League was not a real test of a team's quality, but these sort of sniping comments were silenced as Celtic set out to try to become the first British club to win the European Cup.

They barnstormed into the final with a brand of exciting, attacking football that put to shame those clubs becoming addicted to the drug of defensive football that paralysed so many games in the mid-to-late 1960s. In the final they were to meet the great architects of defence-dominated football, Internazionale Milan, who had captured the European Cup in successive seasons in 1964 and 1965 from the springboard of their sterile *catenaccio* defensive system. They built a human fortress around their goal and then relied on three or four jet-paced forwards to make maximum capital out of carefully constructed counter attacks.

Celtic's style and attitude was the exact opposite. The team that Jock built was geared for flair and adventure.

Goalkeeper Ronnie Simpson was a remarkable last line of defence. He had won two FA Cup-winners' medals with Newcastle in 1952 and 1955. Over a decade later at the age of 36 he was still as agile and alert as ever. Jim Craig, skipper Billy McNeill, John Clark and power-shooting left-back Tommy Gemmell made up a

Billy McNeill, the 'Emperor' of Celtic

formidable back line in front of Simpson. They were encouraged to come forward as auxiliary attackers at all opportunities.

Taking responsibility for the supply of passes from the midfield engine room in Celtic's 4-2-4 formation were the skilful and competitive Bertie Auld and the industrious and inventive Bobby Murdoch.

The four-man firing line was one of the most effective goal machines in football. Jinking Jimmy Johnstone was unstoppable on his day as a quick and clever right winger who could destroy defences with his darting runs. Bobby Lennox patrolled the left wing with a mixture of cunning and power, cutting in to shoot or to feed delicate passes to central strikers Willie Wallace and Steve Chalmers.

The 1967 European Cup final was to be a contest between Inter-Milan's negative, smothering tactics and the up-and-at-'em cavalier charges of Celtic. Neutrals hoped that the positive would beat the negative.

THE TEAMS: **Celtic** Simpson, Craig, Gemmell, Murdoch, McNeill, Clark, Johnstone, Wallace, Chalmers, Auld, Lennox.
Inter-Milan Sarti, Burgnich, Facchetti, Bedin, Guarneri, Picchi, Domenghini, Bicicli, Mazzola, Cappellini, Corso.

THE ACTION: The Milan method was tried and tested. They liked to search for a quick goal and then sit back and barricade their goal behind a fortress defence. So it was no surprise to Celtic when the Italians opened

with a burst of attacking football that could have come out of the Jock Stein manual. Sandro Mazzola, Milan's key player following the late withdrawal of injured schemer Luis Suarez, headed against Ronnie Simpson's legs in the opening raid.

Then in the seventh minute Mazzola triggered an attack that led to the early goal on which Milan had set their sights. He put Corso clear on the left with a penetrating pass. The wingman released the ball to Cappellini, who was in the process of trying to shoot when a crunching Jim Craig tackle knocked him off the ball. It was judged a foul by German referee Herr Tschenscher, and Mazzola coolly scored from the penalty spot.

It had been a magnificent opening spell by the Italians, but by force of habit they shelved their attacking talents and pulled all but two forwards back to guard their goal. It was an invitation to Celtic to attack—and they gladly accepted.

The Scottish champions moved full-backs Craig and Gemmell forward on virtually permanent duty as extra wingers, and the Milan defensive wall buckled and bent under an avalanche of attacks.

Goalkeeper Sarti made a procession of brilliant saves, and when he was beaten the woodwork came to his rescue as first Auld and then Gemmell hammered shots against the bar. Any other team might have surrendered with broken hearts as the Milan goal miraculously survived the onslaught, but skipper McNeill kept brandishing his fist as he urged his team-mates to greater efforts. The

word 'surrender' was not part of the Celtic vocabulary.

At last, after an hour of sustained attack, Celtic were rewarded with an equaliser and it was the exclusive creation of overlapping full-backs Craig and Gemmell. First of all Craig brought the ball forward along the right side of the pitch. The retreating Italian defenders tightly marked every player in a green-hooped shirt, but there was one man that they missed. Craig spotted Gemmell coming through like a train on the left side and angled a pass into his path. Sarti had managed to stop everything to date, but no goalkeeper on earth could have saved Gemmell's scorching shot that was smashed high into the net from 20 yards.

Propelled by panic, Milan tried to get their attacking instincts working but had been back-pedalling for so long that they could not lift the pace and pattern of their play. Celtic maintained their momentum and got the winning goal they so richly deserved six minutes from the end of an emotion-draining match.

Gemmell came pounding forward along the left touchline. The Italians were not sure whether to mark his team-mates or to try to block his route to goal in case he was tempted to take another pot shot. Caught in two minds, they gave too much room to Bobby Murdoch, who accepted a pass from Gemmell and unleashed a shot.

The diving Sarti was confident he had the ball covered, but Steve Chalmers managed to deflect it out of his reach for a winning goal that made Celtic the first British winners of the major prize in club football.

At the final whistle thousands of Celtic fans came chasing on to the pitch to parade their heroes like trophies. Jock Stein waited anxiously in the dressing room, counting his players as they battled their way through the thronging supporters on a night that Lisbon belonged to Glasgow.

Following on behind the last of the Celtic players was Liverpool's larger-than-life manager Bill Shankly, one of the few people who could put his record up against his old Scottish pal Stein.

As he entered the dressing-room Shankly summed up Stein's achievement with one of his typically direct and appropriate statements. 'John,' he boomed, using Stein's Christian name, 'You've just become a bloody legend.'

THE WITNESSES: Jock Stein: 'There is not a prouder man on God's earth than me at this moment. Winning was important, aye, but it was the way that we have won that has filled me with satisfaction. We did it by playing football. Pure, beautiful, inventive football. There was not a negative thought in our heads. Inter played into our hands. It's so sad to see such gifted players shackled by a system that restricts their freedom to think and to act. Our fans would never accept that sort of sterile approach. Our objective is always to try to win with style.'

Helenio Herrera, Inter's controversial and world-famous manager: 'I take my hat off to Celtic. They deserved to win. Their performance was one of courage and daring. The European Cup is in good hands.'

Tommy Gemmell: 'What you saw today was a victory for the game of

79

football. We don't hold with namby pamby tactics. Our objective is to get the ball into the back of the net. The game is about scoring goals rather than stopping them.'

Bobby Murdoch: 'Jock Stein got us in the mood for the match by showing us film of the 1960 European Cup final in which Real Madrid beat Eintracht Frankfurt 7-3. The difference between that game and this one is that two teams wanted to play open, attacking football. Inter did not want to play after their early goal. They just wanted to spoil and to try to cling on to their lead. With an attitude like that they didn't deserve to win.'

Goalkeeper Ronnie Simpson: 'I can't remember when I had a quieter match. The way Inter opened up I thought we were going to have our hands full. They've got some smashing footballers but they are not encouraged to express themselves. They are in reverse gear all the time. This is a thrill of a lifetime for me. If you had told me when I was playing at Wembley with Newcastle back in the fifties that more than ten years later I would be in the first British team to win the European Cup I would have thought you were off your rocker.'

Bill Shankly, who himself entered the land of legend at Anfield: 'This is one of the proudest nights in the history of British football. They should knight John Stein here and now. No, a knighthood is not enough. It's got to be Lord Stein of Parkhead. It would have been a bloody disgrace if Inter Milan had won that match. Aye, a disgrace. There was only one team playing to win and that team got its just reward. Did you see Billy McNeill with the trophy? It was as if it had been made for the big feller. I think he'll be taking it to bed with him tonight, he's that proud of it.'

THE EMPEROR: Skipper Billy McNeill epitomised the spirit and style of Celtic. He was an extension of Jock Stein on the pitch, the driving force who made the team tick and the opponents quiver. There were few harder men in the tackle, and for a big man he was surprisingly quick on his feet and a master of positioning. It was rare for anybody ever to beat him in the air, and his amazing consistency made him Celtic's man for all seasons as he collected a record nine successive League championship medals, seven Scottish Cup winners' medals and 29 full international caps.

Awarded the MBE at the close of his magnificent playing career, the Emperor of Celtic—Caesar to his team-mates—became a demanding manager with Clyde, Aberdeen and Celtic before coming south of the border to Manchester City and then Aston Villa. But his heart was always with Celtic and he got a hero's welcome home when he returned to Parkhead to take up the managerial reins again.

QUOTE: Billy McNeill: 'There was no greater or prouder moment in my life than when I became the first British skipper to lift the European Cup. We knew exactly what we had to do to beat the Italians and went out and did it. Lesser teams would have been demoralised by Milan's early goal, but it just made us more deter-

mined. There was no way we were going to go home to Glasgow without that Cup. Our supporters were just unbelievable. To hear them you would have thought we were back home playing in Glasgow. They made all the difference. There was no way we were going to let them down.'

FOR THE RECORD: For six years, Celtic were the Great Untouchables, winning everything in sight apart from an infamous world championship match with Racing Club of Buenos Aires in which tempers and tantrums overruled the talent of both teams. In 1970 they won the unofficial crown as champions of Britain when they conquered Football League champions Leeds United in the semi-final of the European Cup. In the final they were beaten 2-1 by Feyenoord after extra-time, with Gemmell scoring their goal. Jock Stein, the man who masterminded Celtic's greatest triumphs, sadly died 'in harness' in 1985. Aged 62, he collapsed and died in the players' tunnel moments after Scotland had eliminated Wales from the World Cup in a qualifying match in Cardiff. A light went out in British football. The game had lost one of its finest managers and greatest characters.

JIMMY GREAVES: 'There have been few better sides in the history of British football than Jock Stein's Celtic. They had the perfect blend of skill and power. The way they took Milan apart was magnificent. The Italians were so negative that they hardly ever got out of reverse gear, whereas Celtic were full of adventure. I jokingly take the mickey out of the Jocks, but to be honest I am a secret admirer of the way they play the game. Billy McNeill was a great leader, but I still like to rib him about the time we beat Scotland 9-3. He could have done with his 1967 Celtic team-mates around him that day.'

THE CHAMPIONS OF '67

First Division: Manchester United, 60 pts. Runners-up: Nottm. Forest, 56 pts
Second Division: Coventry City, 59 pts. Runners-up: Wolves, 58 pts
Third Division: QPR, 67 pts. Runners-up: Middlesbrough, 55 pts
Fourth Division: Stockport, 64 pts. Runners-up: Southport, 59 pts
FA Cup Final: Tottenham 2, Chelsea 1
League Cup Final: Queen's Park Rangers 3, West Bromwich Albion 2
Top First Division marksman: Ron Davies (Southampton), 37 goals
Footballer of the Year: Jackie Charlton (Leeds United)
Scottish champions: Celtic, 58 pts. Runners-up: Rangers, 55 pts
Scottish Cup Final: Celtic 2, Aberdeen 0
Scottish Player of the Year: Ronnie Simpson (Celtic)
European Cup Final: Celtic 2, Inter-Milan 1
European Cup Winners' Cup: Bayern Munich 1, Rangers 0 (after extra time)
Inter-Cities Fairs Cup Final: Dynamo Zagreb 2, Leeds 0 (2-0, 0-0)
European Footballer of the Year: Florian Albert (Ferencvaros)

1967-68

Charlton is Wembley master on night of tears and cheers

Scoreline: Manchester United 4, Benfica 1
Venue: Wembley Stadium **Date:** May 29, 1968

THE SETTING: You had to be around in 1958 to understand fully why Manchester United's European Cup final against Benfica at Wembley Stadium had such deep significance. The whole of Britain, and the sympathies and good wishes of most of Europe too, were behind Matt Busby and his team as they set out to fulfill at last a dream that had been shattered in the Munich air disaster ten years before.

Busby and his skipper Bobby Charlton had been survivors of a crash that had cost the lives of eight United players. It was the day a team died, and Busby had silently vowed one day to win the premier prize of the European Cup in memory of those who perished in Munich on the way home from a successful European Cup quarter-final match against Red Star in Belgrade.

It had taken Busby a decade finally to rebuild his squad to the quality and craftsmanship flourished by the pre-Munich team. The side he was sending into action against Benfica was almost in the class of the Busby Babes, who had been setting out a powerful argument to be recognised as the greatest British club team of all time until cruelly decimated in one of the worst tragedies ever to hit British football.

Perhaps the most important part in

Bobby Charlton, the pass master

the Busby jigsaw as he put together a mix of outstandingly skilful and physically powerful players was his purchase in the summer of 1966 of goalkeeper Alex Stepney. He started his career with Millwall and had played just four first-team matches for Tommy Docherty's Chelsea when Busby bought him for what was then a goalkeeping transfer record of £50,000. At £500,000 he would have been a bargain. Stepney brought stability and confidence to a United defence that had been giving away goals like a charitable organisation.

This carelessness was cancelling out the creative work of a stunningly gifted attack that had three shining jewels in Irishman George Best, Scotsman Denis Law and Bobby Charlton, the favourite son of English football. A knee injury forced Law on to the sidelines for this game of a lifetime which he watched from a hospital bed following an operation. His place went to Manchester-born prodigy Brian Kidd, who was celebrating his 19th birthday on the day of the final.

Providing the passes from midfield alongside Charlton was master tactician Paddy Crerand, and operating like a mine sweeper in front of the back line of the defence was the Toothless Tiger Nobby Stiles who had been one of England's heroes in the 1966 World Cup finals. His most impressive performance came in the World Cup semi-finals when he stifled the menace of Portugal's exceptionally talented striker Eusebio. Now United needed a repeat performance from him because Eusebio was the inspiration behind Benfica's climb to their fifth European Cup final in eight years.

Also in the Benfica team from the Portuguese side that gave England a close call in the World Cup were midfield marshal Mario Coluna and quick and clever forwards Jose Torres, Jose Augusto and sparkling left winger Simoes. With the towering 6ft 4in Torres leading the attack, the United defence was going to be tested as never before and all hearts went out to veteran United centre-half Bill Foulkes, another Munich survivor who was coming to the end

of a long and distinguished career at Old Trafford. He was flanked by Irish international full-backs Shay Brennan and Tony Dunne, and utility player David Sadler was delegated to drop back from an attacking role to fill in alongside Foulkes whenever there was pressure from Benfica.

THE TEAMS: **Manchester United** Stepney, Brennan, Foulkes, Stiles, Dunne, Crerand, Charlton, Sadler, Best, Kidd, Aston.
Benfica Henrique, Adolfo, Humberto, Jacinto, Cruz, Graca, Coluna, Augusto, Torres, Eusebio, Simoes.

THE ACTION: Few teams had been under such mental strain as United when they walked out on to the Wembley pitch and into a sea of emotion. The spotlight publicity had been turned on them as never before because of the link with Munich, and the bellowing 100,000 crowd were in a frenzied grip of hope and expectation.

As could only be expected in the circumstances, both teams struggled to settle into their stride and the ball was being moved quickly from player to player as if it were an unexploded bomb. Nobody wanted the responsibility of trying to force the first opening for fear of making a mistake.

All eyes were on United wonder winger George Best, but he was taking a severe buffeting from the Portugese defenders who recalled the way he had destroyed them almost single handedly in a European Cup tie two years earlier. Eusebio was getting similar harsh treatment from the unyiedling Stiles, and the only forward who was making any sort of impression was United's unsung out-side-left John Aston, whose father had won an FA Cup winners' medal with United on this same pitch almost exactly 20 years earlier. Aston was racing past Benfica's defenders in Best fashion, but his team-mates were unable to capitalise on his stunning running in a goalless first half that was wrecked by nervous tension.

Benfica came closest to breaking the deadlock when Eusebio, free for a split second from the fervent attentions of Stiles, clipped the United crossbar with a drive from 20 yards.

The half-time break seemed to steady United's nerves and they began the second half with a spurt of the special sort of football with which this Busby team continually lit up memorable matches during the 1960s. It was the one and only Bobby Charlton, as graceful as a gazelle, who gave them the lead that the crowd were baying for when he sprinted away from his marker to meet a left cross from Sadler with a perfectly placed glancing header.

Aston created a procession of chances for United to seal victory, but the finishing never matched the brilliance of the winger's foundation work. Nine minutes from the end you could almost hear the intake of breath from the suddenly hushed United fans when Graca equalised for Benfica in a breakaway raid.

With just seconds left and extra time looming Eusebio looked certain to destroy United's dream. The deadliest marksman in the world broke free from Stiles and had only Stepney to beat, but somehow the United goalkeeper managed to parry his rocketing

shot with a sensational save. United were still shaking from this heart-stopping escape when the final whistle blew, and Charlton and Stiles found themselves facing the same extra time mountain they had climbed in the 1966 World Cup final.

Matt Busby, the years suddenly heavy on his shoulders, walked urgently on to the pitch and told his players: 'You are being too careless with your passes. Just take a little care and you can win it. Don't throw it away now. Make every pass count and when you get into their box steady yourselves. You are snatching at your shots.'

It was going to take a moment of inspiration to lift the worn-out United players, and it was Best who provided it early in the first period of extra time. He at last managed to escape his Benfica jailers to run on to a headed through ball from Kidd following a long punt upfield by Stepney. Best side-stepped a tackle and nonchalantly dummied his way past onrushing goalkeeper Henrique before side-footing the ball into the net as if in a training match.

This was the goal that settled the match. The spirit and fight disappeared from Benfica like air leaving a punctured balloon, and birthday boy Kidd put the icing on his cake with a determined smash-and-grab goal. He headed the ball against the bar and then beat everybody to the rebound to nod it into the net. As if the match was being plotted by the great script-writer in the sky, it was Charlton—as an 18-year-old boy he had miraculously scrambled out of the wreckage at Munich—who provided the final

telling contribution to give the game a fairytale finish. He volleyed a centre from Kidd high into the Benfica net from the tightest of angles.

Wembley was wild with excitement and awash with tears as Charlton led his team-mates forward to collect the prize of the European Cup. He had tried to talk Matt Busby into receiving it, but the master of managers said: 'No. This is *your* day.'

THE WITNESSES: Matt Busby: 'A lot of special people are in our thoughts tonight. We won this Cup for them. We have played a lot better than we did against Benfica, but in view of all the circumstances the team performed magnificently. Now I know that dreams do come true.'

Bill Foulkes: 'I cannot find words to describe how I feel. We won this for Matt Busby and for all those lads who died at Munich. Little of what Matt said before extra time sank in with me. I was just thinking how I wanted to get it all over and done

Nobby Stiles, the Toothless Tiger

with. There was enormous strain on us throughout the match and I feel totally drained by it all.'

Nobby Stiles: 'I thought the game had got away from us in the last ten minutes of ordinary time. They equalised and started to put some great moves together. God knows how Alex saved that shot from Eusebio. It was unbelievable. When it went into extra time I said to Bobby, 'Here we go again.' Bestie's goal gave us the boost we needed, and from then on there was no stopping us. We all did it for Matt. No man has deserved to win the European Cup more than him.'

Mario Coluna, Benfica skipper: 'If we were going to lose I cannot think of a club I would rather see win the European Cup. It was their destiny, and all of us at Benfica offer our sincere congratulations.'

Eusebio: 'I consider Bobby Charlton a friend and as disappointed as I was to be on the losing side I had the consolation of seeing him collect the Cup. He is a gentleman as well as a great player and is a credit to our game.'

THE FAVOURITE:Ask football fans to name the *greatest* player they have ever seen and Bobby Charlton's name is unlikely to come immediately to mind and tongue. Ask them to nominate their *favourite* footballer of all time…and there is every chance that Bobby Charlton is the name offered instantly.

Charlton was the player everybody loved to love. George Best had more tricks, Denis Law had more dynamism, but Charlton had an indefinable charisma that put him ahead in the popularity polls. Football followers have three faces and three phases of Charlton deposited in their memory bank. There is the teenage Busby Babe of the pre-Munich air disaster with his shock of blond hair and the bombing shots from the left wing. His performances dipped and soared like a barometer on the English weather, sometimes hot with sunshine brilliance; other times caught in the wild wind of inconsistency. Never, ever was he dull...all the way from his opening goals in League football in his debut against, of all teams, Charlton in 1956 and from his first match with England against Scotland at Hampden Park in 1958. He marked his international debut with a gem of a goal, crashing a shot in on the volley from a pass from one of his schoolboy idols, Tom Finney.

The second face, more serious, lean and frowning under a rapidly thinning thatch, came after he had survived the Munich air crash. His game began to gather maturity, consistency and style. He had lost some of his early impudence but showed greater variety and verve as he switched to an inside-forward role.

The third and—for many people —favourite Bobby Charlton face shone in the mid-sixties when he became a strolling midfield player. Wearing the No 9 shirt but rarely as a conventional centre-forward, he plotted openings for team-mates and created goals himself with sudden sprints at the heart of defences, climaxed with rifled shots from either foot.

His greatest moments came in this deep-lying role, plundering vital goals and supplying a succession of precise passes for England's 1966 World Cup winning team and providing the same service for the magnificent United team of that golden era.

Neither side could have succeeded without him. He is the only footballer to win the grand slam of honours in British soccer: World Cup, European Cup, League championship and FA Cup winners' medals. He was European and English Footballer of the Year in 1966 and his collection of 106 England caps is topped only by Bobby Moore.

Born in Ashington, Northumberland, on October 11, 1937, he came from a mining and footballing family that included the talented Milburn brothers. He and his elder brother Jackie played together for England in 35 internationals matches.

Bobby scored 198 League goals for United in 606 games, and added eight more to his collection when playing 38 times for Preston as player-manager. He remains England's top goal scorer with 49, five ahead of Jimmy Greaves.

His first international match was in 1958 and his last against West Germany in the 1970 World Cup quarter-final when Alf Ramsey substituted him with England leading 2-0 so that he would be fresh for the semi-final. England lost the match 3-2 with Bobby looking helplessly on from the touchline bench.

QUOTE: Bobby Charlton: We had lived with the ambition of winning the European Cup for so long that this time we knew we *had* to do it.

When the game went to extra time it was like the 1966 World Cup Final all over again. We had to be professional and not let emotion take over, as it so easily could have done. We owed it to too many people, particularly Matt Busby, not to fail after all the club had been through.'

FOR THE RECORD: United just failed to retain the League championship in the 1967-68 season, finishing runners-up two points behind deadly rivals Manchester City. They saved their greatest efforts for the European Cup and on the way to the final dismissed Hibernian of Malta, Sarajevo, Gornik Zabrze and, in a memorable semi-final, Real Madrid. The victory over Benfica at Wembley was the pinnacle of Matt Busby's managerial career. In 22 years in charge at Old Trafford after distinguished service as a player with Manchester City and Liverpool he managed five League championship winning teams and captured the FA Cup twice. Every team he built played with flair and style. After the European Cup triumph the modest, quietly spoken Scot was knighted. It was a fitting tribute to a man who well earned his unofficial title, Father of Football.

JIMMY GREAVES: 'There was not a dry eye in the house the night United beat Benfica. It was not a classic match but an unforgettable occasion, and United's victory became a wonderful memorial to those players and officials who died in the Munich air disaster. The success at Wembley could not have happened to greater footballing ambassadors than Bobby Charlton, Bill Foulkes and, of course, Matt Busby.'

THE CHAMPIONS OF '68

First Division: Manchester City, 58 pts. Runners-up: Manchester United, 56 pts
Second Division: Ipswich Town, 59 pts. Runners-up: QPR, 58 pts
Third Division: Oxford United, 57 pts. Runners-up: Bury, 56 pts
Fourth Division: Luton Town, 66 pts. Runners-up: Barnsley, 61 pts
FA Cup Final: West Bromwich Albion 1, Everton 0 (after extra time)
League Cup Final: Leeds United 1, Arsenal 0
Top First Division marksmen: George Best (Manchester United) and Ron Davies (Southampton), 28 goals
Footballer of the Year: George Best (Manchester United)
Scottish champions: Celtic, 63 pts. Runners-up: Rangers, 61 pts
Scottish Cup Final: Dunfermline 3, Heart of Midlothian 1
Scottish Player of the Year: Gordon Wallace (Raith Rovers)
European Cup Final: Manchester United 4, Benfica 1 (after extra time)
European Cup Winners' Cup: AC Milan 2, SV Hamburg 0
European Fairs Cup Final: Leeds United 1, Ferencvaros 0 (1-0, 0-0)
European Championship: Italy 2, Yugoslavia 0 (after a 1-1 draw)
European Footballer of the Year: George Best (Manchester United)

1968-69 Arsenal are blown aside by the Wiltshire Whirlwind

Scoreline: Swindon Town 3, Arsenal 1
Venue: Wembley Stadium **Date:** March 15, 1969

THE SETTING: Swindon Town's football history had been more about taking part than winning when they travelled to Wembley for the first time to tackle aristocratic Arsenal in the League Cup final. A year earlier Arsenal had been narrowly beaten 1-0 in the final by Leeds United and few people seriously expected the unfashionable Third Division Wiltshire club to stop the Londoners from winning the trophy at the second time of asking. But perhaps somebody might have pointed out that Arsenal should beware the ides of March. Swindon

Don Rogers, the Wiltshire Wonder

knives were being sharpened for the March the 15th showdown, and they would be buried deep into the Arsenal backs.

Swindon were not burdened with any sort of complex about their Third Division status. They took heart from the fact that just two years earlier Third Division Queen's Park Rangers, inspired by the creative Rodney Marsh, had come from behind to beat West Bromwich Albion of the First Division in the first League Cup final staged at Wembley.

Arsenal were more concerned than Swindon when on the day of the match they found the famous Wembley turf looking a mudheap. Gallons of rain water had been pumped away leaving the pitch ankle-deep in a mixture of sludge and sand. The sight did nothing to improve the mood of the Arsenal players, who were still suffering from the after-effects of a 'flu outbreak. They knew they were on a hiding to nothing and were well aware of the old football cliché that 'the mud is a great leveller.'

Anybody who had seen Swindon purring their way into a promotion challenging position in the Third Division that season would have been able to warn Arsenal that they should not under-estimate a team that had the character to survive four replays on the way to Wembley. They had beaten

Torquay United and Blackburn Rovers at the first go but had needed replays before overcoming Bradford City, Coventry City, Derby County and Burnley.

Their manager Danny Williams, a former Yorkshire miner who had played his heart out for Rotherham for 20 years, encouraged Swindon to play attacking, adventurous football in an era when most teams were putting the emphasis on defence. He had an ace up his sleeve in Don Rogers, a west country winger who was as free as a bird to express his skill in any way he saw fit. 'You don't tell a Goya how to paint a picture or a Caruso how to sing a song,' said Williams. 'I just tell Don to go out and play.'

THE TEAMS: **Swindon Town**
Downsborough, Thomas, Trollope, Butler, Burrows, Harland, Heath, Smart, Smith, Noble, Rogers. Sub: Penman.
Arsenal Wilson, Storey, McNab, McLintock, Ure, Simpson, Radford, Sammels, Court, Gould, Armstrong. Sub: Graham.

THE ACTION: For most of the 90 minutes of ordinary time Arsenal's pedigree showed as they penned Swindon in their own half with football that was as smooth as the heavy conditions would allow but lacking only in goalmouth punch.

When they were able to get past a defence in which full-backs Rod Thomas and John Trollope were outstanding they found goalkeeper Peter Downsborough in inspired form. He saved at least three possible goals before Swindon broke away to take a

shock lead with a goal that had 'made by Arsenal' stamped on it. Centre-half Ian Ure made a mess of an attempted back pass to goalkeeper Bob Wilson and Roger Smart nipped in to score a gift of a goal.

Arsenal charged forward on the churned-up pitch in the second half in a desperate bid to avoid the embarrassment of defeat, but Downsborough was in an even more defiant mood and smothered and saved shot after shot.

He made his one mistake of the match with just four minutes to go when he misjudged a run off his line and was way out of position as battling Bobby Gould powered through the mud to ram in an equaliser.

Arsenal were then faced with the last thing their 'flu-weakened players wanted—30 minutes of extra time on a pudding of a pitch that was making every step a challenge. But one player sensed that this was the time and the place for some west country magic. Enter stage left Don Rogers.

He threaded the ball past a queue of outwitted Arsenal defenders to put Swindon into the lead just before the halfway point of extra time, and then in the closing minutes he raced from the halfway line with the ball at his feet, stopping only to look up and gauge the angle for his shot which he duly placed wide of the oncoming Wilson.

They were two unforgettable moments of footballing genius, and shell-shocked Arsenal had been blown aside by the team that became known as the Wiltshire Whirlwind.

THE WITNESSES: Bertie Mee, Arsenal manager: 'We are not in the business of making excuses. We had our chances to win but did not take them. Don Rogers created two magnificent goals that were good enough to win any game. It is not the end of the world. We shall be back at Wembley, of that I have no doubt.'

Danny Williams, Swindon manager: 'We may be a Third Division club but we play football that is First Division quality. It was our skill and fitness that won it for us…and the genius of Don Rogers.'

THE DON: Don Rogers, born in Midsomer Norton on October 27, 1945, started and ended his career with Swindon for whom he netted 149 League goals. In between he played with mixed success for Crystal Palace and Queen's Park Rangers. He rarely showed his scintillating form in London, mainly because of injury problems. The Don, one of the most talented players ever to come out of the west country, retired in 1973 to concentrate on business interests in Swindon.

QUOTE: Don Rogers: 'Arsenal treated us too lightly. They thought we were just country bumpkins, but we knew that if we could play at anything like our best we were a match for any team in the country.'

FOR THE RECORD: Swindon completed a double in 1968-69 by winning promotion to the Second Division. Arsenal took stock of their situation and started a team rebuilding plan that bore fruit with the winning of the League and FA Cup double two years later.

JIMMY GREAVES: 'I am convinced that if Don Rogers had played for one of the big city clubs early in his career he would have established himself as an outstanding international. He had beautiful close skills and was deadly with his finishing.'

THE CHAMPIONS OF '69

First Division: Leeds United, 67 pts. Runners-up: Liverpool, 61 pts
Second Division: Derby County, 63 pts. Runners-up: Crystal Palace, 56 pts
Third Division: Watford, 64 pts. Runners-up: Swindon Town, 64 pts
Fourth Division: Doncaster, 59 pts. Runners-up: Halifax, 57 pts
FA Cup Final: Manchester City 1, Leicester City 0
League Cup Final: Swindon Town 3, Arsenal 1 (after extra time)
Top First Division marksman: Jimmy Greaves (Tottenham), 27 goals
Footballers of the Year: Dave Mackay (Derby County)/Tony Book (Man City)
Scottish champions: Celtic, 54 pts. Runners-up: Rangers, 49 pts
Scottish Cup Final: Celtic 4, Rangers 0
Scottish Player of the Year: Bobby Murdoch (Celtic)
European Cup Final: AC Milan 4, Ajax 1
European Cup Winners' Cup Final: Slovan Bratislava 3, Barcelona 2
European Fairs Cup Final: Newcastle Uniteds 6, Ujpest Dozsa 2 (3-0, 3-2)
European Footballer of the Year: Gianni Rivera (AC Milan)

1969-70 Banks of England makes the save of the century

Scoreline: Brazil 1, England 0
Venue: Jalisco Stadium, Guadalajara, Mexico **Date:** June 7, 1970

THE SETTING: Can one save warrant a game being included in this gallery of the world's greatest matches? Yes, when it is made by one of the finest goalkeepers of all time against the most phenomenal player of them all and in the most important of all the tournaments.

England were playing Brazil in a vital World Cup group match in the suffocating, capacity crowded Jalisco Stadium in Guadalajara in the heat of the mid-day sun on a scorching Sunday that was ideally suited for a siesta rather than soccer. Only mad dogs and footballers would have gone out in such sweltering 98-degree conditions.

The game was just ten minutes old and goalless when the master of all strikers—Pele—came face to face with the goalkeeping master—Gordon Banks—in a High Noon duel.

THE TEAMS: **Brazil** Felix, Carlos Alberto, Brito, Piazza, Everaldo, Clodoaldo, Cesar, Jairzinho, Tostao, Pele, Rivelino.
England Banks, Wright, Cooper, Mullery, Labone, Moore, Lee, Ball, Charlton, Hurst, Peters. Subs: Astle, Bell.

THE ACTION: Carlos Alberto, Brazilian right-back and captain, pushed a precise pass down the right wing into the path of the skilled Jairzinho who suddenly and dramatically accelerated past Terry Cooper to the by-line. He then stabbed a centre into the goalmouth that seemed to hang invitingly for Pele, who had instinctively read the situation as only he could. He had got himself perfectly positioned beyond his marker Alan Mullery to meet the ball.

Pele climbed above the ball and

Gordon Banks, who made the save of a lifetime against Pele

headed it with ferocious power down—and so he thought—into the net. Mullery later reported that Pele shouted 'Goal!' as the ball flew off his head. So did most spectators in the stadium, including the commentators sending their descriptive phrases around the world to millions of television viewers and radio listeners.

Banks looked rooted on the wrong side of goal but suddenly, with the blurring speed of a panther, sprinted and then dived to his right and somehow managed to get an outstretched hand under the ball to flick it up and away over the bar. Pele stopped dead in mid-celebration to mourn what had somehow become a missed chance.

This moment of astounding gymnastics from Banks inspired England to give the eventual world champions their hardest match of the tournament, but after a magnificent battle they finally succumbed to a superbly drilled shot by Jairzinho on the hour. He cut in from the right to score after Pele and Tostao had combined to rip open the middle of the England defence.

Jeff Astle had a gilt-edged chance to equalise within moments of coming on as a substitute but—yes, even in those heatwave conditions—he was caught cold and shot tamely wide.

Evidence that the England players had given their all is that each of them lost up to ten pounds in weight after running round in the mid-day sun so that the World Cup organisers could satisfy the demands of world-wide television deadlines. The millions tuned into the match will always recall it for having seen one of the saves of the century.

THE WITNESSES: Pele: 'I just couldn't believe it when Gordon stopped my header. It was incredible that he got it and even more incredible that he managed to push the ball over the bar. It was the biggest surprise I have ever had on a football pitch. No doubt about it, this was the greatest save I've ever seen.'

Bobby Moore: 'I was getting ready to pick the ball out of the net when Gordon appeared from nowhere. He swooped across the goal like superman and must have set some sort of world speed record. What a pity we lost the game, because Gordon didn't deserve to be on the losing side after making a save like that. It was out of this world.'

THE HANDY MAN: Born in Sheffield on December 30, 1937, Gordon Banks made a slow start to his football career. He worked first as a coalbagger and then as a bricklayer while playing only on Sundays. Chesterfield signed him when he was 18, but it was not until the 1958-59 season following his National Service that he made the breakthrough into their League team. Within a year his potential had been spotted by Leicester City and from then on he started to establish himself as one of the greatest goalkeepers.

He had nine seasons with Leicester during which he made 293 League appearances and collected two FA Cup runners-up medals. After helping to groom young Peter Shilton as his successor, Banks moved on to Stoke City for £50,000 in 1967. He was voted Footballer of the Year in 1972 after helping Stoke City beat Chelsea in the League Cup final.

Banks played 73 times for England and was an ever-present in the 1966 World Cup winning team. The opposition failed to put the ball past him in 35 of his England appearances. His career was cut short during the 1972-73 season after he lost the sight of an eye in a car smash. He made a comeback in the United States where, despite his handicap, he was elected top goalkeeper in the USA.

QUOTE: Gordon Banks: 'I was too involved in what was happening on the pitch to give a second's thought to the save against Brazil. It was only later when I saw it on television that I realised it was a bit special. It was an instinctive save, but if Pele says it was the greatest he has ever seen, who am I to argue with the king...?'

FOR THE RECORD: England reached the quarter-finals of the 1970 World Cup, but—without an unwell

Banks at the back—they lost 3-2 to West Germany after extra time, surrending a 2-0 lead. Brazil—with goals by Pele, Gerson, Jairzinho and Carlos Alberto—beat Italy 4-1 in the final in Mexico. It was their third World Cup triumph in four tournaments since 1958 and it earned them the Jules Rimet trophy outright. A Wolfgang Overath goal gave West Germany a 1-0 victory over Uruguay in the play-off for third place. West Germany's Gerd Muller was the top scorer in Mexico with ten goals in six games. He also scored nine in six qualifying matches.

JIMMY GREAVES: 'Every time I see that Banks save against Pele on video I shake my head with disbelief. It looked impossible. There has been nobody as safe as the Banks of England. Pat Jennings, Neville Southall and Peter Shilton are the only modern goalkeepers in the same class.'

THE CHAMPIONS OF '70

First Division: Everton 66 pts. Runners-up: Leeds United, 57 pts
Second Division: Huddersfield Town, 60 pts. Runners-up: Blackpool, 53 pts
Third Division: Orient, 62 pts. Runners-up: Luton Town, 60 pts
Fourth Division: Chesterfield, 64 pts. Runners-up: Wrexham, 61 pts
FA Cup Final: Chelsea 2, Leeds United 1 (after extra time and a 2-2 draw)
League Cup Final: Manchester City 2, West Bromwich Albion 1
Top First Division marksman: Jeff Astle (West Bromwich Albion), 25 goals
Footballer of the Year: Billy Bremner (Leeds United)
Scottish champions: Celtic, 57 pts. Runners-up: Rangers, 45 pts
Scottish Cup Final: Aberdeen 3, Celtic 1
Scottish Player of the Year: Pat Stanton (Hibernian)
European Cup Final: Feyenoord 2, Celtic 1 (after extra time)
European Cup Winners' Cup Final: Manchester City 2, Gornik Zabrze 1
European Fairs Cup Final: Anderlecht 3, Arsenal 4 (3-1, 0-3)
European Footballer of the Year: Gerd Muller (Bayern Munich)
World Cup Final: Brazil 4, Italy 1

1970-71 Arsenal are unneighbourly as they win at the double

Scoreline: Tottenham Hotspur 0, Arsenal 1
Venue: White Hart Lane **Date:** May 3, 1971

THE SETTING: Arsenal and Tottenham—like most footballing neighbours—have always had their own private championship. During the sixties it was Tottenham who proved they were the top club in North London. But when Arsenal made the short journey to White Hart Lane for the final First Division match of the 1970-71 season they had a wonderful chance to eclipse their rivals. An over-imaginative Hollywood scriptwriter could not have contrived a more exciting climax to a season, and it has been estimated that more than 150,000 people set off from their homes to see this enticing Monday evening match.

Around 100,00 of them were still pushing and shoving their way to nowhere outside the Tottenham ground when the gates were locked behind 51,192 lucky fans inside.

The fascinating pre-match facts were these: Arsenal, on 63 points, needed only a scoreless draw to win the Championship for a record eighth time by 0.013 of a goal. But a defeat or a goal-scoring draw would concede the Championship to Leeds, football's perennial bridesmaids who had completed their fixtures with 64 points and a top-of-the-table position.

Arsenal were the only club who could overtake Leeds, and to add to the dramatic cocktail of coincidences they were also within shooting distance of the coveted and elusive double—a feat accomplished only once in the 20th century, in 1960-61, by Tottenham. Liverpool were preparing to face Arsenal at Wembley five days later in the FA Cup final.

There was tension in North London, and torture in Yorkshire. 'We have done all we can and now we are helpless,' said Leeds manager Don Revie. 'My players have been magnificent all season. I would hate to see them pipped at the post again. We have got 64 points and there have never been runners-up with a bigger

Frank McLintock, Captain Marvel

collection than that. We are now watching and waiting and relying on Tottenham…'

THE TEAMS: **Tottenham** Jennings, Kinnear, Knowles, Mullery, Collins, Beal, Gilzean, Perryman, Chivers, Peters, Neighbour. Sub: Pearce. **Arsenal** Wilson, Rice, McNab, Kelly, McLintock, Simpson, Armstrong, Graham, Radford, Kennedy, George. Sub: Sammels.

THE ACTION: Charlie George, the inventive young exhibitionist who provided defence-minded Arsenal with necessary moments of brilliance, almost snatched the lead in the opening seconds. Right-back Pat Rice made a deep incursion into Tottenham's left flank before stroking a pass into the path of George who powerfully struck an instant shot. But goalkeeper Pat Jennings, later to extend his glittering career in the service of Arsenal, took off like an Olympic diver attempting a high-tariff dive and turned the ball over the bar.

It was a stupendous save that underlined the fact that Tottenham, League Cup winners and third in the League, were in no mood to do their neighbours any favours. Instead they started stitching together some fast-flowing moves and Arsenal's nerves were apparent. Martin Peters stopped their hearts with a swerving shot that clipped the top of the Arsenal bar with that fine goalkeeper Bob Wilson for once stranded.

Arsenal, missing the midfield snap and bite of injured ball-winner Peter Storey, looked perilously close to a nervous collapse, but skipper Frank McLintock began to pump belief and confidence into them from the back with the sort of inspiring captaincy that earned him the Footballer of the Year title.

The game was ticking like a time-bomb into its closing moments and it looked as if Arsenal's dilemma of playing for a goalless draw or for a victory had resolved itself. Then, with three minutes to go, local hero Charlie George cut in towards goal. Pat Jennings covered his near post ready for a shot that never came. George transferred the ball at shoulder height into the middle and John Radford powered in a header that looked a goal all the way until Jennings intervened, catapulting to his right to push the ball away. Tottenham's confused defenders were still regrouping when George Armstrong calmly lofted the ball back into the goalmouth and Ray Kennedy surged forward to head high into the net off the underside of the bar.

For three minutes Arsenal had to live in fear of an equaliser that would have cost them the Championship, but then retiring referee Kevin Howley blew the final whistle of his career and it was the sweetest sound that many—but not all— North London fans had ever heard.

THE WITNESSES: Ray Kennedy, completing a remarkable first full season in League football: 'Those last three minutes seemed to last for ever. I thought to myself that perhaps it might have been better had my header gone over the bar.'

Jack Charlton, Leeds centre-half: 'What a way to lose the title! Arsenal owe it all to Spurs. They beat us at

Elland Road and now this…'

Don Howe, Arsenal coach: 'You could have cut yourself on the tension in the ground. I have rarely seen a display of captaincy to equal that of Frank McLintock's. He was a real commander out there.'

CAPTAIN MARVEL: Frank McLintock, born in the Gorbals district of Glasgow on December 28, 1939, reluctantly held the title of soccer's best loser for the first ten years of his career. He played in four Wembley finals—two with Leicester and two with Arsenal—and was a runner-up in each of them. Then at the ripe old age of 30 he started to win everything in sight. Switching from swashbuckling wing-half to dependable centre-half, he led Arsenal out of the wilderness to the European Fairs Cup in 1970, and the League and FA Cup double in 1971. He won nine Scottish international caps before winding down

his career with QPR. Frank later masterminded Millwall's climb to the First Division as a coach after up-and-down managerial experience with Leicester City and Brentford.

QUOTE: 'I have never known a night like that at White Hart Lane. We couldn't afford to concede a goal and we knew that to score could give us problems. It was like walking a tightrope over a minefield!'

FOR THE RECORD: Arsenal completed the double five days later, beating Liverpool 2-1 in the FA Cup final thanks to a spectacular goal in extra time by Charlie George.

JIMMY GREAVES: 'That Arsenal team was not a patch on the Spurs double side of 1960-61, but they made up for their lack of flair with efficiency and teamwork. And in McLintock they had a Captain Marvel.'

THE CHAMPIONS OF '71

First Division: Arsenal 65 pts. Runners-up: Leeds United, 64 pts
Second Division: Leicester City, 59 pts. Runners-up: Sheffield United, 56 pts
Third Division: Preston North End, 61 pts. Runners-up: Fulham, 60 pts
Fourth Division: Notts County, 69 pts. Runners-up: Bournemouth, 60 pts
FA Cup Final: Arsenal 2, Liverpool 1 (after extra time)
League Cup Final: Tottenham 2, Aston Villa 0
Top First Division marksman: Tony Brown (West Bromwich Albion), 28 goals
Footballer of the Year: Frank McLintock (Arsenal)
Scottish champions: Celtic, 56 pts. Runners-up: Aberdeen, 54 pts
Scottish Cup Final: Celtic 2, Rangers 1 (after 1-1 draw)
Scottish Player of the Year: Martin Buchan (Aberdeen)
European Cup Final: Ajax 2, Panathinaikos 0
European Cup Winners' Cup Final: Chelsea 2, Real Madrid 1 (after a 1-1 draw)
European Fairs Cup Final: Juventus 3, Leeds United 3 (2-2, 1-1. Leeds United won on the away-goals rule)
European Footballer of the Year: Johan Cruyff (Ajax)

1971-72 Hooligans cause victorious Rangers great pain in Spain

Scoreline: Rangers 3, Dynamo Moscow 2
Venue: Gran Estadia, Barcelona **Date:** May 24, 1972

THE SETTING: It is a sad paradox that one of the greatest performances in the long and proud history of the Rangers Football Club is also one that is considered best forgotten by many Scots.

A magnificent triumph over Dynamo Moscow in the European Cup Winners' Cup Final was overshadowed by the fact that their rioting fans heaped lasting shame on the Ibrox club and caused them to be banned from defending the Cup they had won with such style and panache.

Rangers had deep roots in the Cup Winners' Cup competition. They had reached the first final in 1961 when they were beaten 4-1 on aggregate by Fiorentina. In 1967 they reached the final again, this time going down 1-0 to an extra-time goal by Beckenbauer-inspired Bayern Munich.

It was star-spangled Bayern Munich—including Beckenbauer, Muller and Co—who barred their way to the final in 1972, and Rangers rose to new heights by winning the two-leg semi-final 3-1 on aggregate.

There were 35,000 fans gathered in the Gran Stadia in Barcelona for the final against Lev Yashin's Dynamo Moscow, and more than 20,000 of them were from Glasgow. The rest were neutral Spaniards, with just a handful of supporters allowed to travel from Moscow.

THE TEAMS: **Rangers** McCloy, Jardine, Mathieson, Greig, Johnstone, Smith, McLean, Conn, Stein, MacDonald, Johnston.
Dynamo Moscow Pilgui, Basalev, Dolmatov, Zykov, Dobbonosov, Zhukov, Baidatchni, Jakubik, Sabo, Mahovikov, Evryuzhikin. Subs: Gerschkovitch, Eshtrekov.

THE ACTION: There was a hint of the troubles to come when Rangers fans invaded the pitch to welcome their heroes as they came out for the start of the match. The referee ordered

John Greig, a man for all seasons

97

the teams off while Spanish police persuaded the supporters to return to their seats and places on the terraces. Rangers general manager Willie Waddell, an idol of Ibrox in his playing days, came on to the pitch to help shepherd the fans off. It was obvious that many of them were intoxicated with something other than pre-match excitement, and neutral observers feared there could be serious trouble before the night was out.

The match finally kicked off 15 minutes late, but Rangers wasted no more precious moments and hungrily got on with the job of trying to win the Cup at the third time of asking. Playing positive and flowing football, they hurried into a 2-0 half-time lead with goals from Colin Stein and Willie Johnston.

Each time the ball went into the Russian net hundreds of Rangers fans came stampeding on to the pitch in mass celebrations, and the Scottish players worked hard at coaxing them to go back where they had come from because they knew the match was in danger of being abandoned.

Five minutes into the second half Rangers appeared to have wrapped the match up when Johnston's blinding speed took him past the Moscow defenders to get on the end of a long punted clearance by goalkeeper Peter McCloy and score with an assassin's deliberate aim.

This third goal was the signal for Dynamo to abandon their cautious approach and they started a revival movement that rocked Rangers. Substitute Eshtrekov took advantage of some slack marking to score from close range on the hour, and five

minutes from the end Mahovikov found goalkeeper McCloy out of position and steered the ball into the net to make the score 3-2. Rangers were close to a nervous collapse, but driving skipper John Greig spread calm about him with a real captain's performance.

There was a third pitch invasion by Rangers fans moments after the second Dynamo goal, many of them interpreting the award of a free-kick as the final whistle. The Russians protested as once again the Rangers players pleaded with their fans to clear the pitch.

This had all been a dress rehearsal for the major pitch invasion that followed when the referee did blow the final whistle three minutes later. The ground became a blue sea of scarf-waving supporters as thousands poured on to the pitch in what was supposed to be a celebration. It quickly turned into a war as special riot-police armed with batons beat and battered anybody in hitting distance.

The Rangers fans retreated but only to regroup, and then charged the police using stones and bottles as weapons. It was a full hour before some sort of peace and order was restored, and the presentation of the trophy was staged out of sight and sound of their fans in a sad ceremony inside a stadium building.

THE WITNESSES: Willie Waddell: 'This should have been our finest hour, but it has been ruined by our own supporters. I am not condoning their behaviour, but the treatment they received from some of the police was, to say the least, excessively brutal.'

Lev Yashin, legendary Dynamo goalkeeper elevated to manager: 'Our players could not give the game the concentration it needed because of the hooliganism of the Rangers followers. The match should either be replayed or the Cup taken away from Rangers.'

THE IBROX IDOL: John Greig was Rangers' man for all seasons. He played 496 League games for them between 1962 and 1978 and also had a spell as manager. He was a stylish inside-forward when he first joined the Ibrox staff but it was after his switch to right-half that he really began to make an impact on the game. Awarded the MBE for his services to football, he was twice voted Scottish Player of the Year—in 1966 and again ten years later. He won 44 Scottish international caps between 1964 and 1976.

QUOTE: John Greig: 'It was tragic what happened that night in Barcelona. We played some magnificent football and thoroughly deserved our victory, but the whole thing was spoiled because of the behaviour of a minority of our supporters. Most of them were just celebrating, but those who were looking for trouble damaged the name of a great club.'

FOR THE RECORD: Rangers were allowed to keep the Cup after an emergency meeting of UEFA at which Willie Waddell made an impassioned plea on behalf of his players. But they were banned from Europe for a year.

JIMMY GREAVES: 'After the way English hooligans have scarred our great game I cannot say too much about what happened in Barcelona. I just felt sickened for the Rangers players who performed so brilliantly only to have their great moment ruined by a few hundred morons.'

THE CHAMPIONS OF '72

First Division: Derby County 58 pts. Runners-up: Leeds United, 57 pts
Second Division: Norwich City, 57 pts. Runners-up: Birmingham City, 56 pts
Third Division: Aston Villa, 70 pts. Runners-up: Brighton, 65 pts
Fourth Division: Grimsby Town, 63 pts. Runners-up: Southend, 60 pts
FA Cup Final: Leeds United 1, Arsenal 0
League Cup Final: Stoke City 2, Chelsea 1
Top First Division marksman: Francis Lee (Manchester City), 33 goals
Footballer of the Year: Gordon Banks (Stoke City)
Scottish champions: Celtic, 60 pts. Runners-up: Aberdeen, 50 pts
Scottish Cup Final: Celtic 6, Hibernian 1
Scottish Player of the Year: Dave Smith (Rangers)
European Cup Final: Ajax 2, Inter-Milan 0
European Cup Winners' Cup Final: Rangers 3, Dynamo Moscow 2
UEFA Cup: Wolves 2, Tottenham 3 (1-2, 1-1)
European Footballer of the Year: Franz Beckenbauer (Bayern Munich)
European Championship Final: West Germany 3, USSR 0

1972-73 'Messiah' Stokoe stokes up a miracle by Sunderland

Scoreline: Sunderland 1, Leeds United 0
Venue: Wembley Stadium **Date:** May 5, 1973

THE SETTING: A Second Division team had never won a post-war FA Cup final and few people gave Sunderland a chance when they confronted Leeds United at Wembley in 1973. Leeds were the Cup holders, with ten of the side that had conquered Arsenal 1-0 a year earlier again on duty. All but one of their 12-player squad were internationals. According to the pundits, Sunderland were just there to make up the numbers.

But one man in particular was convinced that Leeds could be beaten. Sunderland manager Bob Stokoe

Jim Montgomery, saved the day

sensed an air of complacency blowing from Elland Road, and he quietly built up the confidence of his players on a foundation of the old saying: 'We've got nothing to lose.' Stokoe had been in charge at Sunderland for just five months but was already being hailed as the 'Messiah of Roker Park.' Once a Cup final hero with Newcastle, he had learned the managerial business with Blackpool, Bury, Carlisle, Charlton and Rochdale before being invited to try to recapture Sunderland's glory days. You needed a long memory to recall when Sunderland were known as the 'Bank of England' club and able to buy success with extravagant raids in the transfer market.

Now it was Leeds who had the aristocratic pedigree, while Sunderland were strictly working class. Yet there was a warning of the quality and character of the Wearsiders in the way they eliminated Manchester City in a fifth-round replay and then toppled Arsenal in the semi-final at Hillsborough. But Leeds supporters comforted themselves by preferring to consider Sunderland's undistinguished performances in the early rounds of the competition when they were taken to replays by Third Division Notts County and Fourth Division Reading.

On paper, it looked as if Sunderland had little or no chance of causing an upset. But out on the pitch...

THE TEAMS: Sunderland Montgomery, Malone, Watson, Pitt, Guthrie, Kerr, Horswill, Porterfield, Hughes, Halom, Tueart.
Leeds United Harvey, Reaney, Madeley, Hunter, Cherry, Bremner, Giles, Eddie Gray, Lorimer, Jones, Clarke. Sub: Yorath.

THE ACTION: Heavy showers had made the Wembley turf slippery and players on both sides struggled to find firm footing in the nervous opening minutes. Sunderland were expected to be overwhelmed in midfield by a Leeds side organised by one of the most talented tandem teams in football in Billy Bremner and Johnny Giles, but it was quickly obvious that they were being effectively contained by Sunderland's driving captain Bobby Kerr and the tenacious Mickey Horswill. The Leeds skills everybody knew about, but it was Sunderland who were taking the eye with unexpected dash and flair from Dennis Tueart, Billy Hughes and Vic Halom that was often stretching the much-vaunted Leeds defence close to breaking point.

Dave Watson, later to become a key player for England, was like a lion in the middle of the Sunderland defence and his ferocious tackling inspired his team-mates and made Leeds suddenly wake up to the fact that they faced a war rather than a walk-over.

After 30 minutes of fast and even competition, Wembley was suddenly rocked by a roar that might have been heard all the way up at Roker. The thundering noise came from the throats of the Sunderland fans celebrating a goal that knocked the life out of Leeds. A Hughes corner from the left flew beyond the far post where Watson's enormous leap distracted the Leeds defence. The ball was deflected back across goal off the knee of Halom to Ian Porterfield, a stylish Scottish midfield player noted for his left foot control. He caught the ball on his left thigh before firing it high into the net with a right foot that, in his own words, he used only to stand on. It wasn't the tidiest goal ever scored at Wembley, but for Sunderland fans it was the greatest they had ever seen.

Leeds were like giants being shaken out of a deep sleep. They struck back with top-quality football, but to no avail against a Sunderland team for which every player was producing the energy and enthusiasm of two men.

Sunderland were protected at the back by Jimmy Montgomery, one of the best uncapped goalkeepers in the game. It was he who literally single handed knocked the heart out of Leeds with an astonishing double save in the 70th minute. He made a stunning reaction save at the near post to push out a diving header from Trevor Cherry. The breathing of Sunderland fans was suspended as the ball dropped at the feet of Peter Lorimer, the man with the cannonball shot. From just six yards he fired in what seemed the equaliser, but Montgomery had other ideas. He threw himself across the goal and somehow managed to divert the ball with his left wrist on to the bar. Sunderland were safe. From that moment on the Cup was theirs because it convinced Leeds that this just wasn't to be their day.

THE WITNESSES: Ian Porterfield: 'To score at Wembley is special, but to have done it with my right foot is beyond belief. I just use my right to stand on usually. Now it's my new secret weapon!'

Bob Stokoe: 'I knew that provided we were ready to compete for every ball and not allow Leeds to dominate in midfield we could win. I ran the length of the pitch at the end to congratulate Monty on his miraculous saves of the second-half. I suppose the whole thing was miraculous really...'

THE MIRACLE MAN: Jimmy Montgomery, born within goal kicking distance of Roker Park on October 9, 1943, played 537 League games for Sunderland before a quick tour of clubs with Southampton, Birmingham and Forest before returning to his beloved Roker. He was an England youth and Under-23 international who would have won promotion to the senior team but for the dominating presence of Gordon Banks, Peter Shilton and Ray Clemence.

QUOTE: Jimmy Montgomery: 'When I die I shall have my left hand embalmed! I have never been prouder of a save than that one from Peter Lorimer Poor old Peter just couldn't believe it. I'm not sure I could either.'

FOR THE RECORD: The FA Cup final victory of '73 was Sunderland's second triumph at Wembley. Raich Carter had collected the Cup for them in '37—a coincidence that really figured with the superstitious men of Leeds. Eleven days later Leeds were beaten 1-0 by AC Milan in the European Cup Winners' Cup final.

JIMMY GREAVES: 'Sunderland's victory was the biggest shock since David beat Goliath. That save of Jimmy Montgomery's was in the same class as the one made by Gordon Banks against Pele in 1970.'

THE CHAMPIONS OF '73

First Division: Liverpool 60 pts. Runners-up: Arsenal, 57 pts
Second Division: Burnley, 62 pts. Runners-up: QPR, 61 pts
Third Division: Bolton Wanderers, 61 pts. Runners-up: Notts County, 57 pts
Fourth Division: Southport, 62 pts. Runners-up: Hereford United, 58 pts
FA Cup Final: Sunderland 1, Leeds United 0
League Cup Final: Tottenham 1, Norwich City 0
Top First Division marksman: Bryan Robson (West Ham United), 28 goals
Footballer of the Year: Pat Jennings (Tottenham)
Scottish champions: Celtic, 57 pts. Runners-up: Rangers, 56 pts
Scottish Cup Final: Rangers 3, Celtic 2
Scottish Player of the Year: George Connelly (Celtic)
European Cup Final: Ajax 1, Juventus 0
European Cup Winners' Cup Final: AC Milan 1, Leeds United 0
UEFA Cup Final: Liverpool 3, Borussia Moenchengladbach 2 (3-0, 0-2)
European Footballer of the Year: Johan Cruyff (Barcelona)

1973-74 Der Bomber Müller makes Holland pay the penalty

Scoreline: West Germany 2, Holland 1
Venue: Olympic Stadium, Munich **Date:** July 7, 1974

THE SETTING: The prospect of the all-European World Cup final between host country West Germany and neighbours Holland whetted the appetite of all football aficionados.

Germany were the European champions and their team was built around a nucleus of players from the brilliant Bayern Munich side that had captured the European Cup just a month before the World Cup finals, chief of whom were skipper Franz Beckenbauer and striker Gerd 'Der Bomber' Müller.

Holland were enjoying the greatest period of their footballing history, with an explosion of talent headed by

Gerd Müller, der Bomber

the artistic Johan Cruyff, a true Dutch master who had helped Ajax win three successive European Cup Finals before taking his golden talent to Barcelona.

It had not been a smooth path to the final for West Germany. They had been beaten 1-0 in their qualifying group in the first ever meeting between East and West Germany, but at least it meant they avoided Holland in the next round. The Dutch had a slight hiccup in their group when held to a goalless draw by Sweden, but they then dismissed East Germany, Argentina and Brazil without conceding a goal and with football that was breathtaking in its skill and simplicity.

Both the Dutch and the Germans had perfected a style labelled 'Total Football' which signified that players were just players rather than forwards and defenders. When on the offensive all players were potential forwards, and all were defenders when the situation demanded it. Something had to give when they came face to face...

THE TEAMS: **West Germany** Maier, Vogts, Schwarzenbeck, Beckenbauer, Breitner, Bonhof, Hoeness, Overath, Grabowski, Müller, Holzenbein. **Holland** Jongbloed, Suurbier, Rijsbergen, Haan, Krol, Jansen, Van Hanagem, Neeskens, Rep, Cruyff, Rensenbrink. Subs: De Jong, R. Van der Kerkhof.

THE ACTION: No World Cup final —indeed, no major match—ever started quite like this one. The Germans were forced to play spot-the-ball as straight from the kick-off Holland put together an unbroken 15-pass move. At first the passes were made in their own half and the German fans jeered what they mistakenly identified as negative possession football. But in the blinking of an eye the ball was suddenly transferred deep into German territory, and as Cruyff made a dramatic break past Bertie Vogts and sprinted goalwards he was tripped by the chasing Uli Hoeness.

English referee Jack Taylor, a master butcher from Wolverhampton, had no hesitation in pointing to the spot for the fastest penalty award in the history of the World Cup. Johan Neeskens calmly steered the spot-kick wide of goalkeeper Sepp Maier. The clock showed just 90 seconds had been played.

Lesser teams than the Germans would have found it difficult to get off their knees after this blitzing start, but —with the majestic Beckenbaueur controlling things from the back like a conductor of an orchestra—they maintained their composure as Holland continued to pass the ball among themselves as casually as if they were in a training session.

It was in this opening 20-minute period when Holland should have sewn the game up. They had almost total possession but lacked a killer thrust.

The Germans realised they were being let off the hook and gradually turned what had been defiant defence into probing attacks. In the 26th minute their growing boldness was rewarded with an equaliser, and again it came from a penalty. Paul Breitner converted the spot-kick after Bernd Holzenbein had been tripped by Jansen after running on to a beautifully placed pass from the elegant Wolfgang Overath.

West Germany were now in command and the Dutch goal had a series of narrow escapes as Hoeness and Beckenbauer teamed up in midfield to dictate the pace and pattern of the game. Holland came briefly back into the match as an attacking force when Cruyff foxed his way past Beckenbauer before setting up a clear scoring chance for Johnny Rep. He hesitated over what looked a simple task of knocking the ball into the net and was finally foiled as Maier dived at his feet. In a retrospective look at the match it was clear that this was the moment when the game, and the Cup, slipped out of Holland's grasp.

Relieved by this let-off, the Germans raised their game to a new peak and non-stop pressure brought what proved to be the winning goal in the 43rd minute. Grabowski, the winger who had run England ragged in Mexico four years earlier, combined with Rainer Bonhof to create a half chance for Gerd Müller. Any other player might have struggled to finish the move off, but the master opportunist dragged the awkwardly bouncing ball back with his left foot and then drilled it low into the net with his right as Arie Haan came clattering in with a tackle that was a split second too late. It was Müller's 68th and most vital goal for his country.

Holland tried desperately to get

back into the match in the second half, but they lost a lot of their rhythm when Robbie Rensenbrink limped off with a pulled muscle. Their best chance of an equaliser fell to Johan Neeskens whose fierce volley from a cross by substitute Rene Van de Kerkhof gave Maier the chance to show why he is rated one of the all-time great goalkeepers. He blocked with ease a shot that had goal written all over it.

Müller celebrated prematurely what he thought was his 69th goal for Germany when he ran through the Dutch defence to beat advancing goalkeeper Jan Jongbloed, but it was ruled offside—a hair-line decision that would have caused a bitter dispute had it affected the result.

One of the most dramatic of all finals ended with the Dutch beaten but not disgraced, and reflecting sadly on how they had allowed the Germans to escape during the first 20 minutes when they produced some of the most dazzling play ever witnessed on any football pitch. It was all very pretty to watch but totally lacking in punch.

THE WITNESSES: Helmut Schoen, West German manager: 'It was a brave decision of the referee to give a penalty so early in the match. We could have been very unsettled by it, but we never lost our composure or our concentration. Once we had equalised I felt confident that we would win. This makes up for the disappointment of our defeat in the 1966 World Cup final and our failure to reach the 1970 final. We had to take a lot of criticism after losing to East Germany in the group match, but the way I

Johan Cruyff, the Dutch master

looked at it was that we had lost a battle but not the war.'

Gerd Müller: 'That was the most satisfying goal of my life. People say that it is an advantage to play at home, but it puts you under enormous pressure. Can you imagine how the supporters would have reacted had I missed that chance? It does not bear thinking about.'

Johan Cruyff: 'We have only ourselves to blame for not winning. For the first 20 or so minutes we could do no wrong, but we have been punished for failing to put the ball into the net. I thought that Franz Beckenbauer was outstanding for the Germans. He always looked so damned confident even when we were running them off their feet.'

DER KAISER: Franz Beckenbauer brought a new dimension to football with his attacking play from a sweeper-base at the back of the defence. An elegant and inventive player, he will always be associated with the great Bayern Munich team of the 1970s. He wound down his distinguished playing career in Hamburg after a spell with New York Cosmos. His 103 international games included the World Cup campaigns of 1966 (runner-up), 1970 (semi-finalist) and 1974 (winning captain). He bravely played on in the memorable 1970 semi-final against Italy despite a painful shoulder injury. Voted European Footballer of the Year in 1972, the player known to his fans as 'Der Kaiser' became a respected coach and took over as the West German team manager.

QUOTE: Franz Beckenbauer: 'In a strange way conceding such a quick goal worked to our advantage. It brought into focus the fear of defeat and it made us sharpen our attention and make a determined effort not to concede another goal. Once we had weathered Holland's opening burst we knew we had managed to live with their best efforts. Once we started to open up their defence with attacking movements of our own I was always confident that we would win.'

FOR THE RECORD: Poland beat Brazil 1-0 in the play-off for third place thanks to a goal by Graegorz Lato who was the tournament's leading marksman with seven goals in seven matches.

JIMMY GREAVES: 'Jack Taylor's decision to give a penalty against the home side in the first minute has to be one of the bravest refereeing decisions of all time. I was hoping to see Holland win because they were such a positive and adventurous side, but you have to admire the way the Germans took the best that they could throw at them and then take charge.'

THE CHAMPIONS OF '74

First Division: Leeds United 62 pts. Runners-up:Liverpool, 57 pts
Second Division: Middlesbrough, 65 pts. Runners-up: Luton Town, 50 pts
Third Division: Oldham Athletic, 62 pts. Runners-up: Bristol Rovers, 61 pts
Fourth Division: Peterborough United, 65 pts. Runners-up: Gillingham, 62 pts
FA Cup Final: Liverpool 3, Newcastle United 0
League Cup Final: Wolves 2, Manchester City 1
Top First Division marksman: Mike Channon (Southampton), 21 goals
Footballer of the Year: Ian Callaghan (Liverpool)
Scottish champions: Celtic, 53 pts. Runners-up: Hibernian, 49 pts
Scottish Cup Final: Celtic 3, Dundee United 0
Scottish Player of the Year: Scottish World Cup squad
European Cup Final: Bayern Munich 4, Atletico Madrid 0 (after a 1-1 draw)
European Cup Winners' Cup Final: FC Magdeburg 2, AC Milan 0
UEFA Cup Final: Tottenham 2, Feyenoord 4 (2-2, 0-2)
European Footballer of the Year: Johan Cruyff (Barcelona)
World Cup Final: West Germany 2, Holland 1

1974-75 Hudson serves up a feast at the Wembley birthday party

Scoreline: England 2, West Germany 0
Venue: Wembley Stadium **Date:** March 12, 1975

THE SETTING: A marriage of the old and the new gave England an exciting dimension when world and European champions West Germany came to Wembley to celebrate the 100th international staged at that famous cathedral of English football.

Artful tactician Don Revie, selecting his third team as England manager, boldly paired Alan Ball and Alan Hudson in midfield and found a devastating double act that promised much for the future.

Ball, the one survivor of England's World Cup winning team that had beaten West Germany in the final at Wembley eight years earlier, was given the extra responsibility of captaincy. Hudson, who had shown precocious skill when a young prodigy at Chelsea, was now the schemer-in-chief for Stoke and was at last being allowed to flourish his creative genius on the international stage.

Hudson—along with defender Colin Todd—had been barred from the England team for refusing to join an Under-23 tour two years earlier. Now the ban had been lifted and both players were ready to show that the two years in the wilderness had been as much England's loss as theirs.

Franz Beckenbauer was the one German survivor from the 1966 World Cup team, and was skippering an experimental side that was being rebuilt following their remarkable successes of the previous two years. There was no Müller, Overath, Hoeness, Grabowski or Breitner, and pass master Gunther Netzer was a spectator on the sidelines. But the Germans were unveiling rich new talent in players like Cullman, Wimmer, Heynckes and Flohe.

Revie had to make his selection without being able to summon players from his old club Leeds because of their FA Cup replay commitments, and so there was no Allan Clarke, Paul Madeley or Norman Hunter.

Alan Hudson, out of the wildnerness

107

Both teams were packed with hungry players keen to establish themselves for the run-up to the 1976 European championships.

THE TEAMS: **England** Clemence, Whitworth, Gillard, Bell, Watson, Todd, Ball, Macdonald, Channon, Hudson, Keegan.
West Germany Maier, Bonhof, Vogts, Koerbel, Beckenbauer, Cullman, Ritschel, Wimmer, Kostedde, Flohe, Holzenbein. Subs: Kremers, Heynckes.

THE ACTION: Alan Hudson stamped his authority on the match right from the start with a performance that has rarely been bettered by a player making his England debut. It was as if he had been patrolling the international arena all his career as he imperiously pointed to where he wanted team-mates to position themselves to receive his arrogantly delivered passes on a pitch soaked by teeming rain.

It was like a display right out of the Gunther Netzer manual, and the English-speaking Netzer asked of the England officials sitting by him: 'Who is this Hudson? Where is he from? What a player!'

With Ball and Bell calling on all their vast experience to dominate in midfield, Hudson had ideal cover to allow himself the luxury of playing the part of a strolling player.

He was feeding Kevin Keegan, Malcolm Macdonald and Mike Channon the sort of dream passes that must have made them wonder if it was their birthday. Behind Hudson, Colin Todd—the other rebel allowed back

into the England fold—was playing like a man possessed. He tackled like a tank and drove his team-mates forward with a passion matched only by demanding skipper Alan Ball.

Hudson's influence was on every England attacking move, and it was his beautifully flighted free-kick that opened the way for Bell to ram in England's first goal in the 25th minute, the diving Sepp Maier managing only to help the ball on its way into the net.

Evidence of England's clear superiority was that the Germans did not force their first corner until an hour had gone by. The ball was scrambled away from the goal-line and this escape prompted Ball to urge extra effort which brought a second match-clinching goal for England when Macdonald rose at the far post to head in his skipper's accurate cross from the right. It was his first goal for England.

THE WITNESSES: Don Revie: 'This is easily the best performance by England since I took over as manager. The England players proved they can hold their own with the best in the world. Ball and Todd were impressive, but the outstanding performance came from Hudson. If he can maintain that sort of form he has the world at his feet.'

Alan Ball: 'It was my proudest moment in football when I led the England team out as captain. Everybody was magnificent, particularly Hudson. All of us in the game know that on his day he is one of the most talented footballers in the world. He proved that against the Germans.'

Franz Beckenbauer: 'We were

experimenting tonight, but that should not be allowed to detract from a fine England performance. I knew that Alan Ball would play his heart out as he always does, but the player all we Germans are talking about is Alan Hudson. Why have we not seen more of him?'

THE IDOL: Alan Hudson, born within sight and sound of Stamford Bridge on June 21, 1951, was cursed throughout his career by injury problems and he won only two more caps after his sensational debut against West Germany. Somewhat undisciplined off the pitch, he was idolised at Chelsea but was allowed to move to Stoke after a personality clash with manager Dave Sexton. After a short spell with Arsenal—his last match was in the 1978 FA Cup final against Ipswich—he joined Seattle Sounders.

QUOTE: Alan Hudson: 'I loved every second of my debut for England, and the way Don Revie reacted I thought I was going to be part of his future plans. But I was frozen out after the next two games against Cyprus. That really hurt but at least I had the satisfaction of getting rave notices for that game against West Germany.'

FOR THE RECORD: England beat Cyprus 5-0 in their next match, with Malcolm Macdonald scoring all five goals. But by the time the following season arrived all the dreams had faded and Hudson and skipper Ball were no longer part of the England squad.

JIMMY GREAVES: 'England, with Alan Hudson looking a million dollars, pulverised the Germans and I thought Don Revie had got the best England team together since the 1970 World Cup. Things looked really promising, but then off-the-pitch personality problems came to the surface and Revie inexplicably broke up the team before it could reach its potential.'

THE CHAMPIONS OF '75

First Division: Derby County, 53 pts. Runners-up:Liverpool, 51 pts
Second Division: Manchester United, 61 pts. Runners-up: Aston Villa, 58 pts
Third Division: Blackburn Rovers, 60 pts. Runners-up: Plymouth, 59 pts
Fourth Division: Mansfield Town, 68 pts. Runners-up: Shrewsbury, 62 pts
FA Cup Final: West Ham United 2, Fulham 0
League Cup Final: Aston Villa 1, Norwich City 0
Top First Division marksman: Malcolm Macdonald (Newcastle U), 21 goals
Footballer of the Year: Alan Mullery (Fulham)
Scottish champions: Rangers, 56 pts. Runners-up: Hibernian, 49 pts
Scottish Cup Final: Celtic 3, Airdrieonians 1
Scottish Player of the Year: Sandy Jardine (Rangers)
European Cup Final: Bayern Munich 2, Leeds United 0
European Cup Winners' Cup Final: Dynamo Kiev 3, Ferencvaros 0
UEFA Cup Final: Borussia Moenchengladbach 5, Twente Enschede 1 (0-0, 5-1)
European Footballer of the Year: Oleg Blokhin (Dynamo Kiev)

1975-76 Geordie Tueart's scissors kick cuts down Newcastle

Scoreline: Manchester City 2, Newcastle United 1
Venue: Wembley Stadium **Date:** February 28, 1976

THE SETTING: Dennis Tueart is a Geordie through and through. He had been born and bred in Newcastle and was one of Sunderland's heroes when they took the FA Cup back to the North East in 1973. Now, having crossed the great divide to join Manchester City in the North West, fate decreed that he should face the home-town club he had supported as a football-daft youngster in the League Cup final.

Newcastle, shaking off the scare of a 'flu bug that at one time put six of their players in doubt for the final, came to Wembley determined to make up for the disappointment of their visit two seasons earlier when they had been generally outplayed by Liverpool in the 1974 FA Cup final.

It was Manchester City's third League Cup final since the competition had gained the Wembley stage in 1967. They beat West Bromwich Albion 3-2 in 1970 and lost 2-1 to Wolves in 1974. Goalkeeper Joe Corrigan and defenders Alan Oakes and Tommy Booth were survivors from the first final and Tony Book, their captain in 1970, was now the City manager. Leading their attack was Joe Royle, the England international centre-forward who had played for Everton in the 1968 FA Cup final.

Newcastle—with a long and proud FA Cup pedigree—were making their first appearance in a League Cup final after beating favourites Tottenham in a thrilling two-leg semi-final. Much of their success was based on the understanding of striking partners, England centre-forward Malcolm Macdonald and Stockport-born Alan Gowling, who had first established himself with Manchester United.

THE TEAMS: **Manchester City**
Corrigan, Keegan, Donachie, Doyle, Watson, Oakes, Barnes, Booth, Royle, Hartford, Tueart.
Newcastle United Mahoney, Nattrass, Kennedy, Barrowclough, Keeley, Howard, Burns, Cassidy, Macdonald, Gowling, Craig.

Dennis Tueart, volley shot specialist

THE ACTION: Newcastle, urged on by an incredible volume of sound from their 'black and white' army of supporters, were first to settle into their stride and the City defence survived several anxious moments in the opening 15 minutes. Yet it was City who snatched the lead when Asa Hartford's perfectly placed free-kick was knocked back across the goal by Mike Doyle. As Newcastle defenders dithered as to which of them should try to clear it, Peter Barnes came speeding in from the left to spring up and strike a mid-air volley that sent the ball crashing into the net off the far post. It was a magnificent goal, but was to be overshadowed by a later effort.

Newcastle shrugged the goal off, just as they had their cold bugs. They struck back with an equaliser that was neatly fashioned and wrapped up with a decisive finish. Alan Kennedy won a tackle out on the left deep in Newcastle territory. The ball was transferred along a conveyor belt of passes from Tommy Craig to Tommy Cassidy and then on to Malcolm Macdonald. SuperMac, desperate to atone for a below-par performance in the 1974 FA Cup final, considered going for goal himself but then spotted his plundering partner Alan Gowling galloping into a better position. He laid the ball back and Gowling drilled it wide of the giant figure of goalkeeper Corrigan.

Just before the end of a fast and even first half Dennis Tueart moved with panther pace to get in a shot that was superbly saved by Mike Mahoney. It was a warning of what was to come.

The second half was barely a minute old when Tueart conjured one of Wembley's great goals. A master of the volley, he had a shot blocked in a raid straight from the kick-off. He was still gathering himself after seeing his shot beaten out when the ball was played back into the goal area by Willie Donachie out on the left. Booth headed the ball towards the far post but there seemed no immediate danger for Newcastle because Tueart had his back to goal. But like a flash of lightning he scissor kicked the ball over his right shoulder and into the net past astonished goalkeeper Mahoney.

Even the Newcastle fans had to applaud this explosion of brilliance and they consoled themselves that the goal had been scored by a player who had learned the footballing arts on the streets and playing fields of Tyneside.

Newcastle refused to surrender but the players who had been suffering from 'flu were rapidly tiring and Asa Hartford began to run the game from midfield with storming support from Dave Watson and Doyle. Macdonald and Gowling both had shots saved by Corrigan in a final flurry by Newcastle but they had to concede defeat. Tueart's scissors shot had cut them down.

THE WITNESSES: Malcolm Macdonald: 'It was a cracking goal by Tueart and brought us to our knees. We came out for the second half determined to get a quick goal and it was a real body blow when City hit us that early.'

Gordon Lee, Newcastle manager: 'I would not dream of making excuses but it is a fact that several of our players were less than fully fit because of the 'flu outbreak. But no matter how fit they had been there was no way anybody could have prevented that goal from Tueart. It was a classic.'

YANKEE DOODLE: Born in Newcastle on November 27, 1949, Dennis Tueart was signed by Manchester City from Sunderland for £275,000 in March, 1974. He won six full England caps while in his first spell at City before becoming a great favourite in the United States with New York Cosmos, who bought him for £250,00 at the age of 28. A quick and incisive player, he netted two goals for Cosmos when they beat Tampa Bay Rowdies in the 1977 Soccerbowl at Meadowlands. In 1980 he returned to League football with his old club Manchester City.

QUOTE:Dennis Tueart: 'I don't want to sound conceited but the goal I

scored against Newcastle was not a fluke. It was the sort of thing I have practised time and again in training, and the ball just happened to drop right for me. I could not have had a better setting for the goal, but what a choker that it had to be against the club I used to support.'

FOR THE RECORD: Newcastle were drawn away to Southport in the second round, but the hard-up Lancashire club elected to play at St James Park. They were beaten 6-0 but were watched by a crowd of 23,000—equal to the total aggregate that had watched their first 18 League matches that season.

JIMMY GREAVES: 'Tueart's goal was a gem. It was the sort of skill that you expect from a Brazilian. The only other British player who might have scored one like it was the one and only Denis Law. I can't give Tueart higher praise than that.'

THE CHAMPIONS OF '76

First Division: Liverpool, 60 pts. Runners-up: QPR, 59 pts
Second Division: Sunderland, 56 pts. Runners-up: Bristol City, 53 pts
Third Division: Hereford United, 63 pts. Runners-up: Cardiff City, 57 pts
Fourth Division: Lincoln City, 74 pts. Runners-up: Northampton Town, 68 pts
FA Cup Final: Southampton 1, Manchester United 0
League Cup Final: Manchester City 2, Newcastle United 1
Top First Division marksman: Ted MacDougall (Norwich City), 23 goals
Footballer of the Year: Kevin Keegan (Liverpool)
Scottish champions (first Premier): Rangers, 54 pts. Runners-up: Celtic, 48 pts
Scottish Cup Final: Rangers 3, Heart of Midlothian 1
Scottish Player of the Year: John Greig (Rangers)
European Cup Final: Bayern Munich 1, St Etienne 0
European Cup Winners' Cup Final: Anderlecht 4, West Ham United 2
UEFA Cup Final: Liverpool 4, Bruges 3 (3-2, 1-1)
European Footballer of the Year: Franz Beckenbauer (Bayern Munich)
European Final: Czechoslovakia 2, West Germany 2 (Czechs won on penalties)

1976-77 — Tommy the Ironman heads to put Liverpool's tails up

Scoreline: Liverpool 3, Borussia Moenchengladbach 1
Venue: Olympic Stadium, Rome **Date:** May 25, 1977

THE SETTING: Liverpool travelled to Italy for their first European Cup final just 48 eight hours after an FA Cup final defeat by Manchester United at Wembley had turned their target of the 'Miraculous Treble' into the impossible dream.

With the League Championship trophy already under lock and key at Anfield, they now had to climb a physical and emotional mountain if they were to conquer European Cup favourites Borussia Moenchengladbach in Rome. Most football experts favoured the Germans and felt that it would take more than three coins in the fountain to get the gods on Liverpool's side.

Liverpool were hardly strangers to European competition. Thirteen successive seasons in the continental cup chase had brought them two UEFA Cup triumphs and a runners-up place in the European Cup Winners' Cup.

But they had fired only blanks in the major tournament, the European Cup. The closest they had come to success was in 1964-65 when they reached the semi-final against Inter-Milan only to be tripped up by two questionable refereeing decisions.

In Borussia they faced a team with an excellent pedigree. Guided by Henness Weisweiler, one of the most respected coaches in the world, they had reached four European finals in the 1970s and had twice won the UEFA Cup. Their impressive record was well known to Anfield fans. The two teams had met in the 1972-73 UEFA Cup final, Liverpool winning their home leg 3-0 and 13 days later managing to hang on to the trophy on aggregate after going down 2-0 in Moenchengladbach. The match that really mattered—the European Cup final—was being staged in Rome five years and two days after the meeting in Germany and, to underline the continuity of the two sides, there were 11 sur-

Kevin Keegan, clinched a transfer

vivors from the game: for Liverpool, Ray Clemence, Tommy Smith, Emlyn Hughes, Kevin Keegan, Steve Heighway and Ian Callaghan; for Borussia, Berti Vogts, Rainer Bonhof, Herbert Wimmer, Jupp Heynckes and substitute Kulik.

Veteran Ian Callaghan had played in all of Liverpool's 13 European seasons, most of them under the banner of the great Bill Shankly who in 1975 had handed the torch on to Bob Paisley after laying the foundation for the power and the glory that was to follow for the Merseysiders.

Paisley had made one of his rare tactical errors by leaving Callaghan on the substitute's bench in the FA Cup final against Manchester United, summoning him into the game too late to turn the tide against Tommy Docherty's adventurous team. But the skilful winger-turned-schemer was selected to start the match against Borussia, triggering a switch in Liverpool tactics from their 4-3-3 formation at Wembley to 4-4-2 in Rome. This meant extra responsibility for Kevin Keegan, the buzz-saw player who was moved to the heart of the Liverpool attack where his injured partner John Toshack usually patrolled. For Keegan, it was the challenge of a lifetime. He was not only playing for a European Cup victory but also to clinch a proposed £500,000 transfer to Hamburg, Borussia's rivals in West Germany.

THE TEAMS: **Liverpool** Clemence, Neal, Jones, Smith, Ray Kennedy, Hughes, Keegan, Case, Heighway, Callaghan, McDermott.

Borussia Moenchengladbach Kneib, Vogts, Klinkhammer, Wittkamp, Bonhof, Wohlers, Simonsen, Wimmer, Stielike, Schaffer, Heynckes. Subs: Hannes, Kulik.

THE ACTION: Liverpool's travelling red army of ee-aye-adioing fans managed to transfer the sight and sound of the Kop to Rome's Olympic Stadium. And Liverpool's players quickly responded to the fanatical support by revealing that they had managed to transfer the skills that made them so dominant on the domestic front.

They were in total control from the first whistle, with Callaghan bossing the midfield like a Napoleonic figure and Keegan running the Borussia defence to the point of panic with a staggering display of perpetual motion. In their one and only telling raid of the first half Bonhof hit the Liverpool post with a snap shot in the 23rd minute. It merely served to make Liverpool go up a gear and in the 27th minute they produced a goal fit for the glittering occasion.

Callaghan gave birth to the majestic move after winning the ball close to the halfway line. He provided a quick pass to Heighway on his right and then made an overlapping support run on the high-stepping Irish international's outside which immediately gave the scampering German defenders problems as to which player to mark, the one with the ball or Callaghan who was moving with such menace down the touchline.

Borussia were so intent on trying to solve the poser set by Callaghan and Heighway that they failed to spot

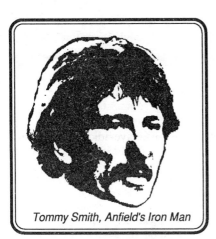

Tommy Smith, Anfield's Iron Man

Terry McDermott moving like an express train on a 50-yard sprint from deep in midfield. Heighway, now cutting diagonally towards goal, knew McDermott would be powering into position because this was a move that had been practised and perfected in dozens of training sessions. He released a perfectly weighted pass between two German defenders and McDermott and the ball arrived together in the penalty area with only goalkeeper Kneib aware of the sudden danger. A German international who knew all about positioning, Kneib did his best to cover his goal as he came forward urgently to narrow the angle but he was beaten all ends up by McDermott's shot on the run that arrowed into the left hand corner of the net. It was a goal fit to hang in an art gallery.

As so often happens after a half-time interval, the team in control lost its rhythm and it was Borussia who started to have the better of exchanges and seven minutes into the second half they were level in a game in which

they had been playing purely a supporting role. Jimmy Case misdirected a headed backpass to the feet of flying Dane Allan Simonsen who needed no second invitation to whip the ball past Clemence for the equaliser.

This was when Liverpool's famous character and spirit were given the severest of examinations. Suddenly spectators were recalling how the Merseysiders had dramatically become brittle after monopolising the FA Cup final against Manchester United four days earlier. Clemence had to risk life and limb as he rushed off his line to save at the feet of the lightning-fast Uli Stielike and there were definite signs of the Liverpool defence starting to buckle in sultry, stamina-sapping conditions.

But the crisis ended as quickly as it had begun. Liverpool were restored to their commanding role when Heighway took a corner from the left in the 65th minute which was met at the near post by, of all people, that redoubtable defender Tommy Smith who sent a thundering header into the net. A Tommy Smith header was as rare as a Penny Black on a postcard from Siberia and it helped push the dynamic 32-year-old Anfield Assassin deeper into the land of Liverpool legend. He had been recalled to the team as a replacement for injured Phil Thompson, and announced it would be his final game before hanging up his boots. But the goal went to his head to such an extent that he decided he was good for another season!

Smith's golden goal calmed Liverpool down and they returned to their flowing football of the first half. They survived one more scare when Clemence had to make another courageous dive towards flying feet, this time to whip the ball off the toes of the dangerous Heynckes.

Then, with seven minutes of a pulsating match left, Liverpool collected the clinching goal that finally knocked all the fight out of battling Borussia. Non-stop Keegan had been giving Berti Vogts, his vastly experienced marker, the sort of run around of which nightmares are made.

Keegan had been unselfishly making chances for others, but he now set off on a run for goal determined to score himself. Even with the ball at his feet he was able to outpace the stocky Vogts as he spurted through the middle of the Borussia defence. In his desperation to stop his tormentor, Vogts tripped Keegan from behind just as he had opened the path to goal. There was no alternative but for the referee to award a penalty. It had been a run of sheer brilliance by Keegan that convinced the watching Hamburg officials that they should tie up his transfer immediately after the match.

The penalty responsibility was left to deadeye shot Phil Neal, who powered the ball into the net to complete the greatest night in Liverpool's history.

THE WITNESSES: Phil Neal: 'I have never felt under such pressure when taking a penalty. I knew that if I scored it would settle the match, but also that if I missed it would give Borussia the momentum for a final effort to force an equaliser. I had scored from the penalty spot in the semi-final in Zurich and had hit the ball to the goalkeeper's left. It was a certainty that the Borussia 'keeper would have studied that kick on television and so I shot to his right. I had won the battle of wits because he dived the wrong way and the ball was suddenly in the back of their net. It was the most important kick of my career.'

Bob Paisley: 'This was a triumph of character. I had to convince the players that our season had not fallen apart because of that one defeat by Manchester United at Wembley. They pushed it out of their mind and produced a team performance that must surely go down as one of the best ever seen in a European Cup final. I have just carried on where Bill Shankly left off. We have tremendous strength in depth and I am not being boastful when I say that this is only the start. There is no team in the world that we need fear.'

Emlyn Hughes, Liverpool skipper: 'Bill Shankly is in all our thoughts. This was as much his triumph as anybody else's . The character and determination that you have all seen was put there by Shanks. Bob Paisley has wisely carried on in the Shankly way. He has let things tick over without trying to make dramatic changes. Tonight he has got his reward for wise management, and he will be the first to admit that the Cup belongs to Shanks as much as to him.'

Tommy Smith: 'I don't think I'll wash my head ever again after that goal. Dixie Dean would have been proud of it. One of the newspapers had dismissed me as a myth and had written an end to my career. Well when did you last see a myth head a goal like that. I think I'll enter it in the

Myth World contest! Seriously though, this is the greatest night of my footballing life. Our supporters made us feel as if we were playing in front of the Kop. We're proud of what we have achieved for them. If anybody deserves to be able to show off the European Cup it's them. They're different class.'

Berti Vogts: 'We have no complaints. The best team on the night won. Kevin Keegan was particularly outstanding. I had been given the task of marking him, but to be honest the mood he was in it needed two men to do the job. He will prove himself a great favourite in Germany, of that I am sure.'

THE YORKSHIRE TERRIER: Kevin Keegan, born in Armthorpe, Yorkshire, on February 14, 1951, was a late developer who was overlooked by the major clubs early in his career. Coventry City rejected him after a trial and he kicked off his professional footballing life down in the bargain basement with Scunthorpe United. Liverpool spotted his potential and Bill Shankly paid £30,000 for him in 1971 after he had scored 18 goals in 120 League games for Scunthorpe. He quickly blossomed with Liverpool where his plundering partnership with John Toshack helped push the Anfield club to a procession of title-winning triumphs.

Keegan scored two goals for Liverpool in their 1974 FA Cup final victory over Newcastle, was voted Footballer of the Year in 1976 and collected three League Championship medals before making his farewell appearance in the European Cup final in Rome. Hamburg shelled out a British record £500,000 for him and he repaid the fee several times over with a succession of outstanding performances that earned him the European Footballer of the Year title in 1979 and again in 1980.

Always a single-minded and surprising personality, Keegan stunned everybody in the game when he elected to return to English football in the summer of 1980 with unfashionable Southampton—which was a major coup for the persuasive powers of manager Lawrie McMenemy. Two years later, after becoming an idol at The Dell, Keegan provided yet another twist in his footballing story when he agreed to sign for Newcastle. He was hailed as a saviour on Tyneside and provided the spark that drove them back to the First Division in his final season. Capped 63 times by England but unable to impress new manager Bobby Robson, he stepped off the soccer stage in 1984 at the age of 33 and after one of the most dramatic careers of modern times. He has since become a media personality, travelling back to England from his base in Spain to give his authoritative comments on matches for the ITV and BBC teams.

QUOTE: Kevin Keegan: 'The nice thing is that I became close friends with Berti Vogts after that match. He is one of the nicest men in football and never once did he try to resort to foul tactics when I was getting the better of him in Rome. The penalty was not malicious. He was just trying too hard to catch up with me. I was under enormous pressure in the match

117

against Borussia because the deal with Hamburg was all but complete. This was common knowledge in Liverpool and quite a lot of fans turned against me as if I was some sort of traitor, choosing to ignore the fact that I had run my legs off for the club for six years. But at least I knew I had not let a soul down at Anfield.'

FOR THE RECORD: Liverpool followed their victory in Rome by retaining the European Cup with a 1-0 victory over Bruges at Wembley in 1978. The winning goal was scored by Kenny Dalglish, the player Bob Paisley bought as a replacement for Keegan. Liverpool won the European Cup again in 1981 (beating Real Madrid 1-0 in Paris with a goal by Alan Kennedy) and in 1984 (defeating AS Roma 4-2 on penalties in Rome after a 1-1 draw) before losing in the 1985 final to Juventus in the miserable match sadly remembered for the Heysel Stadium tragedy.

JIMMY GREAVES: 'There have been more attractive and adventurous Liverpool teams than the one that won the European Cup in 1977, but their performance that night was quite unforgettable. It was particularly memorable for Kevin Keegan, a player whose industry I always admired. There were more skilful and more inventive players, but his remarkable work rate when coupled with his considerable ability lifted him above most of his rivals. Tommy Smith's header was a real collectors' item! Most of all it was a triumph for that great manager Bill Shankly. He always claimed that Liverpool played the best football in Europe and this was proof to support him.'

THE CHAMPIONS OF '77

First Division: Liverpool, 57 pts. Runners-up: Manchester City, 56 pts
Second Division: Wolves, 57 pts. Runners-up: Chelsea, 55 pts
Third Division: Mansfield Town, 64 pts. Runners-up: Brighton, 61 pts
Fourth Division: Cambridge United, 65 pts. Runners-up: Exeter City, 62 pts
FA Cup Final: Manchester United 2, Liverpool 1
League Cup Final: Aston Villa 3, Everton 2 (after extra time, following 0-0 and 1-1 draws)
Top First Division marksmen: Andy Gray (Aston Villa) and Malcolm Macdonald (Arsenal), 25 goals
Footballer of the Year: Emlyn Hughes (Liverpool)
Scottish champions: Celtic, 55 pts. Runners-up: Rangers, 46 pts
Scottish Cup Final: Celtic 1, Rangers 0
Scottish Player of the Year: Danny McGrain (Celtic)
European Cup Final: Liverpool 3, Borussia Moenchengladbach 1
European Cup Winners' Cup Final: Hamburg 2, Anderlecht 0
UEFA Cup: Juventus 2, Atletico Bilbao 2 (1-0, 1-2, Juventus won on away goals)
European Footballer of the Year: Allan Simonsen (B. Moenchengladbach)

1977-78 | Malice in Wonderland as Kempes outshoots Dutch

Scoreline: Argentina 3, Holland 1 (after extra time)
Venue: Buenos Aires **Date:** June 25, 1978

THE SETTING: The 1978 World Cup final can best be summed up as 'Malice in Wonderland.' There were too many nasty, niggling moments for it to be classed a great match, but there has rarely, if ever, been a sporting occasion to compare with it for a cocktail of colour, atmosphere, excitement and controversy.

It was the World Cup final that was almost abandoned before a ball had been kicked. The Argentinians tried deliberately to unnerve Holland by keeping the Dutchmen waiting for seven minutes before they deigned to join them on the pitch where they were greeted with an ecstactic welcome from their frenzied fans who showered the pitch with rivers of blue and white streamers.

Argentina were still not ready to play the game, either physically or in the sporting sense. They caused a further delay by objecting to the light plaster cast that René Van der Kerkhof was wearing on his right wrist. He had worn it from the start of the tournament without a murmur of protest from any of Holland's previous five opponents.

This was nearly the breaking point for Dutch skipper Johan Neeskens, who told rival captain Daniel Passarella: 'If that's how you want it, you can play the World Cup final on your own.'

Mario Kempes, the pace of a panther

Neeskens was just about to lead his players off the pitch when Italian referee Sergio Gonella—a compromise choice following disagreements about who should control the final—ruled that Van der Kerkhof could play with the plaster. The Dutch players, who had been holding an impromptu team meeting on the pitch, were satisfied and lined up for the kick-off. It was hardly the best of spirits in which to start a World Cup final, and over the next two hours there was naked hatred to be witnessed on the pitch as well as some scintillating football.

THE TEAMS: **Argentina** Fillol, Olguin, Galvan, Passarella, Tarantini, Ardiles, Gallego, Kempes, Bertoni, Luque, Ortiz. Subs: Larrosa, Houseman.

Holland Jongbloed, Jansen, Krol, Brandts, Portvliet, Willie Van der Kerkhof, Neeskens, Haan, René Van der Kerkhof, Rep, Rensenbrink. Subs: Suurbier, Nanninga.

THE ACTION: Dutch tempers were still at boiling point as the match started and within the first three minutes of a game scarred by more than 50 fouls two Argentinian players—Bertoni and Ardiles—had been victims of vicious tackles.

Though missing the gifts of striker Johan Cruyff and the guidance of schemer Van Hanegem, Holland were every bit as powerful a team as when they reached the 1974 final. Only magnificent goalkeeping denied them first-half goals when Ubaldo Fillol saved first from Rep and then Rensenbrink.

There were beautifully constructed attacking movements from the Argentinian and Dutch forwards despite the fussy refereeing of Signor Gonella whose inconsistent decisions caused anger and dissent on both sides. It was Mario Kempes, the ace in the Argentinian pack and the most productive forward in the tournament, who broke the scoring deadlock after 38 minutes. He accelerated past Rudi Krol to score with a ruthlessly drilled shot after clever approach work by Osvaldo Ardiles and Leopoldo Luque.

Seconds before half-time Rensenbrink missed a golden chance to equalise when Fillol smothered the close-range shot that the winger should have buried in the net.

Holland were in command throughout most of the second half and the Argentinians resorted to cynical fouls in a bid to stop their progress. The goal the Dutch had always been threatening to score was delayed until seven minutes from the final whistle when towering substitute Dirk Nanninga headed in a cross from René Van der Kerkhof.

Rensenbrink had the chance to write his name into the record books in the final seconds but shot against the post from just five yards after getting into an unmarked position to collect a centre from substitute Suurbier.

Holland had drained themselves of energy with their flat-out performance in the second half and they had no heart for a comeback after Kempes pounced with panther pace to make it 2-1 in the 14th minute of extra time. He wriggled past three challenges before scoring at the second attempt after his first shot had been blocked by goalkeeper Jongbloed.

Argentina put the seal on the victory when Bertoni made it 3-1 six minutes from the end after a Kempes run had cleaved a great hole in the middle of the demoralised Dutch defence.

THE WITNESSES: Cesar Menotti, Argentina's manager who chain smoked so many cigarettes he should have carried a government health warning: 'Holland had the superior physical strength, but it was our skill that told in the end. Mario Kempes

was our hero, but he could not have done it without the assistance of his team-mates who gave him valuable support. We achieved our objective of winning the World Cup in a style that could only be good for the game of football. Nobody could accuse us of being negative or boring.'

Johan Neeskens, Dutch skipper: 'Without Kempes Argentina would have been an ordinary side. He gave them a touch of magic. But for him, we would now be the champions.'

MAGICAL MARIO: Born in Cordoba in 1955, Mario Kempes was 19 when he played in the 1974 World Cup finals but made little impact. His game blossomed when he joined Valencia in Spain from his local club Rosario Central in 1976. He was top scorer for Valencia in his first two seasons, but lost much of his sparkle after his peak performances in the 1978 World Cup. He had signed a five-year contract with Valencia but returned to Argentina to play for River Plate.

QUOTE: Mario Kempes: 'I learnt how to conserve my energy playing in the Spanish League. This was why I was able to give my best in the moments when it really mattered in the World Cup. The final was the greatest experience of my life.'

FOR THE RECORD: Argentina had to beat Peru by at least four goals to reach the final and managed to score six against Argentinian-born goalkeer Ramon Quiroga. Brazil beat Italy 3-1 in the third-place play-off.

JIMMY GREAVES: 'I felt sick for Holland. For the second successive tournament they were the best team but finished runners-up. Argentina had some outstanding players, particularly Kempes and Ardiles, but they were too cynical for my taste.'

THE CHAMPIONS OF '78

First Division: Nottingham Forest, 64 pts. Runners-up: Liverpool, 57 pts
Second Division: Bolton Wanderers, 58 pts. Runners-up: Southampton, 57 pts
Third Division: Wrexham, 61 pts. Runners-up: Cambridge United, 58 pts
Fourth Division: Watford, 71 pts. Runners-up: Southend United, 60 pts
FA Cup Final: Ipswich Town 1, Arsenal 0
League Cup Final: Nottingham Forest 1, Liverpool 0 (after 0-0 draw)
Top First Division marksman: Bob Latchford (Everton), 30 goals
Footballer of the Year: Kenny Burns (Nottingham Forest)
Scottish champions : Rangers, 55 pts. Runners-up: Aberdeen, 53 pts
Scottish Cup Final: Rangers 2, Aberdeen 1
Scottish Player of the Year: Derek Johnstone (Rangers)
European Cup Final: Liverpool 1, FC Bruges 0
European Cup Winners' Cup Final: Anderlecht 4, Austria/WAC 0
UEFA Cup Final: Bastia 0, PSV Eindhoven 3 (0-0, 0-3)
European Footballer of the Year: Kevin Keegan (SV Hamburg)
World Cup Final: Argentina 3, Holland 1 (after extra time)

1978-79 Brady claws the FA Cup from the jaws of United

Scoreline: Arsenal 3, Manchester United 2
Venue: Wembley Stadium **Date:** May 12, 1979

THE SETTING: Can just five minutes of football earn a match the billing of being 'great'? For all those who witnessed the incredible last five minutes of the 1979 FA Cup final the answer has to be a definite yes.

Arsenal were back at Wembley a year after losing to the only goal of the match by Ipswich Town hero Roger Osborne. The game had been a personal nightmare for Irish international midfield master Liam Brady, who had unwisely played when less than fully fit and he had been unable to make any sort of impact on the match. Brady was determined to make up for the heartbreak of 1978 against Manchester United, a team making their third FA Cup final appearance in four seasons. They had been stunned to defeat by Southampton in 1976 and had returned to Wembley the following year to sink mighty Liverpool.

United, with former Arsenal coach Dave Sexton as their imaginative manager, had cleared the Liverpool hurdle again after a replay in the semi-finals to earn a place in the 1979 final. Arsenal had survived a dramatic five-match third-round tie against Sheffield Wednesday and eventually got to Wembley via a 2-0 semi-final victory over Wolves.

THE TEAMS: **Arsenal** Jennings, Rice, Nelson, Talbot, O'Leary, Young, Brady, Sunderland, Stapleton, Price, Rix. Sub: Walford.
Manchester United Bailey, Nicholl, Albiston, McIlroy, McQueen, Buchan, Coppell, Jimmy Greenhoff, Jordan, Macari, Thomas. Sub: Brian Greenhoff.

THE ACTION: Arsenal appeared to have killed the match stone dead as a contest with two first-half goals that gave them a flattering 2-0 lead. Both goals were created by Brady, who wiped out the memory of his misery

Liam Brady, midfield commander

against Ipswich with as commanding an individual performance as has been seen in an FA Cup final. He started the 12th minute move that climaxed with Brian Talbot—on the winning side with Ipswich the previous year—edging out team-mate Alan Sunderland in a race to put the finishing touch to a pass by David Price after inventive work out on the wing by Frank Stapleton.

For the next half hour it was United who played the more constructive and composed football, and goalkeeper Pat Jennings needed to be at his best to keep Arsenal ahead. Jimmy Greenhoff, Lou Macari, Mickey Thomas and Joe Jordan all had scoring attempts before Brady eased the pressure with a quick break down the right from deep in midfield. United's defenders scurried back to cover and were waiting for the Irishman to use his famed and feared left foot, but he fooled them by suddenly crossing the ball with his right foot. Stapleton, his fellow Dubliner, had read the situation perfectly and came dashing round the blindside of the United defence to meet the ball at the far post and head it wide of goalkeeper Gary Bailey.

After a half-time tactics talk from coach Don Howe, Arsenal adopted a what-we-have-we-hold attitude in the second half, and though surrendering territorial advantage rarely looked like allowing United the inspiration of a goal. The game was dying on its feet and many uncommitted fans were leaving the stadium when there was an explosion of action that turned a fairly undistinguished match into an unforgettable one.

With just five minutes to go Arsenal sent on Steve Walford as a substitute for tiring David Price. Walford had not touched the ball when he looked on in horror as United scored two goals in two minutes. Centre-half Gordon McQueen swung a long leg hopefully after Joe Jordan had pushed a Steve Coppell free-kick into the danger area. The ball threaded its way from McQueen's boot past a forest of legs and into the Arsenal net.

Panic suddenly swept through the Arsenal defence like water gushing through a holed ship and two minutes later United scored again when Sammy McIlroy ran on to a pass from Coppell, outpaced David O'Leary and the still-cold Walford and fired the ball positively into the net.

From being down and out jubilant United were now thinking in terms of victory in extra time that was just one minute away. But in their moment of euphoria they committed the cardinal sin of losing their concentration, and they were suddenly mortified to see Brady racing towards their penalty area with the ball at his feet. He drew two defenders out of position and then slipped the sweetest of passes to Graham Rix. Arsenal players piled forward into the United penalty area and were queuing up beyond hesitant goalkeeper Bailey to meet Rix's centre. It was Sunderland who rammed the ball home to give the match an astonishing finish to compare with that of the Stanley Matthews final just over a quarter of a century before. The hardest job the Arsenal players had was catching Sunderland to congratulate him as he took off on a wild celebration run.

THE WITNESSES: Dave Sexton: 'Football can be a cruel game. We were too busy congratulating ourselves on forcing extra time and lost concentration. It was unprofessional but, in the circumstances, understandable. I'm proud that we were part of something as dramatic as this.'

Terry Neill: 'This match will live on in everybody's memory because of that finish. Liam Brady has now proved to everybody that there is not a better passer of the ball in the game.'

THE CLAWMAN: Born in Dublin on February 13, 1956, Liam followed two elder brothers into English League football. Famous for a left foot known as 'The Claw,' he scored 43 goals in 235 First Division matches for Arsenal before taking his talent to Italy where he played for Juventus, Sampdoria, Inter-Milan and Ascoli. He returned to London in 1987 as a West Ham player. A suspension and injury prevented Eire's favourite player from taking part in the Republic's successful 1988 European Championships.

QUOTE: Liam Brady: 'I can now live with the memory of the FA Cup final against Ipswich when I had a nightmare. But I'm not sure how I might have reacted had we not scored that last-minute winner against United. I doubt if there will ever be a finish to match it.'

FOR THE RECORD: Arsenal were back at Wembley in 1980 for a third successive final when they were beaten by a rare headed goal from West Ham's Trevor Brooking.

JIMMY GREAVES: 'Liam Brady is one of the finest midfield players to grace the game in a decade or more, as he proved with his commanding performance against United. That amazing finish served to underline what I have always said—football's a funny old game.'

THE CHAMPIONS OF '79

First Division: Liverpool, 68 pts. Runners-up: Nottingham Forest, 60 pts
Second Division: Crystal Palace, 57 pts. Runners-up: Brighton, 56 pts
Third Division: Shrewsbury Town, 61 pts. Runners-up: Watford, 60 pts
Fourth Division: Reading, 65 pts. Runners-up: Grimsby Town, 61 pts
FA Cup Final: Arsenal 3, Manchester United 2
League Cup Final: Nottingham Forest 3, Southampton 2
Top First Division marksman: Frank Worthington (Bolton W), 24 goals
Footballer of the Year: Kenny Dalglish (Liverpool)
Scottish champions : Celtic, 48 pts. Runners-up: Rangers, 45 pts
Scottish Cup Final: Rangers 3, Hibernian 2 (after 0-0 and 0-0 draws)
Scottish Player of the Year: Andy Ritchie (Morton)
European Cup Final: Nottingham Forest 1, Malmö 0
European Cup Winners' Cup Final: Barcelona 4, Fortuna Dusseldorf 3 (aet)
UEFA Cup Final: Red Star Belgrade 1, Borussia Moenchengladbach 2 (1-1, 0-1)
European Footballer of the Year: Kevin Keegan (SV Hamburg)

1979-80 Francis ends goal famine as Forest clear Berlin wall

Scoreline: Dynamo Berlin 1, Nottingham Forest 3
Venue: Festival Stadion, Berlin **Date:** March 19, 1980

THE SETTING: Has the Nottingham Forest bubble burst? Can Brian Clough pick up his team off the floor? Is this the end of the line for the Nottingham Express? Has the Forest fire gone out?

These were the sort of cliché questions being bandied about in the tabloids as Nottingham Forest prepared to meet Deutschland Democratic Republic champions Dynamo Berlin in the second leg of a crucial European Cup quarter-final tie in East Germany.

After three years of non-stop success the ominous signs were that Forest had suddenly and dramatically

Trevor Francis, million pound man

lost their way. They had surrendered their unbeaten record in the European Cup to Dynamo in the first leg, going down to a 1-0 defeat at Nottingham. This was a sickening enough body blow for Cloughie, their miracle maker of a manager, but worse was to come. Just four days before the return match in Berlin Forest were beaten 1-0 by Wolves at Wembley in the final of the League Cup, the competition they had monopolised and won for the last two years.

Now only their most ardent supporters would have backed them to survive in the European Cup that they had captured at their first attempt in 1979, a year after sprinting away with the League Championship. The previous season they had sneaked into the First Division as third-placed promotion team, and ever since they had been enjoying a sensational success sequence.

One stark reason why Forest had lost their momentum was that Trevor Francis had hit a goals famine. The player Cloughie had made Britain's first £1million footballer when buying him from Birmingham in 1979 had slipped into the sort of worrying form where you would not have backed him to hit the side of a barn with a shot. A lot of people expected Francis—scorer of the goal that won Forest the European Cup ten months earlier—to be

125

dropped for the match against Dynamo. But Brian Clough, the master motivator who is as much a psychiatrist as a manager, cleverly boosted his confidence by letting him know he still had faith in his ability. Now all Clough could do was sit on the sidelines and see how Francis would respond to his support, no doubt wondering at the back of his mind whether it might have been wiser to have selected the enigmatic Stan Bowles, who was sitting alongside him keeping the substitute's bench warm.

THE TEAMS: **Dynamo Berlin**
Rüdwalett, Noack, Trieloff, Strasser, Brillat, Troppa, Terietzkl, Gilrich, Riediger, Pelka, Netz.
Nottingham Forest: Shilton, Anderson, Gray, McGovern, Lloyd, Needham, O'Neill, Bowyer, Birtles, Francis, Robertson.

THE ACTION: The bleak, totally uncovered Berlin stadium was about as welcoming as a barbed-wire handshake and the wind blowing in from the direction of Siberia cut through the Forest players like a sickle. But they were quickly warmed by the early goal for which Cloughie and his right-hand man Peter Taylor had been pleading, and the fact that it was Francis who scored it brought an extra flush of satisfaction to Cloughie as he sat huddled on the touchline.

Dynamo played into the hands of Forest by deciding to sit back and protect their 1-0 lead behind their own version of the Berlin wall. Gary Birtles, who had been as much in the doldrums as Francis, inspired his team-mates with two enthusiastic charges through the wall defence in the opening minutes. The East German defenders started to panic under pressure and when the energetic Ian Bowyer was fouled in the 16th minute Larry Lloyd sent a free-kick high to fellow defender David Needham who had got forward into the Dynamo penalty area. He headed the ball across the face of the goal and Francis, at last showing the rapid reactions on which he had built his reputation, was a thought and a deed ahead of all around him as he moved forward to steer the ball into the net.

A sleeping lion had been awakened. Francis suddenly grew in confidence and stature and started to dictate the tempo of the game. Peter Shilton made one of his magnificent diving saves to keep out a shot from Brillat during a rare Dynamo raid. It encouraged even greater effort from Forest and Martin O'Neill ended a determined run in the 35th minute with a low centre to Francis. He was as nimble as a thimble as he turned past a close-marking defender and all in one movement fired a rising shot into the net off the underside of the bar.

Three minutes later jinking John Robertson was brought down, picked himself up, dusted himself off and planted the penalty kick into the net to make it 3-1 on aggregate.

Skipper Terletzkl scored for Dynamo from the penalty spot in the 49th minute after an alleged foul by Robertson, but Forest—relieved when a shot shook their crossbar—remained commanding and composed as they held out for a famous victory.

THE WITNESSES: Brian Clough: 'It was just a question of maintaining belief in ourselves. We concentrated on doing the simple things well, and all it needed was that early goal from Francis to restore our confidence. This has been a triumph for our strength of character.'

Peter Shilton: 'There was an icy wind blowing that made it difficult to gauge the movement of the ball but once Trevor scored that early goal we all sensed we could win.'

THE MILLION-POUND MAN: Born in Plymouth on April 19, 1954, Trevor has become a have-boots-will-travel footballer since Forest made him British football's first £1million player when signing him from Birmingham City in February, 1979. He spent two summers with Detroit Express and Forest recouped their million pounds when they sold him in 1981 to Manchester City who in turn collected

£800,000 for his services from Sampdoria in 1982. Capped 52 times, Trevor has since played for Rangers in Glasgow and in 1988 became player-manager of Queen's Park Rangers.

QUOTE: Trevor Francis: 'I felt a weight come off my shoulders when I scored the first goal against Dynamo. It gave me just the confidence boost I needed and from that moment on I knew we were going to win.'

FOR THE RECORD: Forest—minus injured Francis—went on to retain the European Cup. John Robertson scored the only goal of the final against Kevin Keegan's Hamburg in Madrid.

JIMMY GREAVES: 'Trevor Francis lost his way for a while at Forest when he started trying to play in a style that didn't really suit him. At his peak, there have been few modern strikers to touch him for quality and control.'

THE CHAMPIONS OF '80

First Division: Liverpool, 60 pts. Runners-up: Manchester United, 58 pts
Second Division: Leicester City, 55 pts. Runners-up: Sunderland, 54 pts
Third Division: Grimsby Town, 62 pts. Runners-up: Blackburn Rovers, 59 pts
Fourth Division: Huddersfield Town, 66 pts. Runners-up: Walsall, 64 pts
FA Cup Final: West Ham United 1, Arsenal 0
League Cup Final: Wolves 1, Nottingham Forest 0
Top First Division marksman: Phil Boyer (Southampton), 23 goals
Footballer of the Year: Terry McDermott (Liverpool)
Scottish champions : Aberdeen, 48 pts. Runners-up: Celtic, 47 pts
Scottish Cup Final: Celtic 1, Rangers 0
Scottish Player of the Year: Gordon Strachan (Aberdeen)
European Cup Final: Nottingham Forest 1, SV Hamburg 0
European Cup Winners' Cup: Valencia 0, Arsenal 0 (Valencia, 5-4 on penalties)
UEFA Cup: Eintracht 3, Borussia Moenchengladbach 3 (Eintracht on away goals)
European Footballer of the Year: Karl-Heinz Rummenigge (Bayern Munich)
European Championship Final: West Germany 2, Belgium 1

1980-81 Second-chance Villa makes it carnival time at Wembley

Scoreline: Tottenham Hotspur 3, Manchester City 2
Venue: Wembley Stadium **Date:** May 14, 1981

THE SETTING: The 100th FA Cup final was a drab, disappointing affair distinguished only by the freak fact that Manchester City's Tommy Hutchison scored both goals in a 1-1 draw with Tottenham. His hero-and-villain act gave birth to a replay that produced a gem of a game rarely bettered

Ricardo Villa, the goal of a lifetime

in the previous century of matches.

Hutchison's first goal—fully intended—was a superbly directed near-post header that ended 30 minutes of stalemate soccer. His equaliser—an unintentional deflection—came ten minutes from the end when a Glenn Hoddle free-kick ricocheted off his shoulder into the opposite corner of the net being guarded by giant goalkeeper Joe Corrigan.

Watching this untidy but gratefully received gift goal was Tottenham's dark and brooding Argentinian Ricardo Villa, who moments earlier had been substituted. He made no secret of being disgusted with manager Keith Burkinshaw's decision and the television cameras followed him as he trudged sulkily around the perimeter of the pitch towards the dressing-rooms. He had just reached the players' tunnel when he turned to see the horrified Hutchison cancel out his goal for Manchester City.

Little did Villa know it then, but Hutchison's nightmare equaliser had opened the door to a dream for the big, bearded man from Buenos Aires.

The uninspiring match finished locked at 1-1 after extra time and everybody gathered back at Wembley five days later for a Thursday evening return encounter—only the second Wembley FA Cup final to need a replay (Chelsea v Leeds in 1970 was

the first). The only thing the replay had in common with the first match is that the players wore the same colour shirts, but this time the football they produced was a feast in comparison with the famine of Saturday's game.

THE TEAMS: **Tottenham Hotspur** Aleksic, Hughton, Miller, Roberts, Perryman, Villa, Ardiles, Archibald, Galvin, Hoddle, Crooks.
Manchester City Corrigan, Ranson, McDonald, Caton, Reid, Gow, Power, MacKenzie, Reeves, Bennett, Hutchison. Sub: Tueart.

THE ACTION: The first ten minutes of the replay produced more excitement and incident than the previous 120 minutes put together. Ricky Villa, selected despite his tantrums after being substituted on the Saturday, determinedly struck an early goal for Spurs from seven yards after his more illustrious countryman, Osvaldo Ardiles, and then Steve Archibald had seen their shots blocked in a feverish opening assault on the City goal. Villa went off on a celebratory run that was to prove just a dress rehearsal for the carnival of joy that was to come later.

Within minutes City had equalised with a goal that can be put up alongside the very best scored at Wembley—or on any other ground, for that matter. The fact that it is now relatively forgotten speaks volumes for the magic and drama that was to follow. The scorer was Steve Mac-Kenzie, the player who had been bought for what was a mind-boggling sum of £250,000 when a 17-year-old unknown at Crystal Palace. Now, two years older, he showed that the then City manager Malcolm Allison had been a good judge with a goal that only a thoroughbred footballer could have created.

Tommy Hutchison directed a headed pass to MacKenzie just outside the penalty area and he struck a blinding right-footed volley into the net with such power that goalkeeper Milija Aleksic did not see it, let alone touch it.

Tottenham quickly composed themselves after this hammer blow and—driven on by their man-for-all-seasons captain, Steve Perryman—they had much the better of the exchanges, yet they found themselves 2-1 down after eight minuts of the second half. City striker Dave Bennett was sandwiched by defenders Paul Miller and Chris Hughton when powering towards goal, and Keith Hackett had no hesitation in becoming only the fifth referee to award a penalty in an FA Cup final at Wembley.

Like George Mutch (Preston, 1938), Eddie Shimwell (Blackpool, 1948), Ronnie Allen (West Brom, 1954) and Danny Blanchflower (Spurs, 1962) before him, Kevin Reeves slotted the penalty home to put City into a flattering lead.

The gifted Glenn Hoddle, missing presumed overawed in the first match, now started to reveal his vast repertoire of midfield magic as he inspired a Tottenham revival movement that had the City defenders as confused and hounded as cats in a dog pound.

Hoddle dropped a lofted pass like a mortar shell into the heart of the City defence in the 70th minute and while

Steve Archibald was trying to bring the ball under control his plundering partner Garth Crooks came steaming alongside him to thump the ball into the net for his 22nd goal of the season. The table was now laid for the highlight of the banquet.

Tony Galvin, patrolling Tottenham's left wing with imagination and flair, released a 76th minute pass to Villa on the left hand side of the pitch some 15 yards outside the heavily populated City penalty area. What followed is the stuff of which fairytales are made. The player who had sulked off the pitch on Saturday was a bright and alert Thursday's man. He set off on a diagonal run towards the City goal, but as there were five defenders ahead of him it seemed a pretty useless exercise and those of us who have no grasp or understanding of an artist's invention assumed that he would be passing the ball to a better-positioned colleague.

Suddenly Villa changed direction and started running across the face of the City goal, side-stepping tackles with the casual grace of a Fred Astaire flying down to Rio, or perhaps Buenos Aires. Two City defenders were so bemused by his unorthodox progress that they ran into each other as they tried to block his path. The hefty Argentinian, suddenly a wild bull of the Pampas, showed strength to go with his skill and survived buffeting challenges before unbalancing the oncoming Corrigan with a pretence at a shot and then shooting the ball right footed into the net from eight yards for a goal in a million.

Now it was South American carnival time, and Villa danced around

Wembley in a tango of delight, with his diminutive countryman Ossie Ardiles as his equally delirious partner. A match that had died on Saturday had been given the kick of life, and it guaranteed that the 100th FA Cup final would be remembered throughout the following century of matches.

THE WITNESSES: John Bond, Manchester City manager: 'Steve MacKenzie's goal was a bit special, but all people will talk about in the future is the winner by Villa. It was completely off the cuff. Nobody could plan a goal like that. Football was the winner because this game proved the quality that there is in our game. I am a great fan of the way Spurs play. They knock the ball about with tremendous style. I said before the season started that they were my fancy for the Cup. For once, I wish I could have proved myself wrong!'

Keith Burkinshaw, Spurs manager: 'I think I have found the way to get the best out of Ricky—get him good and mad! He was upset when I pulled him off on Saturday but once he had cooled down he accepted that I did it for all the right reasons.We did not do ourselves justice in the first match and were a little fortunate to survive to a replay, but in the second game we showed all the attacking qualities that are the hallmark of the Tottenham team.'

ARGENTINIAN CONNECTION: It was Antonio Rattin, remembered as the Argentinian World Cup captain sent off at Wembley in the 1966 quarter-final against England, who

was responsible for Osvaldo Ardiles and Ricardo Villa coming to Tottenham. He tipped off his friend Harry Haslam, then manager of Sheffield United, that two of Argentina's 1978 World Cup squad wanted to play in England. Haslam told Keith Burkinshaw and when the Spurs manager realised that it was Ardiles and Villa who were available he made a secret dash to Buenos Aires to clinch the £700,000 transfers before any rival club could beat him to it. Tottenham got tremendous value for their money, particularly from the exceptionally popular Ardiles.

QUOTE: Ricky Villa: 'On Saturday I so unhappy. Tonight I am happiest footballer in the world. When I run for goal the ball seemed stuck to my feet. I did not think of passing because I enjoy running. My big thanks to the manager for picking me. I repay him with greatest goal of my life. At last I have luck in England, I think.'

FOR THE RECORD: Tottenham were back at Wembley the following year, and again they were taken to a replay—this time by London neighbours QPR, managed by Tery Venables. After a 1-1 draw, the two teams met again at Wembley five days later. Glenn Hoddle scored the only goal of the match when he became the sixth player to convert a penalty in a Wembley FA Cup final.

JIMMY GREAVES: 'The Villa goal was what I call a television director's dream. They have since action replayed it a million times and I never tire of seeing it. It was South American magic. Mind you, I couldn't help feeling sorry for Steve MacKenzie. His goal was good enough to have won any match, but you never hear anybody mention it. All people can talk about is Villa's magical moment.'

THE CHAMPIONS OF '81

First Division: Aston Villa, 60 pts. Runners-up: Ipswich Town, 56 pts
Second Division: West Ham United, 66 pts. Runners-up: Notts County, 53 pts
Third Division: Rotherham United, 61 pts. Runners-up: Barnsley, 59 pts
Fourth Division: Southend United, 67 pts. Runners-up: Lincoln City, 65 pts
FA Cup Final: Tottenham 3, Manchester City 2 (after 1-1 draw)
League Cup Final: Liverpool 2, West Ham United 1 (after a 1-1 draw)
Top Division 1 marksmen: Steve Archibald (Spurs), Peter Withe (Villa), 20 goals
Footballer of the Year: Frans Thijssen (Ipswich Town)
Scottish champions : Celtic, 56 pts. Runners-up: Aberdeen, 49 pts
Scottish Cup Final: Rangers 4, Dundee United 1 (after a 0-0 draw)
Scottish Player of the Year: Alan Rough (Partick Thistle)
European Cup Final: Liverpool 1, Real Madrid 0
European Cup Winners' Cup Final: Dynamo Tbilisi 2, Carl Zeiss Jena 1
UEFA Cup Final: Ipswich Town 5, AZ 67 Alkmaar 4 (3-0, 2-4)
European Footballer of the Year: Karl-Heinz Rummenigge (Bayern Munich)

1981-82 France are gunned down in Russian roulette shoot-out

Scoreline: West Germany 3, France 3
Venue: Sanchez Pizjuan Stadium, Seville **Date:** July 8, 1982

THE SETTING: France had won the hearts of the neutral millions watching the 1982 World Cup on television with football that was inventive, imaginative and free from the sort of malevolence that was contaminating the play of so many teams.

They were through, quite deservedly, to the World Cup semi-finals and they had become the people's favourites following the elimination of the brilliant Brazilians by a mean, miserly and—for some memorable moments—magnificent Italian team.

Blocking the path of France to their first ever final were West Germany, a country that consistently raises peak performances whenever the World Cup is at stake. But this had not been the Germany of the adventurous spirit of 1966, or the flair of 1970, or the Cup-winning mastery of 1954 and 1974. This West German team had won few friends with football that was generally negative, sometimes malicious and quite often mediocre, as for instance in their opening group match when they were humbled by Algeria.

The balance of power was remarkably equal after 15 previous meetings between France and West Germany. They had each won five matches and five had been drawn.

Most observers expected France to go ahead in the results sequence

Karl-Heinz Rummenigge, dangerman

because their World Cup form had been quite exceptional. Every one of their outfield players, including fullbacks Maxime Bossis and Manuel Amoros had attacking notions.

The team was prompted from midfield by Michel Platini, Jean Tigana and Alain Giresse, all of whom had bewitching ball control and provided a high-quality passing service for fleet footed front runners Domin-

que Rocheteau and the gifted Didier Six.

The Germans had come to Spain relying heavily on their most gifted player, Karl-Heinz Rummenigge, but he was struggling to shake off a hamstring injury and the two-times European Footballer of the Year from Bayern Munich started the match on the substitute's bench.

There was a further problem for the Germans in that several of their players had been hit by a stomach bug, including the giant Hans-Peter Briegel, a blond bull of a defender, who insisted on playing despite a touch of sunstroke. It was not the most confident of German teams that lined up for the kick-off.

There was controversy before a ball had been kicked when it was revealed that any semi-final match ending in a draw after extra time would have to be settled by a penalty shoot-out because of the tight playing schedule. But it was widely anticipated that France would win without need of the lottery of penalties simply because they were fielding the finest French side since the 1958 World Cup finals when they defeated West Germany 6-3 in a thrilling third-match play-off.

THE TEAMS: **West Germany** Schumacher, Kaltz, Stielike, K-H Forster, Briegel, Dremmler, B. Forster, Breitner, Magath, Littbarski, Fischer. Subs: Rummenigge, Hrubesch.
France Ettori, Bossis, Janvion, Tresor, Amoros, Tigana, Giresse, Platini, Genghini, Rocheteau, Six. Subs: Battiston, Lopez.

THE ACTION: The Germans shrugged off the negative and nervous attitude that had marked and marred their earlier matches and opened with a blitz of fast, skilful football that had the French defence looking distinctly uncomfortable. Even the marvellous Marius Tresor, a thoroughbred of a central defender from Bordeaux, was having to break sweat for the first time in the tournament. This early German pressure promised a goal and it came in the 18th minute when Klaus Fischer forced an opening for his Cologne club-mate Pierre Littbarski to score an easy goal.

How would the French react to this early set-back? In their opening match of the tournament they had been rocked by an instant goal in 29 seconds by England captain Bryan Robson and had caved in to a 3-1 defeat, although looking the superior side for most of the game. Against the Germans they struck back with power and grace, equalising nine minutes later after Rocheteau had been upended in the penalty area by Bernd Forster. Platini expertly steered the spot-kick past goalkeeper Schumacher.

It was evenly balanced for the rest of the half, with the French showing more flair and the Germans more teeth-gritting fight. There was a let-off for France when Littbarski struck the bar but the 1-1 scoreline at the interval was a fair reflection of the play.

Twenty minutes into the second half there came a sickening incident that brought shame to the World Cup in general and Schumacher in particular. France had been getting on top thanks to their supremacy in mid-field, and chief architect Platini put Patrick

Michel Platini, a midfield maestro

Battiston clear with a precise pass. The Saint Etienne forward, substituting for injured club-mate Bernard Genghini, ignored the oncoming German goalkeeper and coolly released a shot that clipped the outside of a post. Poor Battiston did not see the result of his work. He was knocked unconcious by a crude forearm smash to the face by Schumacher, who charged into the Frenchman like a deranged mugger. Big Daddy would have been proud of it, but this was not acting. Battiston suffered a serious neck injury, lost three teeth and had to be given oxygen to help him breathe as he was stretchered off and out of the World Cup. Incredibly, the Dutch referee Charles Corver awarded Germany a goal-kick when everybody outside the boundaries of Deutschland with reasonable judgement considered it should have been a penalty to France and a sending-off for Schumacher. He was not even cautioned for

one of the most violent fouls ever committed in a World Cup match. Television action replays confirmed what the eye had seen the first time around. It was a coldly calculated foul.

Neutral spectators were now even more firmly on the side of France and right on the stroke of time thousands of voices cheered what they thought was a spectacular French winner. Adventurous full-back Amoros smashed in a shot from 25 yards that hammered against the German crossbar.

But justice appeared to have been done in the second minute of extra time when the talented Tresor volleyed the ball into the net following a Giresse free-kick. Six minutes later the graceful Giresse himself made it 3-1 with a shot that went into the net off a post.

It would need a psychiatrist rather than a football coach to explain why France then proceeded to play as casually as billionaires tossing away coins. They were like men who had broken the bank at Monte Carlo and then returned to the casino to give the money back. With a semi-final place just 15 minutes away, they should have shut up shop and concentrated on protecting their lead. But they seemed intent on humbling and humiliating rather than just beating the Germans.

They came forward in suicidal numbers and the Germans—who never know when they are beaten on a football field (ask the England players of 1966 and 1970)—gratefully reacted to the sudden freedom of space and movement they were being given.

The deadly Rummenigge, who had slipped on almost unnoticed as a

replacement for the unwell Briegel after the Tresor goal, sneaked in at the far post to beat goalkeeper Ettori and centre-back Janvion to a low cross in the 103rd minute and he whipped it into the net with the speed of a striking cobra. It was a masterpiece of finishing, particularly considering he had only just picked up the pace of the match a few minutes earlier.

The earlier arrogance of the French players was now replaced by panic as they dropped back into deep and desperate defence, but the Germans sensed that they could save the game with one more mighty effort and they threw everybody but goalkeeper Schumacher forward in search for an equaliser which, when it came, forced applause even from the devastated French fans.

It was scored in the 108th minute by Klaus Fischer, and it was a goal that deserved to be hung in the Louvre. Hrubesch headed a cross back into the goalmouth and Fischer took off like an Olympic springboard diver and netted with a dazzling overhead bicycle kick—the sort of goal that had become his trademark with Cologne.

From having one foot in the final France now suddenly felt legless and were confronted with the Russian roulette game of alternate penalties to decide which team would go forward to play Italy for the World Cup.

Players on both sides had run themselves to the edge of exhaustion in the stifling heat of Seville, and the 12-yard penalty shot looked as difficult as a mountain climb.

Alain Giresse was first to shoot and sent Schumacher the wrong way before planting the ball in the left hand corner of the net. Then, in turn and with the eyes of the world trained on them, Kaltz, Amoros, Breitner and Rocheteau all succeeded in converting their penalties. Then came the first miss. Uli Stielike looked on in horror as goalkeeper Jean-Luc Ettori stretched across goal to save his shot. The tormented Stielike dropped to his knees as if he had been punched in the solar plexus and Schumacher consoled him before taking his position on the goal-line to face Didier Six's penalty. Six had been one of the most consistent players throughout the tournament but, suffering from dehydration along with several other players, he failed to get any real power into his shot and Schumacher saved with ease. Then Littbarski coolly made the shoot-out score 3-3.

Platini and Rummenigge each completed the mandatory five penalties and the teams were deadlocked at 4-4. Now it was sudden death. As this was the bullfighting world of Seville, thoughts centred on who was going to make the kill.

You could almost touch the tension as Maxime Bossis drove the ball to the right of Schumacher who—a villain in most eyes—became a German hero as he flew across the ground to make an excellent save. This was not so much a miss by the distraught Bossis as a piece of marvellous goalkeeping by Schumacher.

Horst Hrubesch, a veteran of many European nights with Hamburg, had just the right temperament for the job in hand. He convinced Ettori he was going to shoot to his right and then firmly powered the ball into the opposite corner of the net to bring to a sudden end the first penalty shoot-out in the history of the World Cup.

Many people—particularly French supporters—thought it should be the last. It is hardly a satisfactory way to decide a match in the most important football tournament on earth. What a cruel way for France to lose an unforgettable match to which they had contributed most of the quality and flair. But even the most ardent French fan had to admit grudging praise for the way the Germans had hung in and refused to concede defeat.

THE WITNESSES: Michel Hidalgo, French manager: 'It cannot be right to settle a match of this importance in this way. Four years' work has been wrecked by one penalty save. It is said that we have the consolation of a play-off for third place, but this is a meaningless match. It is of no interest and should not exist. We were interested only in a place in the final. The referee should have given us a penalty after that appalling foul on Battiston, then we would have won.'

Michel Platini: 'I'm sure the world knows that the best team lost. But in a way we have only ourselves to blame. If the Germans had led 3-1 they would have closed the game up. But it is just not in our nature. We like to be adventurous. Perhaps this was one time when we should have defended.'

Jupp Derwall, West German manager: 'You must give our players credit for showing great character. We have had all sorts of problems with injury and illness, but we refused to lie down. The penalty system is a cruel way to decide a match but at least it is the same for both sides. For us, it is consolation after losing on penalties against Czechoslovakia in the 1976 European Championship final. As for the incident with Battiston, Schumacher insists that he was going for the ball and his momentum was such that he could not avoid the collision. He is very upset over what happened, but it was an accident.'

SUPER SUB: Team captain Karl-Heinz Rummenigge was used sparingly throughout the tournament by the Germans to avoid aggravating his damaged hamstring. According to reports, his emergency treatment included injections of calf's blood and hot pepper poultices. Despite his injury, Rummenigge still managed to score five goals including a hat-trick against Chile and that's not counting his penalty in the semi-final shoot-out. His goal just minutes after coming off the substitute's bench against France turned the game Germany's way just as they looked down and out. It was typical of his deadly marksmanship for Bayern Munich, where he took over the mantle of star striker from the one and only Gerd Müller. Though not as powerful and consistent as Müller, he had better close control of the ball and could make as well as take goals. His performances for Bayern earned him the European Footballer of the Year title in 1980 and again the following year, and it was his finishing strength that made West Germany virtually unbeatable on their way into the World Cup finals. They won all eight of their qualifying matches, scoring 33 goals and conceding only three.

QUOTE: Karl-Heinz Rummenigge: 'It was much harder watching the game from the touchline than playing in it. I died a thousand deaths before I decided I should risk further injury by going on to the pitch after France had scored their second goal. The gamble paid off when I managed to squeeze in our second goal. France played some beautiful football, but they were naïve with their tactics after going 3-1 into the lead. They gave us a chance to get back into the game and we took it.'

FOR THE RECORD: Italy, captained by 40-year-old goalkeeper Dino Zoff, won the World Cup for a third time by beating West Germany 3-1 in the final in Madrid on Sunday, July 11. Paolo Rossi, the player reinstated after being banned following a bribery scandal, scored Italy's first goal which made him the top marksman with six goals. Italy, negative and cynical in their early matches, produced their best performance in their second group match when beating Cup favourites Brazil 3-2 in a classic contest. Diego Maradona was ordered off in the group match against Brazil in which Argentina were beaten 3-1. Poland beat a virtual reserve French team 3-2 in the third-place play-off.

JIMMY GREAVES: 'I fancied Italy to win the tournament right from the off. They did not have the flair of Brazil or France, but they were strong and ruthless in defence and had Rossi in peak form. It was sad for football when West Germany beat France. The Germans had a terrible tournament yet fluked their way through to the final. What I will never understand is how Schumacher was allowed to stay on the pitch after his disgraceful foul on Battiston. It was a real mugging job and probably robbed us of an Italy-France final that would have been a real spectacle.'

THE CHAMPIONS OF '82

First Division: Liverpool, 87 pts. Runners-up: Ipswich Town, 83 pts
Second Division: Luton Town, 88 pts. Runners-up: Watford, 80 pts
Third Division: Burnley, 80 pts. Runners-up: Carlisle United, 80 pts
Fourth Division: Sheffield United, 96 pts. Runners-up: Bradford City, 91 pts
FA Cup Final: Tottenham 1, QPR 0 (after 1-1 draw)
League Cup Final: Liverpool 3, Tottenham 1 (after extra time)
Top First Division marksman: Kevin Keegan (Southampton), 26 goals
Footballer of the Year: Steve Perryman (Tottenham)
Scottish champions: Celtic, 55 pts. Runners-up: Aberdeen, 53 pts
Scottish Cup Final: Aberdeen 4, Rangers 1 (after extra time)
Scottish Player of the Year: Paul Sturrock (Dundee United)
European Cup Final: Aston Villa 1, Bayern Munich 0
European Cup Winners' Cup Final: Barcelona 2, Standard Liege 1
UEFA Cup Final: IFK Gothenburg 4, SV Hamburg 0 (1-0, 3-0)
European Footballer of the Year: Paolo Rossi (Juventus)
World Cup Final: Italy 3, West Germany 1

1982-83 Red for danger as Gordon sinks Real in Swedish lake

Scoreline: Aberdeen 2, Real Madrid 1
Venue: Ullevi Stadium, Gothenburg **Date:** May 11, 1983

THE SETTING: There could not have been a greater contrast between Real Madrid and Aberdeen, the two teams contesting the European Cup Winners' Cup final under a grey Swedish sky that appeared to have saved a season's rain for the occasion.

It was Real's 11th European final, Aberdeen's first. Real were a costly assembly of experienced professionals, two of whom—Metgod, of Holland, and Stielike, of West Germany—had been imported at great expense. Aberdeen, with an average age of just 23, were a home-grown side with 12 of their 16-man squad having come up through their youth ranks. There was also a contrast between the two managers, both of

whom were former centre-forwards. Real were under the guidance of perhaps the greatest of them all, the one and only Alfredo di Stefano who as a player had been all skill and style. In charge of Aberdeen was Alex Ferguson, who in his playing days had been such an aggressive competitor that he had been sent off six times. He had brought his determination into management and the fact that he had ended the 14-year hold on the Scottish championship by the 'auld firm' Celtic and Rangers proved he had instilled the will-to-win attitude into his players.

It was touch-and-go whether the final would be staged as scheduled because of cascading rain that saturated the ground. A heavy tarpaulin cover protected the grass, but the moment it was removed the pitch was turned into a lake that shimmered under the floodlights like a boating pool. The Aberdeen players were warming up in hooded tracksuits as the referee splashed through a pitch inspection and, surprisingly, passed it fit.

THE TEAMS: **Aberdeen** Leighton, Rougvie, Miller, McLeish, McMaster, Cooper, Strachan, Weir, McGhee, Black, Simpson. Sub: Hewitt.
Real Madrid Augustin, Metgod, Bonet, Camacho, Juan Jose, Angel, Gallego, Stielike, Juanito, Santillana, Isidro. Subs: San Jose, Salguero.

Gordon Strachan, red for danger

THE ACTION: Aberdeen settled to the atrocious conditions quicker than their illustrious opponents, and almost snatched a sensational lead in the opening moments. Gordon Strachan trapped a mishit clearance by Johnny Metgod on his chest and chipped a perfect pass to Eric Black. The 18-year-old striker, with the impudence of youth, leant back and struck a bullet of a volley from 20 yards that goalkeeper Augustin finger-tipped against the bar with an instinctive save.

It was Black's first shot in football in nearly a month because of an injury lay-off, but he gave further proof that he had shaken off any rust in the seventh minute. Strachan sent a corner to Alex McLeish who came splashing through the puddles from a deep position to head the ball down into the goalmouth. Black reacted quicker than the Real defenders and prodded the ball into the net from close range.

The rain continued to pour down and mistakes were inevitable in conditions that made every single step a challenge. Willie Miller, one of the most dependable defenders in British football, watched in agony as his attempted 15th minute back pass to goalkeeper Jim Leighton stopped dead in the mud. Real skipper Santillana ploughed past Miller and was driving towards the net with the ball at his feet when Leighton caught his legs. Juanito levelled the scores from the penalty spot.

Strachan, his fiery red hair plastered to his face, was playing a storming match in midfield and it was red for danger every time he got the ball.

He started and finished a 50-yard passing movement in the 55th minute that deserved the reward of a goal, but his shot hit the legs of the diving Augustin, who moments later made a fully intended save from the lively Black.

Real were fortunate to survive to extra time and the winning goal that Aberdeen had always been promising finally came in the 113th minute, just as the press photographers were beginning to plan their positions for the anticipated penalty shoot-out. John Hewitt, a substitute who had made a speciality of dramatic goals, topped them all when he climbed out of the muddy Real goalmouth to score with a glancing header following clever combination on the left wing between McGhee and the tireless Weir.

It was Scotland's first win in the European Cup Winners' Cup final since Rangers had captured the Cup in 1972. That night had been ruined by the behaviour of the Scottish fans, but the 15,000 Aberdeen supporters who had made the trip to Sweden were a credit to their club and their country.

THE WITNESSES: Alex Ferguson: 'I instilled it into our players that they had no need to feel inferior to the Real Madrid team. Real have such a pedigree that you can easily be in awe of them, but I got the message across that it is the present that counts not the past...and our present team can be a match for any club side in Europe. Considering the appalling conditions I thought we gave a magnificent team performance. Gordon Strachan had the match of a lifetime. He was perpetual motion.'

139

Alfredo di Stefano: 'Aberdeen were the more positive and deserved their victory. But they were fortunate in that the conditions suited them better. We just could not get our precise passing game to flow. Perhaps it would have been best if the game had been postponed until the pitch was perfectly playable. It was fit only for swimming!'

GREAT SCOT: Born in Edinburgh on February 9, 1957, Gordon Strachan first made an impact with Dundee before joining Aberdeen for whom he scored 55 goals in 183 League matches. He was elected Scottish Player of the Year in 1980 at the end of a season in which he won the first of more than 40 caps for Scotland. Manchester United bought him for £500,000 in 1984 and he was a key player in the United team that won the FA Cup by beating Everton 1-0 at Wembley in 1985.

QUOTE: Gordon Strachan: 'It was exhausting playing on that pitch in Gothenburg. We should have been fitted with water skis. It would have been an injustice if we had lost because we created nearly all the chances. Even Real's goal was given to them.'

FOR THE RECORD: Aberdeen won the Premier Division championship in the next two seasons and in defence of the Cup Winners' Cup reached the semi-finals.

JIMMY GREAVES: 'That was a cracking Aberdeen team and they brought tremendous prestige to Scotland. Gordon Strachan reminds me of that compulsive competitor Alan Ball. Like Alan, he is a red-headed dynamo who refuses to accept defeat until the final whistle. Mind you, whether the game should have been played on that pitch is another issue.'

THE CHAMPIONS OF '83

First Division: Liverpool, 82 pts. Runners-up: Watford, 71 pts
Second Division: QPR, 85 pts. Runners-up: Wolves, 75 pts
Third Division: Portsmouth, 91 pts. Runners-up: Cardiff City, 86 pts
Fourth Division: Wimbledon, 98 pts. Runners-up: Hull City, 90 pts
FA Cup Final: Manchester United 4, Brighton 0 (after a 2-2 draw)
League Cup Final: Liverpool 2, Manchester United 1 (after extra time)
Top First Division marksman: Luther Blissett (Watford), 27 goals
Footballer of the Year: Kenny Dalglish (Liverpool)
Scottish champions: Dundee United, 56 pts. Runners-up: Celtic, 55 pts
Scottish Cup Final: Aberdeen 1, Rangers 0 (after extra time)
Scottish Player of the Year: Charlie Nicholas (Celtic)
European Cup Final: SV Hamburg 1, Juventus 0
European Cup Winners' Cup Final: Aberdeen 2, Real Madrid 1 (after extra time)
UEFA Cup Final: Anderlecht 2, Benfica 1 (1-0, 1-1)
European Footballer of the Year: Michel Platini (Juventus)

1983-84 Barnes nets Brazilian-style goal in wingers' paradise

Scoreline: Brazil 0, England 2
Venue: Maracana Stadium, Rio de Janeiro **Date:** June 10, 1984

THE SETTING: The Maracana, the cathedral of Brazilian soccer erected for the 1950 World Cup, is the world's biggest football stadium with a capacity of 200,000. Only three teams had beaten Brazil there, and the last defeat had been 27 years before Bobby Robson's England squad arrived in wondrous Rio for the first match of their South American summer tour.

The confidence of the England team was low following a discouraging 2-0 defeat by the USSR at Wembley eight days earlier. It was hardly the ideal preparation for what was considered just about the most difficult date on the football calendar.

There were raised eyebrows and muttered cynical comments when Robson revealed at a pre-match press conference that he was selecting a side that would *attack* Brazil. It was like a tugboat captain saying he was going to take on a destroyer.

Robson said he would be looking to Mark Chamberlain and John Barnes to play as conventional wingers. More exchanged glances. This was, after all, Brazil—home of Jairzinho, Rivelino, Garrincha; a wonderland of wingers. And Chamblerlain and Barnes just happened to be up against Junior and Leandro, two of the finest attacking full-backs in the world.

But Robson was convinced that the way to beat Brazil was to take them on at their own game. It was his view that to try to play defensively would be inviting trouble. Most people quietly thought that England were about to commit soccer suicide.

John Barnes, a classic goal

THE TEAMS: **Brazil** Roberto Costa, Leandro, Mozer, Ricardo, Junior, Pires, Renato, Zenon, Roberto, Assis, Tato. Subs: Vadmir, Rinaldo.
England Shilton, Duxbury, Sansom, Wilkins, Watson, Fenwick, Chamberlain, Robson, Hateley, Woodcock, Barnes. Sub: Allen.

THE ACTION: The fears of a humiliating defeat for England proved to have a good foundation in the opening ten minutes when the Brazilians tore apart the English defence with almost contemptuous ease. Three times Peter Shilton, in an all-grey kit that seemed suitably funereal, came to England's rescue as forwards glided past tackles like ghosts of Brazilians past.

Renato was whipping outside Kenny Sansom with Jairzinho-like power and grace, and the early indications were that Brazil's wingers were the ones to watch and admire. The yellow-shirted Brazilians were coming forward like a swarm of bees, and it was England who seemed certain to get badly stung.

But, almost to their surprise, England did not concede a goal during this opening blitz, and after 15 minutes of chasing shadows they began to get the confidence to follow Bobby Robson's advice to take on the Brazilian defenders. Mark Hateley, playing his first full international, nearly caught goalkeeper Roberto Costa napping with a powerful header, and then he fed Barnes with a sweeping pass. The Watford winger dribbled Brazilian-style past two challenges before releasing the ball. The move did not produce a goal, but it gave Barnes the appetite to assert himself on the match and just before half-time he started off on a run that will be remembered for all time by those lucky enough to witness it.

Hateley won the ball with a strong challenge and delivered it to the feet of Barnes out on the left touchline. He started cutting infield and tricked his way past three tackles and was suddenly into the Brazilian penalty area where he shimmied past two more challenges before wrong footing the goalkeeper and virtually walking the ball into the net. English onlookers rubbed their eyes to make sure they had seen a goal by a player in an England shirt. The goal just conjured by Barnes like a footballing magician was the kind of gem usually associated with players wearing the yellow of Brazil.

England grew visibly in stature after this moment of brilliance from Barnes and throughout the second half Bryan Robson and Ray Wilkins played to the peak of their form to master the midfield. They fed the ball continually out to the wings where Barnes and Chamberlain did all that was ambitiously asked of them by Bobby Robson.

Brazil were rushed off their feet in defence and unable to get into the game as an attacking force. The second goal that England richly deserved came just after the hour when Wilkins and the lively Tony Woodcock worked the ball down the left to Barnes, who gave the Brazilians the jitters every time he was in possession. Instead of dribbling this time, he fired an instant cross to the far post where Hateley rose high to head in a goal that was a throwback to the old England glory days of Matthews and Lawton. It clinched one of the most memorable—and unexpected—victories in the history of England international football.

THE WITNESSES: Bobby Robson: 'I have not had a more satisfying moment in football than when John

Barnes ran through the entire Brazilian defence to score. It was everything you dream about. I am proud of the efforts of the entire team. This victory has filled us all with a new optimism and will send shock waves around the world of football.'

Peter Shilton: 'I wondered what we were in for at the start when Brazil hit us with everything, but that unbelievable goal from John Barnes knocked the life out of them. The only time I've seen a goal like it was when Jimmy Greaves once ran the ball round our entire Leicester defence before walking it past me. This was every bit as good, if not better.'

THE BLACK DIAMOND: Born in Jamaica in on November 2, 1963, John Barnes scored 65 goals in 233 League games for Watford before joining Liverpool for £900,000 in 1987. He had a sensational first season at Anfield and his partnership with

Peter Beardsley was an outstanding feature in Liverpool's Championship-winning season of 1987-88.

QUOTE: John Barnes: 'I did not make up my mind to go for goal until I had gone past two or three challenges. I realised the goal was not that far away and so I just kept going. The Maracana Stadium could not have been a better setting for the goal.'

FOR THE RECORD: England lost 2-0 to Uruguay and were held to a 1-1 draw by Chile in their remaining matches on the South American tour.

JIMMY GREAVES: 'I remember seeing the goal live on television. There had been a hold-up in joining the match and we got the picture on our screen just as Hateley passed the ball to Barnes. I couldn't believe what I was seeing. I shouldn't think even Pele scored a better goal at the Maracana.'

THE CHAMPIONS OF '84

First Division: Liverpool, 80 pts. Runners-up: Southampton, 77 pts
Second Division: Chelsea, 88 pts. Runners-up: Sheffield Wednesday, 88 pts
Third Division: Oxford United, 95 pts. Runners-up: Wimbledon, 87 pts
Fourth Division: York City, 101 pts. Runners-up: Doncaster Rovers, 85 pts
FA Cup Final: Everton 2. Watford 0
League Cup Final: Liverpool 1, Everton 0 (after a 0-0 draw)
Top First Division marksman: Ian Rush (Liverpool), 32 goals
Footballer of the Year: Ian Rush (Liverpool)
Scottish champions: Aberdeen, 57 pts. Runners-up: Celtic, 50 pts
Scottish Cup Final: Aberdeen 2, Celtic 1 (after extra time)
Scottish Player of the Year: Willie Miller (Aberdeen)
European Cup Final: AS Roma 1, Liverpool 1 (Liverpool won 4-2 on penalties)
European Cup Winners' Cup Final: Juventus 2, Porto 1
UEFA Cup Final: Spurs 2, Anderlecht 2 (1-1, 1-1; Spurs won 4-3 on penalties)
European Footballer of the Year: Michel Platini (Juventus)
European Championship Final: France 2, Spain 0

1984-85 Gray's smash-and-grab goal triggers a Rapid decline

Scoreline: Everton 3, Rapid Vienna 1
Venue: Feyenoord Stadium, Rotterdam **Date:** May 15, 1985

THE SETTING: Everton arrived in Rotterdam hoping to negotiate the second leg of a unique hat-trick of honours. They had already clinched the League Championship and were now bidding to become the first English club for 14 years to win the European Cup Winners' Cup. Three days later they were due to meet Manchester United in the FA Cup final at Wembley.

The day before leaving for Holland Everton had sufffered their first defeat in 29 matches when Nottingham Forest beat them 1-0 in their final League match of the season. They had been minutes away from defeat in the sixth round of the FA Cup against Ipswich and again against Luton in the semi-final, battling back each time to snatch dramatic victories. Bayern Munich seemed certain to beat them in the semi-final of the Cup Winners' Cup, but again a late flourish took Everton into the final.

In Rapid Vienna they were facing another team that had specialised in Houdini-style escapes. They had come back from the dead in the Cup Winners' Cup after being eliminated by Celtic in the second round. Rapid produced medical evidence to prove that one of their players had been injured by a flying bottle in the second leg in Glasgow. A replay was ordered and Rapid won.

Andy Gray, strong and fearless

The Austrians came from three goals behind to conquer Dynamo Dresden in the quarter-finals and they beat Dynamo Moscow in the semi-finals after being a goal down and missing a penalty. Their most prominent player was Hans Krankl, a vastly experienced international striker who had helped Barcelona win the European Cup Winners' Cup in 1979.

Everton were fired by the ambition of wanting to keep pace with their neighbours and arch rivals Liverpool who just the previous season had completed the treble of League Championship, European Cup and League Cup.

THE TEAMS: Everton Southall, Stevens, Van den Hauwe, Ratcliffe, Mountfield, Reid, Steven, Sharp, Gray, Bracewell, Sheedy.
Rapid Vienna Konsel, Kienast, Garger, Weber, Lainer, Hristic, Kranjcar, Weinhofer, Brauneder, Pacult, Krankl. Subs: Panenka, Gross.

THE ACTION: The Rapid goal enjoyed a charmed life throughout a first half in which Everton proved themselves superior in all departments. Trevor Steven and Kevin Sheedy were providing skilful touches to balance the driving power of Peter Reid, and Andy Gray and Graeme Sharp might have had two goals each as they cleaved great holes through the middle of a hesitant Rapid defence.

Skipper Kevin Ratcliffe was a commanding figure at the heart of an Everton defence that snuffed out virtually every attempt at an attack by the Austrian forwards. But Everton, paralysing their opponents with the speed and accuracy of their passes, did not have a goal to show for all their supremacy at half time. The fear was that the Austrians might reveal the great recovery powers that had lifted them through to the final after looking down and out so many times.

Rapid opened the second half with a surge of their best football to date, but they found goalkeeper Neville Southall as wide as a Welsh mountain at the back of the Everton defence. It was the Merseysiders who went into a deserved lead in the 57th minute. Sharp, living up to his name with the alertness of his actions, took full advantage of slackness in the Rapid defence, racing on to a back pass and then laying the ball back into the path of fellow-Scot Andy Gray, who hammered a volley into the net.

There was now a flood of flowing football from Everton, who were doing themselves and their country proud with the style and elegance of their play. Steven tapped in goal number two in the 72nd minute after Derek Mountfield had confused the Rapid defenders by making a pretence at a shot following a Sheedy corner.

There were just six minutes left when Rapid managed yet again to pull one foot out of the grave. Hans Krankl, their veteran Austrian international who had gunned down many defences in his time, snatched a typical opportunist goal. But hopes of a Rapid recovery were quickly shot down when just a minute later Sheedy tricked his way past two challenges before scoring an excellent third victory-clinching goal for Everton.

THE WITNESSES: Howard Kendall, Everton manager: 'This was a very special performance. In terms of possession football you will not see anything better. We got as close to perfection as you can get and thoroughly deserved our victory.'

Hans Krankl, Rapid's famous striker: 'Everton were the better team and outplayed us at times. We were not at our best and just could not cope with their speed and aggression. Nobody can dispute that they are worthy winners of the Cup.'

Kevin Ratcliffe: 'Once Andy Gray knocked in our first goal we knew we were on our way to winning. That was the all-important goal because we were then able to relax and play the sort of football that has destroyed a lot of teams this season.'

HANDY ANDY: Born in Glasgow on November 30, 1955, Andy Gray scored 36 goals for Dundee United before being snapped up by Aston Villa for whom he netted 54 goals in 113 League games. Wolves paid a then British record £1,175,000 for him in 1979. He was in League Cup winning teams with Villa (1977) and Wolves (1980), netting the deciding goal for Wolves against Nottingham Forest. He also scored for Everton in the 1984 FA Cup final win against Watford. Andy had a spell back at Villa after scoring 14 goals in 49 First Division matches for Everton, and he then made a surprise move back to Scotland with Rangers. An aggressive centre-forward, he was capped 20 times by Scotland and became a key striker for every club that signed him.

QUOTE: Andy Gray: 'The night we beat Rapid was as good a team performance as I have ever experienced. We played them off the park. On that form, we would have beaten any team in the world.'

FOR THE RECORD: The FA Cup final against Manchester United three days later was a bridge too far for the worn-out Everton players. They were beaten 1-0 in extra time by a Norman Whiteside goal.

JIMMY GREAVES: 'Andy Gray was the ideal partner for the clever and under-rated Graeme Sharp. He is a throwback to the old-style centre-forwards, diving in bravely where others fear to tread. Everton's performance that night in Rotterdam reminded me of Tottenham's European Cup Winners' Cup final victory there in 1963. It was a marvellous advertisement for British football.'

THE CHAMPIONS OF '85

First Division: Everton, 90 pts. Runners-up: Liverpool, 77 pts
Second Division: Oxford United, 84 pts. Runners-up: Birmingham, 82 pts
Third Division: Bradford City, 94 pts. Runners-up: Millwall, 90 pts
Fourth Division: Chesterfield, 91 pts. Runners-up: Blackpool, 86 pts
FA Cup Final: Manchester United 1, Everton 0 (after extra time)
League Cup Final: Norwich City 1, Sunderland 0
Top First Division marksman: Kerry Dixon (Chelsea), 24 goals
Footballer of the Year: Neville Southall (Everton)
Scottish champions: Aberdeen, 59 pts. Runners-up: Celtic, 52 pts
Scottish Cup Final: Celtic 2, Dundee United 1
Scottish Player of the Year: Hamish McAlpine (Dundee United)
European Cup Final: Juventus 1, Liverpool 0
European Cup Winners' Cup Final: Everton 3, Rapid Vienna 1
UEFA Cup Final: Videoton 1, Real Madrid 3 (0-3, 1-0)
European Footballer of the Year: Michel Platini (Juventus)

1985-86 Maradona's handiwork puts England out of World Cup

Scoreline: Argentina 2, England 1
Venue: Aztec Stadium, Mexico City **Date:** June 22, 1986

THE SETTING: England recovered from a neurotic start to the 1986 World Cup to battle their way through to the quarter-finals where they were confronted by Argentina, the only unbeaten team left in the topsy-turvy tournament.

Portugal beat England 1–0 in the opening match and then a surprisingly fluent and inventive Moroccan team held them to a goalless draw. It looked as if Bobby Robson's squad would be making an early exit, but a hat-trick from Gary Lineker lifted England to a 3-0 victory over Poland and squeezed them through to the second round where they comfortably eliminated Paraguay.

England's quarter-final match with Argentina, witnessed by a massive gathering of 114,580 spectators in the Aztec Stadium built for the 1968 Olympics, was heavy with tension because of the overspill of feeling from the Falklands War. Squads of military police brandishing white batons patrolled the ground, but apart from a few isolated skirmishes the rival English and Argentinian fans gave all their attention to a game that was electric with action and atmosphere.

England manager Bobby Robson won a psychological battle before a ball had been kicked. Carlos Bilardo, manager of Argentina, was concerned

Diego Maradona, the handy man

that England would pack their midfield in a bid to stifle his forwards and he countered this anticipated tactic by omitting the adventurous forward Pasculli and selecting in his place the more defensive Enrique. But Robson stuck with the adventurous team that had paralysed Poland and Paraguay, apart from recalling Terry Fenwick in

147

place of Alvin Martin at the heart of the defence. England were quietly confident they could repeat the 1966 World Cup quarter-final victory over the Argentinians, but as the game started under a boiling mid-day sun the one player they knew they had to beware was the dynamic Diego Maradona.

THE TEAMS: **Argentina** Pumpido, Ruggeri, Cuciuffo, Olarticoechea, Brown, Giusti, Batista, Burruchaga, Enrique, Maradona, Valdano. Sub: Tapia.
England Shilton, Stevens, Sansom, Hoddle, Butcher, Fenwick, Steven, Reid, Lineker, Beardsley, Hodge. Subs: Barnes, Waddle.

THE ACTION: He might have been the shortest man on the field at 5ft 4in, but the chunky, wide-shouldered Maradona paraded across the pitch like a giant among pygmies. England's defenders noticeably quivered every time he took possession, which was often because he was continually demanding the ball the moment it reached the feet of any team-mate. When he had the ball on his left foot, he would glide past tackles with the ease of a Rolls Royce overtaking a Robin Reliant; and when he did not have the ball the Argentinian captain was still a menace because of the speed with which he ran into areas of space.

Terry Fenwick, an uncompromising defender out of the retaliate-first school of football, decided that a physical assault might be the best way to keep Maradona quiet. All he got for his clumsy effort was a booking and a cold stare from the Master that could be interpreted as meaning that he would pay for his attempted ambush before the match was much older.

But despite the almost overwhelming presence of Maradona, it was England who nearly snatched an early lead—courtesy of goalkeeper Pumpido. He deserted his penalty area in an unnecessary chase to meet a mishit through ball from Glenn Hoddle. As he approached the ball he stumbled and Peter Beardsley looked as surprised as a poacher suddenly finding himself being handed a gift by the gamekeeper. He took the ball wide of the panicking Pumpido and released a curling shot on the turn that swerved into the side netting.

Both defences looked uncertain under pressure, and it was like watching two heavy-hitting boxers who had suspect chins. England wobbled against the thrusts of Maradona and the centre of Argentina's defence buckled several times in the first half under the direct attacks of fast-moving partners Lineker and Beardsley.

England might have fared better in the goalless first 45 minutes had they been more adventurous, but they were so conscious of Maradona's match-winning ability that they cautiously kept players back in defence who might have been better employed supporting raids against an Argentinian back line that looked vulnerable under attack.

Whichever way you looked at it, the second half belonged to Maradona and the two goals that he scored became the major talking point of the entire tournament. The first will

always be remembered for its controversy, and the second for its marvellous, mind-blowing quality.

Six minutes had gone of the second half when Maradona swept the ball to the feet of Valdano. As he raced through the centre to meet the return some England defenders were appealing for offside. But the linesman's flag stayed down as Valdano's centre was deflected across the face of the England goal by Steve Hodge. Peter Shilton came off his line prepared to punch clear. There seemed no way that the stocky Maradona, dwarfed by the powerfully built England goalkeeper, could outjump Shilton. But spectators looked on in amazement as the ball cannoned into the net off Maradona with the airborne Shilton stretching out to thrash at empty air. All eyes in the Press box swivelled towards the action replay television screen for confirmation of what they thought their eyes had seen and there was the instant evidence. No doubt about it, Maradona had pushed the ball into the net with his left hand.

Shilton led a posse of protesting players trying to persuade referee Ali ben Naceur that the goal had been illegal, but from the angle that the Tunisian official saw it Maradona appeared to have scored with his head. He pointed to the centre circle and the Argentinian went on a dance of celebration that should really have been a skulk of shame.

Four minutes later, with the aggrieved England players still trying to regain their composure, two-faced Maradona unveiled the genius in his game that had prompted Napoli to buy him from Barcelona for a world

Gary Lineker, top marksman

record £6.9 million in 1984. To say he ran rings round England would be too simple a description of a goal that stands comparison with the very best scored anywhere and at any time. Running with the ball at his feet from close to the halfway line, Maradona drew England defenders to him like a spider luring its prey. Kenny Sansom, Terry Butcher and then Terry Fenwick all came into his web and were left in a tangle behind him as he glided past their attempted tackles.

Again, it was Maradona versus Shilton, this time on the ground. Maradona did not have to cheat his way past the England goalkeeper. He sold him an outrageous dummy that left Shilton scrambling for a shot that was never made, and then he nonchalantly prodded the ball into the empty net for a goal of breathtaking beauty. It was a moment of magnificence that sweetened the sour taste left by Maradona's first goal.

Too late, England manager Bobby Robson decided that attack was the best form of defence against the Argentinians. He pulled off Everton midfield partners Trevor Steven and the limping Peter Reid and sent on wingers John Barnes and Chris Waddle with instructions to attack down the flanks.

This spirit of adventure was rewarded with a goal in the 80th minute. Barnes spurted to the by-line and pulled the ball back into the middle where the razor-sharp Lineker turned it into the net from close range for his sixth goal of the tournament. Suddenly England were filled with belief that they could save a game that had looked beyond rescue.

Out of necessity, England were now so committed to attack that they were leaving themselves exposed at the back. Tapia unleashed a sniper shot that hit the post and Fenwick risked being sent off with a crude tackle that halted a Valdano run.

There were just moments to go when Lineker raised one more gallop and he was within inches of netting an equaliser which, frankly, would have flattered an England team that paid the price for being too cautious in the first half.

As they walked exhausted off the bakehouse of a pitch, the England players—led by Peter Shilton—found the energy to continue their complaints to the referee about the first Maradona goal. But most of the capacity crowd were only talking about his second goal as they filed out of the ground at the end of an eventful quarter-final that would always be remembered as 'Maradona's Match.'

THE WITNESSES: Bobby Robson: 'We were beaten by one goal that was, to say the least, dubious and another that was miraculous. We can hold our heads up high. We lost, but only just, to a very good team. They managed to compress our midfield in the first half so that our men at the front got few passes. There is no question that Maradona is a very special player, and quite unstoppable when he makes up his mind to take on defenders. His second goal was as good as you will ever see, but every England player close to the incident insists that he put the first goal in with his hand. That was the way I saw it, too.'

Peter Shilton: 'There is not a shadow of doubt that Maradona pushed the ball into the net with his hand for the first goal. It's a joke that anybody could believe that he beat me to the ball and headed it into the net. I was a foot above him as the ball came across and the only way he could possibly have reached it was with his hand. All of us accept that his second goal was brilliant. But it does nothing to ease our disappointment about the first goal.'

Carlos Bilardo, Argentinian manager: 'I am sure that any neutral spectators would agree that the best team won. England were very physical and some of their tactics were questionable. I am surprised more of their players were not cautioned by the referee. Maradona's second goal was the work of a genius. His first? I could not see clearly from where I was sitting, but the referee thought—as I did—that the ball went into the net off Maradona's head.'

GOLDEN BOY: Born in Argentina on October 30, 1960, Diego Maradona was a boy wonder from a football-daft family who was hoping to play for his country in the 1978 World Cup finals at the age of 17, but manager Cesar Luis Menotti decided he was too young. Maradona played in the 1982 tournament that turned into a personal nightmare when he was sent off for a wild foul in the match against Brazil. He had agreed to sign for Barcelona before the finals in a £5 million transfer deal that rescued his club, Boca Juniors, from bankruptcy. Two years later he moved to Napoli for 15,895 million lire (£6.9 million).

QUOTE: Maradona: 'Yes, the ball did go into the England net off my hand. It was not deliberate and so I do not feel guilty claiming it as a goal. Would an England player have gone to the referee and said, "Don't award the goal. The ball hit my hand?" Of course not. Anyway, why all the controversy? Surely my second goal ended all arguments.'

FOR THE RECORD: Argentina duly won the 13th World Cup final at the Aztec Stadium on June 29, 1986, when they beat West Germany 3-2. Argentina beat Belgium 2-0 in the semi-finals with two goals from Maradona. West Germany beat France 2-0. In the play-off for third place France beat Belgium 4-2. Gary Lineker was the tournament's top scorer with six goals.

JIMMY GREAVES: 'I wonder if it ever entered Maradona's head that he could have made himself the idol of every kid in the world if he had owned up straight away to the referee that he handled the ball. But instead of being remembered as a hero, many people will think of him first and foremost as a cheat.'

THE CHAMPIONS OF '86

First Division: Liverpool, 88 pts. Runners-up: Everton 86 pts
Second Division: Norwich City, 84 pts. Runners-up: Charlton Athletic, 77 pts
Third Division: Reading, 94 pts. Runners-up: Plymouth Argyle, 87 pts
Fourth Division: Swindon Town, 102 pts. Runners-up: Chester City, 84 pts
FA Cup Final: Liverpool 3, Everton 1
League Cup Final: Oxford United 3, QPR 0
Top First Division marksman: Gary Lineker (Everton), 30 goals
Footballer of the Year: Gary Lineker (Everton)
Scottish champions: Celtic, 50 pts. Runners-up: Heart of Midlothian, 50 pts
Scottish Cup Final: Aberdeen 3, Heart of Midlothian 0
Scottish Player of the Year: Sandy Jardine (Heart of Midlothian)
European Cup Final: Steaua Bucharest 0, Barcelona 0 (Steaua on penalities)
European Cup Winners' Cup Final: Dynamo Kiev 3, Atletico Madrid 0
UEFA Cup Final: Real Madrid 5, Cologne 3 (5-1, 0-2)
European Footballer of the Year: Igor Belanov (Dynamo Kiev)
World Cup Final: Argentina 3, West Germany 2

1986-87 Bold Coventry put a smile back on the face of football

Scoreline: Coventry City 3, Tottenham Hotspur 2
Venue: Wembley Stadium **Date:** May 16, 1987

THE SETTING: Few people gave Coventry City a hope of becoming the first Midlands club for 19 years to capture the FA Cup. They were at Wembley for the first time in their 104-year history and facing them were North London giants Tottenham, bidding for their eighth victory in eight FA Cup finals.

Spurs, managed with flair and intelligence by outstanding tactician David Pleat, had sparkled all season with fluent football that flowed from a fountain of passes provided by midfield partners Glenn Hoddle and Osvaldo Ardiles, two of the world's most graceful and skilful players.

For the enigmatic Hoddle, it was a match of extra special significance. He had decided on a move to France and was holding his passing out parade after a decade of bewitching and at times bewildering performances for Tottenham. Feeding hungrily off the passes of Hoddle and Ardiles in attack was Clive Allen, who had been banging in goals with staggering regularity. His tally for the season stood at 48 goals, a record that surpassed even anything Jimmy Greaves achieved with Spurs after he replaced Clive's father, Les Allen, in the Tottenham firing line. Allen arrived at Wembley weighed down with individual honours, including the award of Footballer of the Year

Keith Houchen, a classic goal

and Players' Player of the Year. Aiding and abetting him in the dismantling of defences was England winger Chris Waddle, who when in the right mood could monopolise any match.

But Coventry were anything but overawed by the all-star names on the Tottenham team-sheet. Neutral fans might have considered them like workhorses in competition with thoroughbreds, but anybody who had closely watched their progress to Wembley would have noted that they could turn on the style to go with their sweat. Managerial partners George Curtis and John Sillett had instilled enormous confidence and self belief into their players, and they went into the match convinced that they could prove the pundits wrong.

THE TEAMS: Coventry City Ogrizovic, Phillips, Downs, McGrath, Kilcline, Peake, Bennett, Gynn, Regis, Houchen, Pickering. Sub: Rodger.
Tottenham Hotspur Clemence, Hughton, Thomas, Hodge, Gough, Mabbutt, Clive Allen, Paul Allen, Waddle, Hoddle, Ardiles. Subs: Claesen, Stevens.

THE ACTION: Coventry could not have got off to a more discouraging start to their first Wembley final. Clive Allen sprinted to the near post in the second minute to head the ball into the net from close range for his 49th goal of the season.

It could easily have unhinged a team with less character than Coventry, but they struck back with a boldness and daring that brought its reward in the shape of an equaliser by Dave Bennett. The Tottenham defence dithered as Keith Houchen nodded on a lob from Greg Downs and Bennett swayed round goalkeeper Ray Clemence with a snake-hip movement before steering the ball into the net.

Lloyd McGrath, an England youth international who had served his apprenticeship at Coventry, was given the job of shadowing Glenn Hoddle and the evidence that he was doing his job lay in the fact that Hoddle's farewell appearance for Spurs was muted and uninspiring.

Hoddle made a rare impact on the match six minutes before half-time when he curled in a free-kick that drew giant goalkeeper Steve Ogrizovic off his line. His intent was correct but his timing hopeless and as he grasped at thin air the ball was deflected into the net by Coventry skipper Brian Kilcline after Gary Mabbutt had stabbed it goalwards.

Tottenham were flattered by their lead, and it was only justice when Houchen threw himself into a spectacular full-stretch dive to head in a second equaliser on the hour from a cross by the energetic Bennett.

Clive Allen chose this second half suddenly to start missing the sort of chances he had been snapping up all season, and two got away in the closing minutes as the final drifted into extra time for the fifth time in seven years.

It was Coventry who had the strength and the desire to go all out for a winner and Mabbutt, as always playing his heart out for Tottenham, had the misfortune to turn a cross from McGrath into his own net six minutes into extra-time. There have been neater winning goals scored at Wembley but rarely one more deserved. Coventry had put the smile back on the face of football with their attitude and endeavour.

THE WITNESSES: John Sillett, Coventry coach: 'We were determined to be positive and to make it an occasion to remember. It was not just our intention to stop Spurs from playing, but to prove that we could play some pretty useful stuff ourselves. I don't think anybody can begrudge us our victory. The winning goal was something of a fluke, but we deserved it. We have made a lot of people eat their words.'

David Pleat: 'I was terribly disappointed by the input of several of our players. They just did not get into the game. My heartiest congratulations go to Coventry because I appreciate the mountains they have climbed to achieve this success.'

Glenn Hoddle: 'I am disappointed in my personal performance. I was so keen to leave Spurs on a winning note, but I just couldn't get my game together. McGrath did a good job marking me, but it's always easier to destroy a picture than paint one.'

THE HEAD MAN: Born in Middlesbrough on July 25, 1960, Keith Houchen had been a have-boots-will-travel footballer plying his trade in the lower divisions with Chesterfield, Hartlepool, Orient, York and Scunthorpe. He had played just nine League matches for Scunthorpe United when Coventry snapped him up for £60,000 in July, 1986. Just ten months later it was looking the bargain of the decade when he dived to head his classic goal that took the FA Cup final into extra time. At 26, Houchen had finally arrived as a star player on English

football's premier stage.

QUOTE: Keith Houchen: 'The goal at Wembley and my winners' medal have made all the lean years worthwhile. I've been down at the bottom in this game, and I appreciate what we have achieved better than most. Now I am convinced that this Coventry team can go on to even bigger things.'

FOR THE RECORD: Coventry were also taken to extra time in the semifinal before beating Leeds 3-2. Tottenham beat Watford 4-1.

JIMMY GREAVES: 'I was willing Coventry to win even though it was against my old club. John Sillett was my best pal in our playing days at Chelsea and he stands for all that is good about the game. If Spurs had won it would have been remembered as just another final. But Coventry's magnificent victory brought a touch of romance and magic to the Cup.'

THE CHAMPIONS OF '87

First Division: Everton, 86 pts. Runners-up: Liverpool, 77 pts
Second Division: Derby County, 84 pts. Runners-up: Portsmouth, 78 pts
Third Division: Bournemouth, 97 pts. Runners-up: Middlesbrough, 94 pts
Fourth Division: Northampton Town, 99 pts. Runners-up: Preston NE, 90 pts
FA Cup Final: Coventry City 3, Tottenham Hotspur 2
League Cup Final: Arsenal 2, Liverpool 1
Top First Division marksman: Clive Allen (Tottenham), 33 goals
Footballer of the Year: Clive Allen (Tottenham)
Scottish champions: Rangers, 69 pts. Runners-up: Celtic, 63 pts
Scottish Cup Final: St Mirren 1, Dundee United 0 (after extra time)
Scottish Player of the Year: Brian McClair (Celtic)
European Cup Final: FC Porto 2, Bayern Munich 1
European Cup Winners' Cup Final: Ajax 1, Lokomotiv Leipzig 0
UEFA Cup Final: IFK Gothenburg 2, Dundee United 1 (1-0, 1-1)
European Footballer of the Year: Ruud Gullit (AC Milan)

1987-88   Hat-trick hero Marco piles on the agony for England

Scoreline: Holland 3, England 1
Venue: Rheinstadion, Dusseldorf   **Date:** June 15, 1988

THE SETTING: England desperately needed a victory over Holland in their second European Championship finals group match to rescue themselves from the wreckage of a humiliating defeat by the Republic of Ireland.

The match with Holland had come down to a sudden-death duel because whichever team lost would be making an early exit from the tournament. The Dutch were coming into the game on the back of a 1-0 defeat by Russia, but at least they could claim bad luck for their loss.

England could offer no excuses for the 1-0 defeat in their opening group match by a spirited Ireland side pumped up for peak performances by former England World Cup hero Jack Charlton. Their finishing against the Irish had been appalling, with the usually deadly Gary Lineker the main culprit as he continually fired blanks.

Shouldering the blame along with Lineker were Liverpool duo John Barnes and Peter Beardsley, both of whom had been in devastating form on the domestic front but looked stale and lacking in total commitment against Ireland. Barnes, the double Footballer of the Year, and Beardsley —at £1.9million the English game's most expensive player—were given a Nelsonian 'England expects' pep talk by manager Bobby Robson.

Glenn Hoddle, banished to the substitute's bench for much of the match against Ireland, was recalled to the team along with Trevor Steven in a bid to give better balance in midfield.

One of the most important matches in England's recent history was co-inciding with goalkeeper Peter Shilton's 100th international selection, and he had not faced a tougher task in his previous 99 games. Included in the Dutch attack were the supremely gifted European Footballer of the Year Ruud Gullit and his AC Milan partner Marco Van Basten. Both of them had the ability to destroy England if allowed time and space in which to manoeuvre.

Peter Shilton, a century of caps

THE TEAMS: **Holland** Van Breukelen, R. Koeman, Rijkaard, Van Tiggelen, Van Aerle, Wouters, Vanenburg, E. Koeman, Gullit, Muhren, Van Basten. Subs: Kieft, Suvrijn. **England** Shilton, Stevens, Wright, Adams, Sansom, Steven, Hoddle, Robson, Barnes, Lineker, Beardsley. Subs: Waddle, Hateley.

THE ACTION: England were twice within inches of taking the lead during a first half in which they must have wondered what they had done to upset the soccer gods. In the eighth minute Gary Lineker chased a loose ball and from an acute angle on the right hit the near post. Thirty minutes later Hoddle struck a curling shot against the inside of the same post after Bryan Robson had teed up a free-kick for him.

It was the last time that England could claim to be in control of the match. As if inspired by their second narrow escape, Holland stepped on the accelerator and raised the pace of the game to a level that stretched England's defence to breaking point.

Two minutes before half-time Frank Rijkaard relieved Lineker of the ball with a block tackle and threaded it past Gary Stevens to Gullit, who raced deep into England territory before releasing a swerving pass to the feet of Van Basten. Tony Adams was marking him tightly but the Dutchman swivelled and shot past Shilton all in one stunning movement.

England hopes rose of at least holding Holland ten minutes into the second half when skipper Bryan Robson made an inspired run through the middle of the Dutch defence, ex-changed passes with Lineker and forced the ball over the line for a grittily earned equaliser.

Hoddle started to match the guile of Gullit and just as England were beginning to think in terms of trying to win the match they were flattened by two goals in four minutes by Van Basten.

Gullit almost arrogantly brought the ball under control after a mishit shot by Wouters in the 72nd minute and when he transferred it to Van Basten he had it in the back of the net in the twinkling of an eye.

England were rocking and rolling under a series of attacks and Van Basten was too quick for them in the 76th minute when he pounced to volley the ball into the net after substitute Kieft had headed on a corner from Erwin Koeman.

THE WITNESSES: Bobby Robson: 'We were unlucky when we hit the woodwork twice in the first half, but we can have no complaints about the final score. We had to play well to keep the score down to 3-1. If we'd played badly it could have been 5-1.'

Bryan Robson: 'Van Basten's finishing was devastating, but it might so easily have been a different story if the two shots that hit the post had gone in. There were about 20 minutes in the second half when we had them going, but Van Basten's second goal was the real killer.'

Peter Shilton: 'I'm proud to have become the first England goalkeeper to have won 100 caps, but the edge has been knocked off it because of our defeat. We don't have to feel ashamed of ourselves. We lost to a first-class

side. I wouldn't be surprised to see them go on and win the Championship.'

Ruud Gullit: 'England put a lot of effort into the match, but they were let down by their tactics. They are very predictable. It is as if they are living in the past.'

THE HAT-TRICK MAN: Born in 1965, Marco Van Basten first established himself as an international striker with Ajax Amsterdam before teaming up with Ruud Gullit at AC Milan in a £3.3million transfer. He was on the point of walking out on the Dutch squad in protest at not being selected for the opening match against the USSR. His idol, Johan Cruyff, talked him out of defecting and he stayed to become the talk of the tournament. He fractured a cheekbone in Milan's final League match of the season and was still feeling the effects of the injury when the European Championship kicked off.

QUOTE: Marco Van Basten: 'I can now go back to Italy with my head high. My first season there was miserable because of injury problems, but now I have proved to everybody that I can score goals in the best company.'

FOR THE RECORD: Van Basten scored the winning goal that lifted Holland to a 2-1 victory over host country West Germany in the semi-finals. He then laid on the first goal for Gullit against the USSR in the final and scored the match-clinching goal himself with a superb volley. England were beaten 3-1 by the USSR in their third and final group match.

JIMMY GREAVES: 'Van Basten's finishing was as lethal as anything ever seen in a major championship. Everybody started screaming that Bobby Robson should be sacked, but he did as well as he could with the players available. We simply weren't good enough.'

THE CHAMPIONS OF '88

First Division: Liverpool, 90 pts. Runners-up: Manchester United, 81 pts
Second Division: Millwall, 82 pts. Runners-up: Aston Villa, 78 pts
Third Division: Sunderland, 93 pts. Runners-up: Brighton and HA, 84 pts
Fourth Division: Wolverhampton W, 90 pts. Runners-up: Cardiff City, 85 pts
FA Cup Final: Wimbledon 1, Liverpool 0
League Cup Final: Luton Town 3, Arsenal 2
Top First Division marksman: John Aldridge (Liverpool), 29 goals
Footballer of the Year: John Barnes (Liverpool)
Scottish champions: Celtic, 72 pts. Runners-up: Heart of Midlothian, 62 pts
Scottish Cup Final: Celtic 2, Dundee United 1
Scottish Player of the Year: Paul McStay (Celtic)
European Cup Final: PSV Eindhoven 0, Benfica 0 (PSV won on penalties)
European Cup Winners' Cup Final: Mechelen 1, Ajax 0
UEFA Cup: Bayer Leverkusen 3, Espanol 3 (0-3, 3-0, Bayer on penalties)
European Footballer of the Year: Marco Van Basten (AC Milan)
European Championship Final: Holland 2, Russia 0

1988-89 Liverpool are hammered as Paul becomes a Pele clone

Scoreline: West Ham United 4, Liverpool 1
Venue: Upton Park **Date:** November 30, 1988

THE SETTING: West Ham had not got the better of mighty Liverpool in a sequence of 13 matches spread across six seasons. Few of the sell-out 26,971 crowd shoe-horned into the compact Upton Park stadium for this fourth round Littlewoods Cup tie could realistically have expected the Merseyside monopoly to be broken.

West Ham were struggling down in the dumps of the First Division, while Liverpool were in the running for their seventh League Championship of the decade.

There had been signs that the 'Anfield Assassins' were not quite the force of previous years, but the defiant way they had outlasted Arsenal in a marathon tie in the previous round of the Littlewoods Cup suggested they were returning to something like their best form.

West Ham have a long and proud tradition of playing purist football that makes them a delight to the eye even when they are caving in to defeat. But going into this cup tie against Liverpool they were stretching the patience of their supporters to the limit. They had won only two of 14 League matches, and there was a gathering chorus of disapproval aimed at manager John Lyall, the longest-serving of all the First Division managers, who is an idealist standing for everything that is good about the game of football.

Paul Ince, every inch a winner

It was going to need something special from West Ham to placate their fans and puncture Liverpool's domination. What they provided was beyond the wildest dreams of even their most optimistic followers as they gave the Merseysiders their biggest hiding in a domestic cup match for nearly 50 years.

THE TEAMS: **West Ham United** McKnight, Potts, Dicks, Gale, Martin, Devonshire, Brady, Kelly, Rosenior, Dickens, Ince.
Liverpool Hooper, Ablett, Venison, Nicol, Whelan, Spackman, Beardsley, Aldridge, Staunton, Houghton, McMahon. Subs: Watson, Durnin.

THE ACTION: Right from the first whistle West Ham produced football of a quality and style unrecogniseable from the scrambling, neurotic soccer that had sent them plummeting towards the basement of the First Division. It was as if they were relieved to be playing without the burden of having to worry that a defeat could send them deeper into the relegation rat race.

With veteran Irish international Liam Brady pulling the strings from midfield West Ham pinned Liverpool in their own half under an avalanche of attacks. The Anfield defenders, masters at covering and then countering, were reduced to making panic clearances as the East Enders unwrapped the sort of flowing football that had made Upton Park an academy of soccer science.

The non-stop first-half pressure produced two goals in three minutes that were works of art by the unheralded Paul Ince, who suddenly had commentators and reporters reaching for the sort of adjectives reserved for the likes of Pele and Maradona.

Brady opened the path for the first goal with a teasing cross that the Liverpool defence could only half clear. The ball was at shoulder height in the middle of the penalty area when Ince rose like an Olympic high jumper and volleyed the ball into the net. As he came down to earth he was lifted again, this time by team-mates celebrating one of the great goals of the year.

The name Pele was on many lips when Ince struck again three minutes later with another spectacular goal. This time he came bounding in from the back of the penalty area to meet a corner-kick from Alan Devonshire, and the way he headed it down and into the corner of the net was like an action replay of a memorable goal Pele scored for Brazil in the 1970 World Cup final.

West Ham, with the cushion of a two-goal lead, continued to tear the Liverpool defence apart and striker Leroy Rosenior might have doubled the score with steadier finishing.

It is no exaggeration to say that Liverpool were being outplayed and they could hardly believe their good fortune when they were awarded a penalty during a rare raid on the Hammers goal in the 34th minute. Central defender Alvin Martin and striker John Aldridge went up together to meet a high ball and, to everybody's amazement, the referee pointed to the spot as Aldridge tumbled to the ground after what looked a 50-50 challenge.

Aldridge picked himself up and steered the ball coolly into the net to bring Liverpool back into a game that was beginning to look all over bar the shooting.

The confidence began to leak out of West Ham and in the opening moments of the second half Liverpool started to dictate the pattern and the pace of the play. But West Ham's self-belief and control of the match was restored by a gift of a goal in the 58th minute. David Kelly sent what appeared a harmless cross into the Liverpool penalty area. There was no West Ham player with any hope of reaching the ball as Liverpool defender Steve Staunton head-flicked it to where he thought goalkeeper Mike

Hooper was waiting. But Hooper had dashed off on a different route to gather a ball that never arrived, and he could only look on helplessly as it struck the inside of the post and bounced into the unguarded net.

Liverpool hopes of salvaging the game disappeared ten minutes later when key defender Steve Nicol was helped off the pitch with damaged ribs. Steve McMahon followed him off soon after and the substitution had hardly been made when Tony Gale hammered a 25 yard free kick into the net to seal a sensational victory.

THE WITNESSES: Kenny Dalglish, Liverpool manager: 'West Ham were far superior to us, and we got what we deserved—which was nothing at all. On the evidence of this performance it is hard to understand why West Ham are stuck near the bottom of the table. I don't think they will be there for long if they can maintain anything like this form.'

John Lyall: 'We have tried hard not to lose belief in ourselves. Our objective is always to play good, technical football and to make sure we do the simple things well. Tonight we got our reward and we must build on this to get the motivation we need to start climbing up the First Division table. Paul Ince is one to watch for the future. He has been promising this sort of performance for some time. Now he must seek consistency.'

Liam Brady: 'I have never seen a Liverpool team taken apart like this before. Those two goals from Paul Ince were world class, and confirms my belief that he is an England international player of the future.'

THE INCH MAN: Born in West Ham territory at Ilford on October 21, 1967, Paul Ince joined Hammers on the Youth Training Scheme in the summer of 1984. He is a versatile player who since making his League debut at Newcastle on November 30, 1986, has appeared as a sweeper and in attacking and defensive roles in midfield. It is as an attacking left-sided midfield player that he has made the greatest impact. His passes are inch-perfect and he is competitive as well as skilful.

QUOTE: Paul Ince: 'I'm grateful to John Lyall for giving me the chance to achieve my ambition of playing for West Ham. The two goals I scored against Liverpool were just what I needed to boost my confidence. To have scored them against one of the greatest clubs in the world was like a dream come true.'

FOR THE RECORD: It was Liverpool's heaviest cup defeat in domestic competition since the 4-1 FA Cup fifth round loss against Wolves in 1938-39. West Ham surpassed their performance against Liverpool in the third round of the FA Cup when they beat Arsenal in a replay at Highbury after a 2-2 draw in a classic confrontation at Upton Park. But their relegation battle overshadowed their cup conquests.

JIMMY GREAVES: 'It was an extraordinary performance by West Ham. In that mood they would have taken apart any team. Paul Ince looked like a clone of Pele! But they became labelled the Jekyll and Hyde team of the First Division because of their form in the League.'